FIRST CLASS

CHARACTER EDUCATION
ACTIVITIES PROGRAM

Ready-to-Use Lessons & Activities
for Grades 7-12

Michael D. Koehler · Karen E. Royer

JOSSEY-BASS
A Wiley Imprint
www.josseybass.com

Copyright (c) 2001 by Michael Koehler and Karen Royer.

Published by Jossey-Bass
A Wiley Imprint
989 Market Street, San Francisco, CA 94103-1741 www.josseybass.com

Jossey-Bass books and products are available through most bookstores. To contact Jossey-Bass directly call our Customer Care Department within the U.S. at 800-956-7739, outside the U.S. at 317-572-3986 or fax 317-572-4002.

Jossey-Bass also publishes its books in a variety of electronic formats. Some content that appears in print may not be available in electronic books.

Library of Congress Cataloging-in-Publication Data

Koehler, Mike
    First Class character education activities program : ready-to-use lessons & activities for
grades 7–12 / Michael D. Koehler and Karen E. Royer
        p.   cm.
    ISBN 0-13-034081-2
    ISBN 0-13-042586-9 (Layflat)
    1. Moral education (Secondary)—United States—Handbooks, manuals, etc. 2.
Character—Study and teaching (Secondary)—United States—Handbooks, manuals, etc. 3.
Education, Secondary—United States—Activity programs—Handbooks, manuals, etc. I.
Royer, Karen E. II. Title

LC311.K62 2202
373'.01'14—dc21
                                                                                                    2001036120

FIRST EDITION
PB Printing 10 9 8 7 6 5 4 3 2

ACKNOWLEDGMENTS

Thanks to Arthur "Tee" Newbrough, the Superintendent of Mundelein High School, for his commitment to the school's First Class program. His stewardship throughout the process provided the administrative support and the conceptual input that contributed to the character education of so many students.

We are also grateful to a number of teachers who contributed so much of their time, energy, and creativity to the development of activities as well as to the organization of the entire First Class program at Mundelein High School. They are committed and dedicated professionals. The Mundelein community should be proud of them. Every school in this country would be pleased to enjoy the services of such complete professionals. We are thankful to: John Algrim, Jose Acosta, Jodi Cusack-Acosta, Kathy Bell, Mary Jane Chiado, Karen Chilcote, Dave Ekstrom, Kathy Hajek, Karen Hall, Judy Juske, Alexander Kapotas, Lillian Medina, Brian Swanson, Susan Theotokatos, and Jodi Wirt.

Finally, we want to thank good friend Lou Adler for his concept, "It's Your Call," which was used periodically throughout the book.

ABOUT THE AUTHORS

Michael D. Koehler, Ph.D., was a teacher, counselor, and coach at Deerfield High School in Deerfield, Illinois for 31 years and an adjunct professor of educational administration at Northeastern Illinois University's graduate school for 23 years. He has written more than a dozen books with Prentice Hall, the most recent being *First Class Character Education Activities Program* (2001, with Karen Royer), *Counseling Secondary Students with Learning Disabilities* (1998, with Marybeth Kravets), *The Athletic Director's Survival Guide* (1997), *Advising Student Athletes Through the College Recruitment Process*, and *Building the Total Athlete* (1995, with Bruce Hanson).

Mike has also authored more than 30 articles for professional publications, including the *NCAA News* and the *Olympian*, written and narrated a videotape for the College Board, a newspaper column, the radio show of prominent radio personality John Doremus, and even the episodes for Dial Santa Claus and the Cinnamon Bear, which enjoyed millions of phone calls in Chicago, New York, and Philadelphia. He has been asked to speak scores of times for the College Board, the nation's high schools and events sponsored by the United States Olympic Committee, usually on behalf of his grandfather, Jim Thorpe.

Persons wishing to contact Mike to provide in-service presentations or speeches are asked to write or call him at:

8246 Voss Road
Minocqua, Wisconsin 54548
(715) 358-8802

OR

15380 N. 100th Street
Unit 1116
Scottsdale, Arizona 85260
(480) 661-4818

Karen E. Royer, M.A., is a former teacher at Mundelein High School, where she taught all levels of French including AP French and spearheaded the writing of a five-year French curriculum, one of the first "immersion" curricula in the State of Illinois. In recognition of her work, Royer was the recipient of the Illinois Board of Education Those Who Excel Award of Merit in 1997 and appeared on a teacher training film produced by Dr. Grant Wiggins, an international authority on authentic assessment. She was one of the faculty who worked with students to initiate First Class—the program described in this resource which emphasizes basic social principles including respect for self and others.

ABOUT THIS RESOURCE

No one is more influential in the lives of children than their parents. Character development starts logically with the family, probably from the day infants are brought home. That influence continues, to a lesser or greater extent, whenever children have contact with their parents. It is unrealistic, therefore, to assume that even the most enlightened program of character education in schools will dramatically affect the attitudes and behavior of all students.

But it will help—a lot. Schools exert profound influence on children. Peer groups, counselors, favorite teachers, and coaches all help to shape the belief systems that result in student attitudes and behaviors. Activities like the ones in this book provide the experiences and the dialogue for all students that promote an exchange of ideas, an interaction with role models, and the analysis and reflection that influence student values, attitudes, and behavior. Character development results.

Why has character education become so important in our nation's schools? Consider recent developments. Senseless violence is escalating because some children are unable to control their anger. Prominent athletes, especially in professional sports, are teaching our children that "It's good to be bad." Chest-bumping, trash-talking, and gratuitous violence have transformed media and sports role models into role *muddles*. High-ranking politicians are giving new meaning to "public affairs" and to the notion that absolute power corrupts absolutely. Talk shows and soap operas are redefining what is normal in our society. We seem to be creating more characters than character.

How can we even hope to explain the senseless cruelty in our nation's schools? How do we account for evident increases in immature, irresponsible, and inconsiderate behavior everywhere else in society? It may be that our unprecedented economic growth has created increasing numbers of "Me first" mentalities who have little time for anyone else. It may be that technology has created distances between us that we are unable to bridge. It may be that the media have warped our social principles and our perceptions of reality by populating the sports and entertainment industries with more and more role muddles.

Or it may be that the traditional cultural principles that were rejected during preceding decades resulted in a vacuum that left much of this country rudderless. Although most of the people who rebelled against those principles were well-intentioned and, to a large extent, justified, our nation may still be struggling to find new or rediscover old social principles that reaffirm a sense of moral and ethical direction for ourselves and our children.

The challenge to these principles may have confused parents and schools about their responsibilities to children, made them hesitant to act firmly and confidently, at times even afraid to risk the anger of children who have learned defiance from media role muddles. Adolescence is tough enough on kids. But when they are denied consistent help from significant adults in their lives, they fail to understand and surmount the developmental milestones that confuse and anger them and that contain the potential for future tragedy.

First Class Character Education Activities Program suggests ways to provide such help. It contains a range of activities that develop character in our children and regards character as something everyone can learn. As defined in this book, character is the quality of "knowing what is right, desiring what is right, and doing what is right." As such, it involves not only an understanding of integrity, morality, and spirituality, but also the willingness to behave accordingly. Children must *know* and then *do* what is right—and they need our help.

This book addresses such issues. The activities and materials range from behavior in the auditorium and corridors to attitudes regarding a variety of personal and social issues. Section One defines character, describes one particular program, and discusses how it was developed in the school and community. It shows how the program started and explains the problems that had to be overcome to get everyone committed to an all-school program of character education.

Section Two looks at student behavior and the related issues of motivation, communication, and parent involvement. It provides a range of reproducibles that will help get your program started and a series of activities that promotes improved student behavior. The activities in Section Three explore student and family principles as they engage students in the analysis and discussion of specific issues such as sex and drugs.

Section Four's activities explore anger management, stress reduction, dealing with failure, impulse control, distinguishing between wants and needs, leadership, and decision making.

Social issues are the focus of Section Five. The activities consider family roles, violence, the impact of television and the rest of the media, and cooperation vs. competition.

Section Six analyzes the specific issues of prejudice, discrimination, stereotyping, and sexual harassment. The activities help students become aware of these issues and better able to deal with them.

Section Seven focuses on the understanding and acceptance of oneself. It engages students in activities that promote reflection, self-criticism, friendship, and self-acceptance. Section Eight looks at the environment. Its activities explore caring about the school, working with the elderly, maintaining effective communication, using appropriate language, maintaining personal appearance, and engaging in volunteer activities.

Finally, the Epilogue addresses teachers specifically, acknowledging that their involvement is critical to the success of the program. It provides activities that promote ownership of the program, teacher evaluation, and processes for promoting change.

The character development activities in this book are equally useful in homerooms, advisories, or regular classrooms. Teachers can use them to establish a specific focus on character education and/or to complement related areas of the curriculum. The book contains a great many reproducibles that promote classroom discussion and that can be incorporated into daily or weekly activities in any junior high school or secondary school classroom.

Why is this book so important? Teachers and others in the school need a resource that promotes student exploration and assimilation of positive influences, the kind that lead to healthy character development. An activities book that provides these experiences and addresses the topic of Character Education is important to many educators, not just to administrators but to classroom teachers and counselors, all of whom share the crucial task of positively influencing the character development of their students.

This book recognizes that problems in our society result not just when bad people act but when good people *fail* to act. There are no "victimless" crimes. All of us, especially young people, are influenced by everything we see and hear. How children develop character and eventually understand and practice the virtues of self-restraint depend on the willingness of good people to reflect these same virtues in their own behavior and in the learning experiences they provide for all students.

Counselors and teachers realize there is no such thing as a "self-made" person. Each of us is the embodiment of life's influences. Everyone who has been kind to us or spoken a word of encouragement or, for that matter, has hurt us has influenced our character development. Character isn't created in a vacuum. Intellect and talent may be formed in relative isolation, but character is created only in the excitement, challenge, and occasional stress of human interaction. *First Class Character Education Activities Program* promotes such interaction.

Michael D. Koehler
Karen E. Royer

INTRODUCTION

First Class Character Education Activities Program defines character as "the quality of knowing what is right and doing what is right." Self-knowledge and awareness may give us an understanding of the right thing to do, but character *causes* us to do it. We will not distinguish between good character and bad character. We regard character as a positive quality. It not only understands morality and principles, but behaves in ways that are consistent with that understanding. In street parlance, character is "walking the walk," not just "talking the talk."

The Six Facets of Character

People are likely to behave in this positive way when they have developed the following six characteristics:

- **Being unconditionally friendly most of the time**. The person who, by nature, is cold, indifferent, and self-focused fails to see people around him or her as worthwhile in their own right and to reach out to others as a helpmate and friend. Character is "other-focused" and cheerfully opens itself up to outside experience.

- **Being free from inner anger.** Even those of us who ostensibly reach out to others may be distracted or compromised by inner resentment, prejudice, or jealousy. Such resentments and jealousies inevitably cause us to say one thing and often do another. Character is evidenced consistently when people are free of such inner hostility.

- **Committing to worthwhile causes and events vigorously and confidently**. Spontaneous commitment reflects a genuine and positive desire to help. Such help is given without the expectation of something in return or because of a nagging, neurotic guilt. Character is a healthy awareness of social responsibility and a willingness to accept it without any expectation of personal gain.

- **Being self-controlled**. Some of us accept responsibility and react to adversity willingly but only if someone else is watching. We need an outside incentive to do what we know is right. Others of us are governed by inner controls and follow them because they are well-integrated with our behavior. Character is doing the right thing when no one else is watching.

- **Complying with rules and regulations**. Most of us conform happily to reasonable rules and regulations. Others of us see them as impositions and interferences. Character is having the inner strength to seek harmony with the world around us.

- **Understanding the consequences of behavior**. Some of us behave inappropriately with little regard for the implications of our actions. Others of us are self-aware and capable of self-reflection and self-evaluation. Character is developing appropriate personal standards and behaving consistently within them.

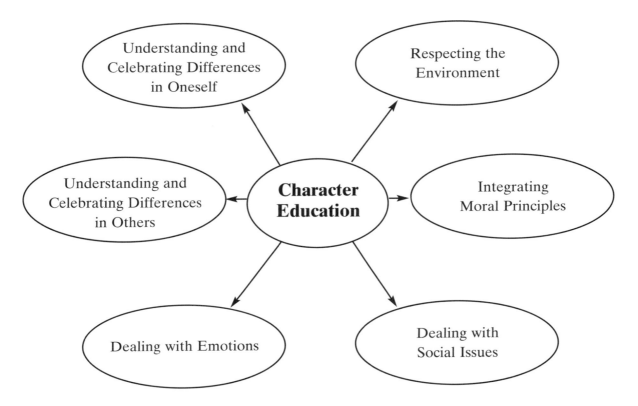

How the Activities in This Book Help Develop Character

Asking students to decide what they will do the next time they get angry at their parents promotes an objective and dispassionate exploration of reasonable alternatives and consequences to such anger. It enables students to understand *why* they get angry and to determine a reasonable and effective set of behaviors before they actually *get* angry. When all of us know how to respond to provocative situations, we tend to control ourselves and to react with less passion.

The same can be said of students' reactions to their friends and teachers, even to other drivers on the highway. Knowing *how* to respond to any given situation is critical to control oneself and maintain satisfying relationships with others. When students consider such situations and their likely responses to them *before* being forced to make decisions, the decisions tend to be reasoned and much more effective. Section Four of this book, "Dealing with Emotional Issues," provides a range of such experiences for students.

The point is, thought process is the focus of all classrooms, from freshman English to Advanced Placement calculus. It is also the focus of most of the activities in this book, all of which explore moral issues and principles that transcend religious proscriptions and seek only to promote comfortable interpersonal relationships among all of us.

Exploring the Context of Character Education

The essential context of character education is critical to the success of the program. One predominant principle applies: The school must demonstrably care about kids. The needs of students must be foremost in the minds of teachers, administrators, counselors, and others in the building. Everyone in the building must recognize that their task is to help students satisfy their needs in order to develop strong self-concepts and feelings of belonging. This is the operational context of character education.

The situational context involves the way the school chooses to deliver the program. The situational context is influenced by a variety of factors: the nature of the school's schedule; the availability of staff; the availability of space; the perceptions of the staff regarding the value of the program; the financial, time, and moral support of the school's administration; the support of the board of education; the degree of involvement of the parent community; opportunities to train and monitor student leaders; and the general philosophy of the school regarding character education.

There are probably more factors, depending on the size and location of the school. Fortunately, a program of character education can be implemented in a variety of ways. Mundelein High School chose to train student leaders and give them primary responsibility to lead discussions and oversee activities. Obviously, teachers can assume such responsibilities, or the program can be organized and run by counselors.

We make these statements advisedly! We recognize that teachers and counselors are already performing a variety of important and time-consuming tasks. Although most of them acknowledge the value and the need for character education activities, many will be resistant to the additional time and preparation such a program requires. We understand their concerns, most of which are legitimate.

That's why schools must collaborate with teachers and counselors to explore the development and implementation of such a program. The staff must feel a sense of ownership of the program in order to commit to it. They can also benefit from the use of a group of student leaders who assume the primary task of delivering the program. This aspect of the program relieves the teachers of additional preparation and time commitments, and offers a significant number of students the opportunity to develop their leadership skills and to help promote the program throughout the building.

Mundelein High School also chose to organize advisories that were added to the school schedule one day a week for 40 minutes to deliver the program. These advisories were composed of each grade level in the building, freshman through senior.

Schools that choose not to organize special advisories can use existing homerooms that can serve the same function. Or they might want to integrate many of the activities in this book within their curricula and offer the program to students through regular classroom activities.

Schools might choose to provide character education activities just to sixth or seventh graders or only to freshmen. By so doing, the activities can be used from one year to the next. The activities might only be refined periodically and/or complemented by new activities. It's also important to recognize that some of the activities in this book are more appropriate for certain grade levels than for others. Similarly, some may be inappropriate for your school. Schools are well-advised to review the entire book and then to pick and choose the activities that meet your needs. Fortunately, the vast majority of them are appropriate in any circumstance.

These are the activities used in one of the most successful programs of character education in the country. Their value to schools that are interested in similar programs is pronounced. Mundelein High School took years to develop many of these activities. That aspect of the task is already done for you. All that schools have to do is promote dialogue in the building about the importance and the value of a character education program.

We admit that the statement "All you have to do is" camouflages a whole lot of hard work. Sometimes it even completely misses the point. We also admit that securing a commitment from teachers, students, and parents for such a program can be challenging, but we also know that it can be done. We did it. We knew that teachers are genuinely interested in doing whatever they can to help students develop into wholesome and responsible young adults and that they will commit to such a program, whatever its situational context, if given the opportunity to explore, develop, and implement it.

The What and Why of the Activities

We have chosen these activities for several important reasons. Regarding prejudice, for example, research has proven consistently that general education may help transform certain notions about minority groups, but that it does little to create tolerant attitudes or a warmer personal acceptance of minority group members. Certain researchers even discovered that revealing the humanity and achievements of certain groups did little to change attitudes about them. What was needed to reduce prejudice, these researchers discovered, was an overt discussion of prejudice.

These activities engage students in not only the discussion but the experience of prejudice. As such, they influence the emotions as well as the intellects of most students. Early researchers Peterson and Thurstone, as far back as 1933, have made clear that highly charged emotional experiences can provoke changes in attitude about other nationalities and ethnic groups.

Other researchers, such as Hovland and Mandell, however, are quick to warn teachers that a subtle approach to the facts is generally ineffective. Schools cannot allow the facts to speak for themselves. Teachers must be aggressive in pointing out morals or conclusions, no matter how obvious they seem. In addition, one researcher, Manis, in 1961 revealed that students must understand and accept the authority and competence of the speaker. Obviously, this principle applies to a range of situtations that extend beyond prejudice and discrimination.

As with all the other units in this book, therefore, the teachers are critical to the success of enabling students to reflect on and influence their own character development. With the exception of a few very intelligent and dynamic students—all of whom we try to get involved in the program—no one in the school is more qualified than teachers to speak authoritatively or competently about character and the need for more self-discipline in our society.

Considering Anchor Points

An anchor point is the core of a person's accepted, even cherished beliefs. To modify those beliefs, arguments on behalf of different behaviors can't be too far removed from the student's anchor points. If arguments or new information are too far removed from anchor points, students will aggressively reject them. If the information, however, introduces a gray area and causes uncertainty, students will accept the new position as possible. This acceptance may eventually result in a new anchor point.

Again, teachers are most capable of moving anchor points. When they use activities like the ones in this book, they are more likely to introduce gray areas for student consideration and to convince them of the possibilities of new perceptions and new behaviors. Most students may have preconceptions, but such preconceptions are generally flexible. Teachers, therefore, can create socially acceptable anchor points in students with few predispositions to be immoral, lazy, prejudiced, or angry.

A Final Consideration

Character is a learned behavior. Little boys learn early in their lives that you can't trust your dog to watch your food. They don't associate it with the dog's needs or its impulsivity. They just learn to be careful. Little girls learn early that when Mommy's mad, never let her comb your hair. They know little about dealing with someone else's anger or controlling their own. They, too, just learn to be careful.

A cognitive understanding of impulsivity and anger are unnecessary to children. They are important, however, as we grow older. Widely recognized educator and author, Art Costa, suggested years ago that people who can control their impulsivity are intelligent people. He asserted that impulse control is one of several signs of intelligence. It follows that if we teach youngsters to control their impulsivity, we teach them to act intelligently. Such intelligent behavior leads to greater learning and to improved interpersonal relationships.

The same can be said of anger. Youngsters who learn to deal with their own anger as well as the anger of others develop a sense of comfort and control that makes life more predictable and satisfying. Children who understand the abstractions of impulsivity, anger, and the others in this book function more successfully in school, at home, and in the community. They tend to be more self-disciplined—and self-discipline invariably leads to character.

It's safe to say that self-discipline and moral reflection were not the strong points of the two boys who introduced tragedy to Columbine High School or of the 13-year-old who shot and killed a popular teacher at the Palm Beach County Middle School. It's also safe to say that their character was questionable. Certainly, we're not claiming that the activities in this book will prevent a recurrence of such tragedies. We *are* claiming that such activities will help.

Consider recent developments. The media report that the Cincinnati Police Division has recently created a team that has the exclusive responsibility of entering schools where violence is occurring to immediately apprehend the shooters. They are to disregard everything else, even wounded children, in order to stop the shooting as quickly as possible. This is probably a good idea. In fact, several other states are exploring the program. Any intention to stop further violence is essential in a school being victimized by senseless rage.

But it's also disturbing to many of us who see schools as unlikely places for SWAT team intervention. Even a superintendent of schools in one Cincinnati district responded to the strategy by saying, "It's a sad commentary on our society when it comes to having SWAT teams storm an elementary school." We agree with him.

But it seems to have come to that. Further disturbing, however, is the fact that such an intervention strategy, no matter how necessary, responds only to the *symptoms* of the problem. Acts of overt violence are symptoms in our society that something is terribly wrong. As important as it is to deal with these symptoms, such a tendency will never solve the problem. Ask any doctor. Treat only the symptoms of a disease and the patient dies. Our job is the same as any doctor's: Relieve the symptoms—but cure the disease.

To begin to cure the disease, we have to find its causes. We are convinced that one of the causes of violence, even of cheating and vandalism in our schools, is an absence of first-class behavior, the kind of behavior that accompanies character. With that thought in mind, we offer the activities in this book to promote character development in your students and to start your school on its way to the creation of its own First Class program.

Mike Koehler and Karen Royer

CONTENTS

Section 6: Understanding and Celebrating Differences in Others / 227

SECTION 1

IN THE BEGINNING . . .

"Talent develops in quiet,
Character in the torrent of the world."
JOHANN WOLFGANG VON GOETHE

First, a Quick Story *(More of the story will unfold in succeeding sections.)*

Mundelein High School is unique among many of the nation's schools. Its superintendent, Art Newbrough, students like Bill Zasadil, and teachers like Karen Royer, are routinely challenging traditional notions of student, teacher, even administrator roles in schools. The time-sanctioned notion that "We teach, you learn" has been complemented by a "We're all in this together" philosophy that is promoting remarkable changes in their school.

They have brought collaboration to life. A recurring subject in textbooks and university classrooms and a desirable but elusive concept in many schools, collaboration among administrators, teachers, and students is alive and well at MHS. The teachers are so open to the opinions of students that many of the students feel free to suggest and develop needed changes. Consider one of their most exciting and innovative programs, one that is currently receiving national attention.

They call it their First Class program. It is student-developed and largely student-run. Interestingly, it is responsive not only to student concerns but to teacher and administrator concerns about student misbehavior. This is not to say that Mundelein High School was out of control. It simply was experiencing problems similar to other schools: occasional cheating and vandalism, class cutting, evident increases in inconsideration and swearing, and a rising disrespect for teachers and the school building.

Events during Mundelein High School's Homecoming activities crystallized many of these concerns. En route to the auditorium to watch the selection of that year's Homecoming queen, students observed that corridor floors were strewn with decorations: streamers and signs that had been hung just that morning. But it was not until they watched the announcement of the Homecoming queen that many of the students experienced their greatest disappointment.

The five candidates for the honor were sitting on stage, and each was given a bowl of chocolate ice cream. The candidates were told to start eating their ice cream and the girl who found a cherry in her bowl would be the Homecoming queen. One girl found the cherry almost immediately, and her schoolmates in the audience congratulated her with cat calls.

The reaction angered many students. What happened next angered and embarrassed many of them even more. One of the senior students conducting the program asked the queen to stand, hugged her, and placed the bowl of ice cream upside down on her head. Laughter and a few shouts of derision broke out on stage and in corners of the auditorium, and flash bulbs and cameras captured the humiliation of Mundelein High School's new Homecoming queen.

The next day the local papers contained pictures of the spectacle: five or six laughing senior boys pointing at the Homecoming queen, a bowl of ice cream on her head, chocolate dripping down her face. One angry student brought a newspaper the next day to his French class and asked his teacher what could be done to avoid such an embarrassment in the future. The conversation that followed was the first of several, both in class and out, that helped create the First Class program at MHS.

Following that initial conversation with the teacher, the students developed and circulated a questionnaire among their schoolmates to determine how many others in the school shared their concerns about the apparent lack of character that was becoming increasingly evident throughout the school. Three hundred fifty questionnaires were returned, the vast majority sharing the students' concerns.

One of these students, Bill Zasadil, was striking evidence that our nation's schools *are not* populated by more airheads than eggheads. He was a concerned and mature young man, a co-captain of the football team, and one of the most accomplished and respected students in the junior class. Like so many bright and involved students across the country, Bill and his friends were fed up with the blatant insensitivity of growing numbers of students in his school.

Again at his teacher's suggestion, Bill and his friends took the results of their questionnaire to the principal and the superintendent to discuss their findings and to determine their next steps. The superintendent suggested that Bill, his friends, Karen, and a couple of other interested teachers organize three open-forum meetings with the faculty and students to share the results of the students' questionnaire and to discuss possible solutions to their concerns. The meetings were to be held before and/or after school.

During their first meeting, one of the teachers mentioned that character education has become an issue in a few neighboring schools. He mentioned that the behavior of several students in these schools was underscoring the belief of many teachers that character development is just as important as the cognitive development of students. This emphasis on character gave the teachers and students a focus and a sense of direction.

It also provided a mission for the school. It was decided at this meeting that the school would focus on *the 3 Rs:*

- **Respect** for Self and Others
- **Respect** for How We Communicate
- **Respect** for Our Environment

Those at the meeting hoped that a focus on the 3Rs would promote first-class behavior among the students, even many of the teachers. The newly formed committee wanted the school to be a first-class place, and they realized that to change the school, they would have to change themselves and each other. "First Class" became the goal for everyone in the building. "Am I behaving in a first-class way?" became the new standard for all behavior at Mundelein High School.

They knew that such a focus was their best way to promote character development in everyone. Karen recalls how one of the students during their first meeting synthesized everyone's thoughts when she said, "Character is a container that's never full. Each of us can always develop more." It was an insightful comment and further underscored the intelligence and commitment of the students. How to establish a process that would help develop more character in all students, even many teachers, became the exclusive focus of the Steering Committee.

Index of Activities for In the Beginning . . .

Activity 1-1: Assessing Student Needs

PURPOSE: To find out what kids really need to talk about and reflect upon. First Class is like the family dinner table. There is an adult member (faculty facilitator) who, like a parent, qualifies remarks, provides historical background, and offers an adult point of view when needed. Juniors and seniors, like older siblings, do most of the talking. Freshmen and sophomores, like younger brothers and sisters, often listen a lot and once in a while offer an astounding and interesting point of view. First Class is *not* a club or an organization. No one holds an office or a grade over someone else's head. All discussions take place in a safe and secure environment where students are not afraid of being laughed at or put down for their opinions and thoughts.

MATERIALS: Worksheet 1-1; pencils

PROCEDURE:

- Divide the class into groups of three or four.
- Give each group one worksheet and one pencil.
- Have the groups complete the worksheet.
- Allow each group to share the results of its worksheet with the whole class.
- Come to consensus as a whole class on the five things the students are most proud of in their school and the five main student issues they feel need to be discussed.
- Have a student record the class consensus on a separate worksheet and send the list to the First Class steering committee for development into:
    1. ways of viewing what students are most proud of (i.e., a mural, a banner, a collage, an all-school picture, a video)
    2. activities for discussing the main student issues in your school community

Students' Names _____   **Date** _____

_____

1-1   ## Student Needs

I.   List in order of importance the five things that make you proud to be a member of your school community.

    1._____

      _____

    2._____

      _____

    3._____

      _____

    4._____

      _____

    5._____

      _____

II. In your opinion, the five main student issues that need to be addressed are:

    1._____

      _____

    2._____

      _____

    3._____

      _____

    4._____

      _____

    5._____

      _____

Activity 1-2: Identifying the Essentials

PURPOSE: To identify the essentials of good character. This activity can be fun as well as creative. It can also be quite serious, especially if a student has lost a family member or a friend. The essential question "How do you want to be remembered?" directs thinking to character education.

MATERIALS: Worksheets 1-2A, 1-2B, and 1-2C; pencils

PROCEDURE

- Read Worksheet 1-2A aloud.

- Use the discussion questions on Worksheet 1-2B. Allow students time to complete the discussion questions individually and then discuss as a whole group.

- Have students use Worksheet 1-2C to write their epitaph.

- Allow each student to share his or her epitaph with the class. (Sharing resolutions aloud with friends often makes them more binding.)

- Ask students to put their epitaphs in a place where they will see them regularly.

Identifying the Essentials:
Start with Yourself

In the book *Chicken Soup for the Soul* by Jack Canfield and Mark Victor Hansen, the words on the tomb of an Anglican Bishop in the Crypts of Westminster Abbey underscore how important it is in life to "walk the talk."

"When I was young and idealistic and my imagination had no limits, I dreamed of changing the world. As I grew, however, I discovered the world would not change. I then altered my sights and decided to changed only my country.

But it would not change.

As I grew much older I settled for changing only my family and those closest to me. It was a last desperate attempt, but they would have none of it.

Now on my deathbed, I suddenly realize: If *only I had changed myself first*, my example would have changed my family.

From their inspiration and encouragement, I would then have been able to better my country and possibly even have changed the world."

Anonymous

1-2B

Identifying the Essentials:
Discussion Questions

Complete the following questions before you begin to write your epitaph.

1. How do you want to be remembered after you die?

   _____

   _____

   _____

2. What does the expression "walk your talk" mean?

   _____

   _____

   _____

3. Think about people who walk their talk. How do you feel about them?

   _____

   _____

   _____

4. Think about people who don't walk their talk. How do you feel about them?

   _____

   _____

   _____

5. How do you feel about people who say one thing and do another?

   _____

   _____

   _____

6. How does thinking about how you want to be remembered guide you in living your daily life?

   _____

   _____

   _____

1-2C   ## Identifying the Essentials

Activity 1-3: Good Character*

PURPOSE: To help students realize that character (who you really are) is more important than reputation. To encourage students to think about the aspects of their reputation that don't match their character. This activity also helps them understand more of what the First Class initiative is aiming for. A goal of First Class is not only to know what is right, but also to do what is right, even when no one else is watching.

MATERIALS: Worksheet 1-3; pencils

PROCEDURE:

- Divide your class into groups of three. (Groups of two don't provide enough variety of opinions. Four can be more easily distracted from the focus of the activity.)
- Have each group write a definition for *reputation* and *character*.
- Have a spokesperson from each group read the group's definitions aloud.
- Appoint a student to record on the board the characteristics of each group's definition of the words.
- Read the *Random House Dictionary of the English Language* definition for each word aloud.

  REPUTATION: (1) the estimation in which a person or thing is held, especially by the community or public generally; (2) favorable repute.

  CHARACTER: (1) the aggregate of features and traits that form the apparent individual nature of some person or thing; (2) moral or ethical quality; (3) good repute.

- Hand out a copy of Worksheet 1-3 to each group.
- Instruct each group to choose a recorder to write down the group's answers on the worksheet.
- Have a spokesperson from each group share his or her group's answers to the questions with the entire class. Be sure not to force anyone to answer questions aloud.
- Wrap it up with the following "food for thought." Fitting in during high school may seem crucial, but developing what you are is more important to your future. In the long run, a person's character determines how far he or she goes in life. Dr. Steve Farrar, author of *Point Man: How a Man Can Lead a Family*, said, "Reputation is what people think you are. Character is what you are when no one is around."

*Thanks to Briana Sprague for this activity.

Students' Names _____ Date _____

1-3   # Good Character

Answer the following questions as a group. Choose one person from the group to record your answers on the worksheet.

1. How are the two words (reputation and character) alike?

   _____

   _____

   _____

   _____

2. How are they different?

   _____

   _____

   _____

   _____

3. Think about people who have a good reputation and bad character or vice versa. (Draw examples from the political world, the sports world, history, literature, the movie industry, and the corporate world.) Does your opinion of someone change when you find out he or she is really a different person from the one his or her reputation suggests? Explain.

   _____

   _____

   _____

   _____

4. How could an incorrect reputation help someone?

   _____

   _____

   _____

   _____

5. How could an incorrect reputation hurt someone?

_____

_____

_____

_____

_____

6. Do you think reputation or character is more important to teenagers? Why?

_____

_____

_____

_____

_____

7. Do you think people try to form a reputation to cover up their character?

_____

_____

_____

_____

_____

8. Are you pleased with your character right now?

_____

_____

_____

_____

_____

Activity 1-4: Good Character: What Is It?

PURPOSE: To establish the personal characteristics of a first-class individual. Kids are exposed to so many "role muddles" in today's world that their idea of what constitutes good character is also muddled. This activity will enable your students to identify character traits, to associate them with people who exemplify those traits, and then to discuss why they associated certain characters with the given character traits.

MATERIALS: 22 self-adhesive nametags that you have filled in with the names of the people on the Answer Key; Worksheet 1-4; pencils

PROCEDURE:

- Place one of the prepared nametags on the back of each participating student.

- The students will go around the room asking questions about the individual on the nametag on their backs. They may speak to the same person only if they get a "yes" response to their question. If they get a "no" response, they must move on to another person. Examples of questions to ask here:

    Am I fictional?

    Am I human?

    Am I still alive?

- As a student guesses the name of the individual on his or her nametag, place that name on the board and have the student sit down. If the students could not guess their nametag identity, the name of their individual is still placed on the board.

- Allow about 15 minutes for the activity and 10 to 15 minutes for the discussion.

- With all the characters on the board, instruct students to use Worksheet 1-4 to match the individuals now listed on the board with the personal characteristics they possess. There will be no more than three in each group.

- Conclude with a discussion of what categories the particular individuals fit into and why.

ANSWER KEY

Loyalty

Lassie
R2D2
Boy Scout

Wisdom

Albert Einstein
Alexander G. Bell

Wealth/Power

Bill Gates
Donald Trump
Ted Turner

Honesty

Judge Judy
Abraham Lincoln

Respect for Others

Mother Teresa
The Pope

Patriotism

George Washington
Franklin D. Roosevelt

Integrity

Colin Powell
Luke Skywalker

Creativity

Walt Disney
Steven Spielberg
John Lennon

Personal Responsibility

Ghandi

1-4   # Good Character: What Is It?

Loyalty   *Wisdom*   *Wealth/Power*

Honesty   **Respect for Others**   *Patriotism*

Integrity   *Creativity*   ***Personal Responsibility***

Activity 1-5: Good Character: The Next Step

PURPOSE: To identify first-class characteristics in those we know and to determine how we can become more like those individuals. This activity, a continuation of activity 1-4, enables your students to reflect upon the traits that constitute first-class character. What they need to consider is which of the character traits in the game they played will foster an environment of ethical decision making and social responsibility, and how this can be accomplished.

MATERIALS: markers or pencils; Worksheets 1-5A and 1-5B for each participating student; sheets of newspaper; glue or tape

PROCEDURE:

- Give Worksheet 1–5A and a marker or pencil to each participating student.
- In the center of the circle on the worksheet, have each student write the name of a person he or she knows personally and would consider to be a first-class individual.
- Next, have them list on the lines the characteristics of that person that qualify him or her to be considered first-class.
- While the students are working, list on the board the character traits from Worksheet 1-4. Ask students if any of their first-class individuals possess any of these character traits. List any additional character traits that their first-class individual possesses.
- Collect the worksheets.
- On the newspaper, create a collage of Worksheets 1-5A and attach with glue or tape. Display the collage of the character traits of a first-class individual. Remind students that people may not always remember everything we say, but they will remember what we do.
- Follow up with the discussion questions on Worksheet 1-5B.

1-5A   # Good Character: The Next Step

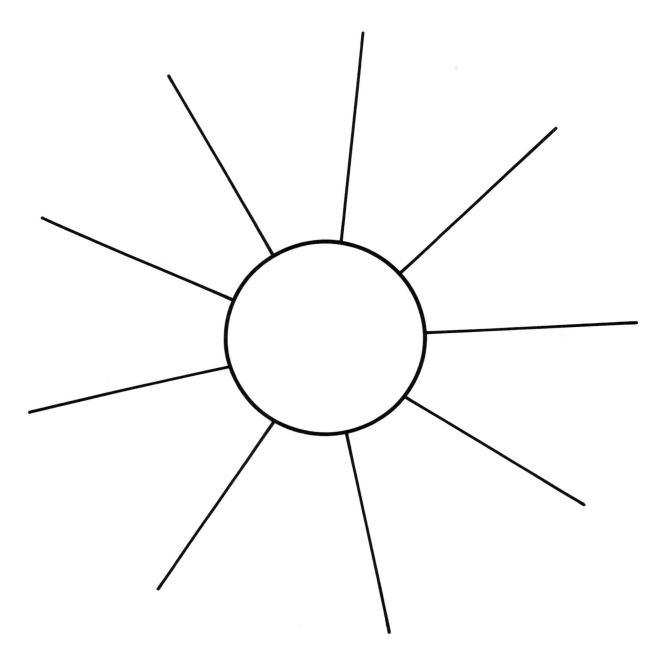

1-5B

Good Character: The Next Step
Discussion Questions

1. How do you show respect for others, specifically for the person on your worksheet?

   _____

   _____

   _____

   _____

2. How has this person changed your behavior, your values, and your life?

   _____

   _____

   _____

   _____

3. How will you know when someone respects you?

   _____

   _____

   _____

   _____

4. What specifically must you do (how must you behave) to earn someone else's respect?

   _____

   _____

   _____

   _____

5. Why do you want the respect of others?

   _____

   _____

   _____

   _____

Activity 1-6: The Facets of Good Character

PURPOSE: To highlight the facets of good character. In the world of "role muddles," students need to be encouraged to reflect upon the facets of *good character* and to focus on honing those facets. To be internalized, the behaviors we wish to promote require repetition and encouragement. Catch kids doing something good and reward it.

MATERIALS: Worksheets 1-6A, 1-6B, and 1-6C; pencils; reward passes (optional); piece of 8½ × 11-inch heavy-duty paper or card stock

PROCEDURE (At the beginning of each month):

- In groups of three, have students define the character connector of the month. (See Worksheet 1-6A.)

- Have a spokesperson for each group read the group's definition aloud to the class.

- Come to a consensus as a whole class on a complete definition for the character connector of the month.

- Have a student write or print the class definition on an 8½ × 11-inch sheet of heavy-duty paper or card stock. It is important to have a student write or print the class definition in his or her own handwriting so that students entering each classroom in the building see different student definitions of the same character word displayed in student handwriting.

- Display the definition in the classroom, allowing room for the remaining character connectors of the month to be added.

- Revisit the character connectors of the month at least two times in your advisory during the month. You could ask students for examples of the behavior they have noticed in their own lives (personal, in classes, in their studies) or in the world (TV, movies, politics).

- Ask students to share from their worksheets examples of actions they intend to take in order to develop the character connector of the month. (See Worksheet 1-6B.)

- Ask students to share examples of when they recently practiced a particular character connector. (See Worksheet 1-6C.)

- Reward the practice of first-class character connectors with reward coupons. An example is shown here.

First-Class Character Connectors of the Month

Month	*Character Connector*
SEPTEMBER	INTEGRITY
OCTOBER	HONESTY
NOVEMBER	COURTESY
DECEMBER	RESPECT
JANUARY	RESPONSIBILITY
FEBRUARY	LOYALTY
MARCH	FAIRNESS
APRIL	CARING
MAY/JUNE	COMMUNITY

Character Connectors

Complete the chart with the actions you will take to develop the first-class character connectors.

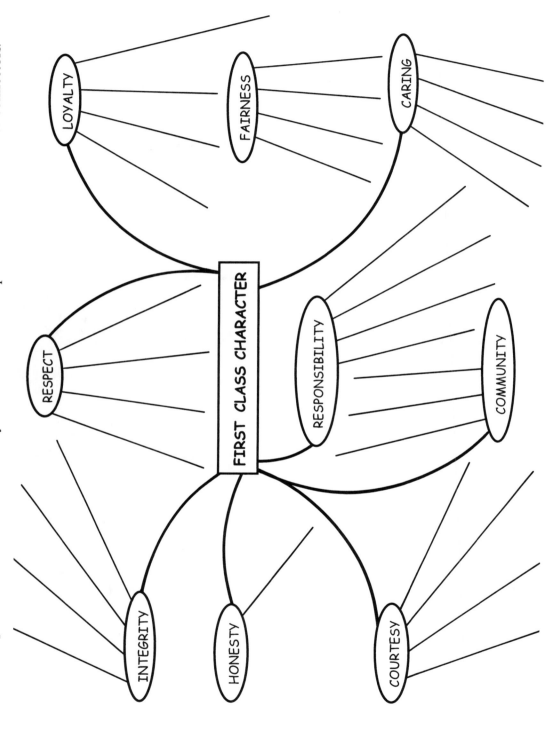

1-6C   # Good Character

1. The character trait I would like to work on developing is _____.

    The actions I will take are: The results of my actions will be:

    _____   _____

    _____   _____

    _____   _____

    _____   _____

    _____   _____

    _____   _____

2. The character trait I would like to work on developing is _____.

    The actions I will take are: The results of my actions will be:

    _____   _____

    _____   _____

    _____   _____

    _____   _____

    _____   _____

    _____   _____

Activity 1-7: The Test

PURPOSE: To encourage moral reflection. There are no easy solutions to moral dilemmas. This activity should be used in a group that has been able to establish bonds of trust among its members. Students are reluctant to share their innermost feelings with others they do not know well enough to trust. Doing the activity in small groups provides students with a safer setting to share their true thoughts and feelings.

MATERIALS: Worksheets 1-7A and 1-7B; pencils

PROCEDURE:

- Divide the class into groups of three.
- Give each group a copy of Worksheet 1-7A to read.
- Allow time for each group to discuss the dilemma and come to a consensus about the right thing to do in the situation. (See Worksheet 1-7B.)
- Have each group share its outcomes with the other groups in the class.
- After hearing the result of each group's discussion, decide as a whole class what is the right thing to do in this situation and why.
- Have a student record the right things on the board.

The Test

Jessica and Betsy had been best friends since first grade. They did everything together and knew they could always count on each other. Jess, who was already a cheerleader, had worked everyday after school for weeks with Betsy to help her get ready for tryouts. Much to the joy of both girls, Betsy made the squad. Jess also helped Betsy everyday in resource period with math, her most difficult and confusing subject.

One day Jessica caught Betsy as she was heading to her biology class for a unit test. Jess look tired and seemed panicked. she explained to Betsy that she had been up until 3:00 A.M. working on the final group project that was due for French class that morning. It had taken more time than anyone in the group had guessed or planned. As a result, Jess hadn't had time to study for the biology unit test. She asked Betsy to write down the answers to the multiple-choice test as the teacher went over the test in class and give them to her at lunch time. She explained she could memorize them during lunch and be ready for the test because her biology class was right after lunch. Betsy didn't know how to respond. Jessica was a top student and always well prepared for class. Yet, she was asking Betsy to cheat for her. Still, Jess was her best friend and had always done anything she could to help Betsy. What should Betsy do?

1-7B　　　　　**The Test: Questions and Alternatives**

TWO QUESTIONS:

1. As Betsy, was it normal to be confused in this situation? Explain your answer.

_____

_____

_____

_____

2. Jessica is just asking for help from her best friend. What do you think of this way of looking at the situation? Explain your answer.

_____

_____

_____

THE SEARCH FOR ALTERNATIVES:

As Betsy, write down the alternatives available to you. Under each alternative, write at least two consequences of that decision.

ALTERNATIVE 1: _____

_____

　　　CONSEQUENCE: _____

　　　_____

　　　CONSEQUENCE: _____

　　　_____

ALTERNATIVE 2: _____

_____

　　　CONSEQUENCE: _____

　　　_____

　　　CONSEQUENCE: _____

_____

ALTERNATIVE 3: _____

_____

    CONSEQUENCE: _____

_____

    CONSEQUENCE: _____

_____

MORE ALTERNATIVES AND CONSEQUENCES? Write them here.

_____

_____

_____

_____

_____

TWO MORE QUESTIONS:

1. Consider your principles, the core of who you are as a person, the image of who you want to be in life. within the framework of that belief system, what is the primary issue here? What belief or principle of yours is most affected?

_____

_____

_____

_____

2. Based on the above belief or principle, what is the right thing to do? Explain.

_____

_____

_____

_____

Activity 1-8: Take Your Pick

PURPOSE: To promote moral reflection and critical-thinking skills. Students need opportunities to reflect on moral issues and to make appropriate decisions about their relationships with others. This real-life experience gives them that opportunity and helps them examine their core principles. *Note:* You might want to give students the Peer Pressure Quiz in activity 5–4. Then arrange your students in groups of three based on the scores they earned on the quiz. One student in the group should have scored 10–16 points on the quiz; the second student should have scored 17–23 points, and the third student should have scored 24–30 points on the quiz.

MATERIALS: Worksheets 1-8A and 1-8B; pencils

THE PROCESS:

- Hand out one copy of Worksheet 1-8A to each group and give students time to read and discuss the worksheet.

- Hand out Worksheet 1-8B and give students time to complete it as a group.

- Have a spokesperson from each group share the results of the group's discussion with the entire class.

- Discuss the group answers as a whole class and try to determine the best answer.

Megan's Story

Megan, the president of Student Council, decided to invite Juan to the Prom. She had known him since he had arrived at school from Mexico in their freshman year. He was quiet and rather shy because his English wasn't so advanced as the English of the cousins with whom he lived. Megan found out his parents were in the United States illegally and worked at menial jobs in the community in order to support the family.

Even though Juan was shy, Megan thought he had an endearing personality. He was kind and thoughtful. He often helped her with Student Council volunteer projects even though he himself was not a member of the group. Upon occasion, he would present Megan with a flower for no apparent reason at all.

When Megan announced to her friends that she was thinking of inviting Juan to the Prom, the reaction was disturbing. Her friends wanted to know why she would do that when there were so many other great guys in their class. They said their dates probably wouldn't want to share a limo with Megan and Juan or go to dinner with them before the Prom. They told her she should do what she wanted, but they knew Megan's best friends' parents wouldn't be very interested in having Juan come to the after-Prom party at their home. They also said they didn't see how she could expect to bring him to the picnic the next day. Some of them even started gossiping about Megan behind her back.

1-8B   # TAKE YOUR PICK

As a group, consider the essential question and Alternatives A, B, C, D. Choose one person from your group who will serve as the recorder to write down at least two consequences for alternatives A, B, and C. Alternative D will be your group's own solution to Megan's dilemma and the consequences of your solution.

THE ESSENTIAL QUESTION: What would you do if you were Megan?

ALTERNATIVE A: Forget the idea of inviting Juan to Prom

    CONSEQUENCE: _____

    _____

    _____

    CONSEQUENCE: _____

    _____

    _____

ALTERNATIVE B: Find some acquaintances to go to the Prom with you who would accept Juan, even though they were not your best friends.

    CONSEQUENCE: _____

    _____

    _____

    CONSEQUENCE: _____

    _____

    _____

ALTERNATIVE C: Tell your friends you are very disappointed in them and go to the Prom with Juan as you have decided.

    CONSEQUENCE: _____

    _____

    _____

    CONSEQUENCE: _____

    _____

    _____

ALTERNATIVE D: (your suggestion): _____

_____

_____

    CONSEQUENCE: _____

    _____

    _____

    CONSEQUENCE: _____

    _____

    _____

WRAP IT UP

1. Consider your principles, the core of who you are as a person, the image of who you want to be in life. Within the framework of that belief system, what is the primary issue here? What belief or principle of yours is most affected?

    _____

    _____

    _____

    _____

2. Based on the above belief or principle, what is the best solution? Explain.

    _____

    _____

    _____

    _____

    _____

    _____

SECTION 2

STUDENT BEHAVIOR AND CHARACTER

"I have always thought the actions
of men the best interpreters of their thoughts."
JOHN LOCKE

More of the Story:

Most of the teachers and administrators at Mundelein High School acknowledge the uniqueness of the student body. They couldn't help but notice the personality and moral strength of Bill and his friends. They were also aware of the characterless behavior that was becoming increasingly evident in some corners of the building. Swearing among some students, especially the girls, was becoming disturbingly evident. Vandalism in the form of gang "tagging" was just starting, and disrespect among and between students and teachers was evident in the cafeteria and corridors, even the classrooms.

These were among the reasons why Bill and his friends were pleased to attend faculty meetings to talk to the teachers about the results of their questionnaire and to secure support from them to develop a program that responded to the students' concerns. They were additionally pleased to watch and hear the overwhelming support they received from the faculty during their first meeting. In fact, on the very next day of the first faculty meeting, the teachers nominated 100 students to serve as the student leaders for the school's 100 advisories, pledging their support to work with the leaders to present the programs.

In addition, most of the faculty responded to a survey that sought their opinions about the problems that seemed to be confronting Mundelein High School. What specific issues and topics required the attention of the Steering Committee, and what suggested activities might address these issues? Again the faculty responded enthusiastically, this time with a wide variety of topics and recommendations.

Some people suggested early in the planning stages of the program that it be turned over to the Dean of Students' office. They reasoned that if the program was concerned with student behavior, it should be under the direct control of the dean. The Steering Committee disagreed and worked hard to remind these few people, along with the rest of the faculty and administration, that the program focused on student *self*-discipline. They reminded everyone that character results only incidentally from punishment, that it is created when students learn to reflect on, evaluate, and modify their own behavior.

Most of the administration and faculty agreed with them. As a result, the program, still in concept, remained independent of the Dean's office. But a few problems persisted. Segments of the faculty resisted the program because they regarded it as another covert administrative attempt to foist more work on the staff by a "front group" of teachers and students. As such, they resisted the idea of additional responsibilities, no matter how desirable they seemed. They even aggressively criticized the Steering Committee as being dupes of the administration.

The Steering Committee redoubled their efforts to educate the students and faculty about the what and why of the program. They started with the students. During the following summer, the 100 students who had been nominated by the faculty spent three days in summer school studying conflict management and team building and preparing for their leadership responsibilities when school resumed. Much of their time was spent studying dialoguing techniques and learning to facilitate most of the activities that were being developed by the Steering Committee.

They also learned to respect and to work within the cultural behaviors of prevalent ethnic groups in the school. For example, the school enjoyed a large and growing Hispanic population. The Steering Committee recognized the importance, therefore, of familiarizing the student leaders with the Hispanic inclination to engage passively in group discussions out of respect for the others in the group. The summer training sessions, then, not only emphasized valuable leadership skills for the 100 students, but also increased their cultural awareness and appreciation of the characteristics of many of their classmates.

While the students were learning leadership skills and cultural awareness, the Steering Committee was creating activities designed to accommodate the issues and recommendations made by the respondents to the most recent faculty survey. Following the development of the activities and the training of the student leaders, the program had taken shape. The Steering Committee couldn't wait for school to start to get the program off the ground.

Their opportunity came during a faculty inservice meeting in August just before school started. The 100 recently trained students were introduced to the faculty, and a meeting of student leaders and faculty partners subsequently was held in the school's cafeteria. When the cafeteria doors opened, students and teachers alike swarmed into the cafeteria, sat together in pairs, and discussed the First Class activities and discussion strategies.

This proved to be a very powerful session, in retrospect one of the primary reasons for the program's initial success. For days afterward, teachers praised the enthusiasm, commitment, and knowledge of the student leaders. Any school interested in such a program, therefore, should carefully consider a training program for the student leaders and familiarize them with the activities in this book and the strategies needed to use them successfully.

In addition, the Steering Committee recommended that Mundelein High School:

- Review their behavioral code with the student body early in the school year. Discuss it in classrooms, advisories, homerooms, or in large-group meetings. Be sure to encourage teachers to discuss it positively with frequent explanations of the what and why behind the rules and regulations. (See Activity 2-8, *Student Evaluation of the Rules*.)

- Give all MHS students the opportunity to recognize and reward the evident character of other students. Two of the reproducibles (Figures 2-1 and 2-2) at the end of this section enable students to acknowledge the First Class behavior of another student or teacher. This is an especially effective element of the program. It not only rewards the positive behavior of one student, but it also encourages others to watch for evidence of character throughout the building. First Class behavior thus becomes an important and continuing issue throughout the school.

  Notice how the referral and the recognition reproducibles mention the specific behavior being recognized. General praise is less motivating and satisfying than specific recognition. Telling someone "Nice job" or "Thanks for the act of kindness" is less fulfilling than saying "The hard work you put in on the Home-coming float helped us get the job done on time" or "Your first-class behavior of helping Melissa Hanson pick up her books the other day when they fell out of her locker is appreciated by Melissa and everyone in the school."

- Post framed statements of First Class expectations throughout the building and refer to them periodically when discussing behavior with students.

Deerfield High School in suburban Chicago posts multiple copies of First Class expectations in every corridor, every gymnasium, the cafeteria, the auditorium, the lobbies, sporting venues, and every office and classroom in the building. Some of the students come close to memorizing the behaviors because they see them so often. Following are the behaviors posted throughout the building:

- We treat each other with dignity and respect.
- We know our audience when communicating and always use appropriate language.
- We keep our school neat and clean.
- We solve our problem creatively by stopping, thinking, and discussing our actions.
- We believe character begins with honesty, integrity, personal responsibility, and respect for others.

- We share the commitment to recognize, model, and nurture character in the school community.
- We will create an atmosphere that encourages ethical decision making and fosters social responsibility.

QUESTIONS OF MOTIVATION

While seeking psychological principles to guide the development of the program, members of the Steering Committee at MHS learned that schools and homes are blessed by an intriguing reality. The motivations of students are affected by ego and social needs that complement the needs of the home or the school. In essence, we realized that what we expect of kids regarding proper behavior is precisely what they want to do anyway. The ego needs of students, as identified by psychologist H. A. Murray decades ago, require that they:

- Accomplish something difficult.
- Overcome weaknesses.
- Put things in order.
- Ask questions in order to understand.
- Take part in sports or games.
- Experience their worlds.

Further, Murray indicated that the social needs of students require that they:

- Admire or yield to a superior.
- Work closely with people they like.
- Receive help from an ally or protector.
- Accept blame.
- Impress or amuse others.
- Be independent and free to follow impulses.
- Control or direct others.
- Help the young or the unfortunate.
- Oppose unfairness.
- Avoid or dismiss disliked persons.

These are intriguing insights, not just because they help describe the motivations of young people, but because they identify needs that are so complementary to the needs of our teachers and parents when teaching character. In essence, enlightened attempts to help students satisfy these motivational needs also helps them develop character and behave in First Class ways, yet another reason for our program of character education and the activities in this book.

To further satisfy these needs, we encourage any school interested in promoting character development to use the referral forms in Figures 2-1 and 2-2. They officially acknowledge First Class behavior and reward it. We know a school that used such forms and rewarded students by giving them a free school lunch after three such referrals, a free ticket to a special school event after four, and a $10 gift certificate after five. Schools interested in using a similar concept obviously can change the award system; the important point is to take the time to acknowledge such behavior.

Some teachers complain about the imposition of such additional responsibilities. They ask, "Who's going to fill out such forms?" "Who's going to keep track of the number of such referrals?" They say, "I don't have time for this kind of thing given the volume of my other classroom responsibilities." These are legitimate observations, but to us they were insufficient to disregard a school's willingness to catch kids being good.

The very predisposition of some teachers to think that we don't have time for this kind of thing is itself a big obstacle to helping our students develop First Class behaviors. Our Steering Committee decided to *make time* to acknowledge and reward positive behavior, just as we organize banquets, press releases, and all-school assemblies to recognize and reward academic and athletic excellence. We say this for one simple reason: *Personal excellence* is more important!

We decided to accommodate such a referral process by giving one or more teachers released time to organize and maintain the process or by having students do it. Students involved in the National Honor Society, for example, are always looking for volunteer activities to satisfy the requirements of NHS. Helping to coordinate such a referral process is a perfect fit for them as well as the school.

ASSURING THAT STUDENTS FEEL A PART OF THE PROCESS

"Catch 'em being good" is a valuable piece of advice because it helps satisfy the students' motivational needs as well as the school's organizational needs. When we satisfy motivation, we promote self-discipline in young people. Self-discipline is the essential element within any program of character education. Having said this, however, we must acknowledge the importance of external standards and reasonable consequences when such standards are violated.

Mundelein High School has a well-conceived and complete Code of Student Behavior. It contains a clear mission statement and a well-defined set of objectives. The roles of students and staff and the behaviors of students are clearly defined. Figure 2-4 contains sample pages from the school's handbook. We make no claims that these statements are the best in the business, but they do a nice job establishing the parameters of appropriate student behavior.

What is important is that schools establish such parameters by encouraging input from each of the school's constituencies: students, staff, and parents. Having developed the Code, schools can then provide activities, such as Activity 2-7, *Guidelines for Appropriate Public Behavior*, and Activity 2-8, *Student Evaluation of the Rules*, to involve everyone in the development of the standards and to help them *own* the behavioral expectations of the school.

Index of Activities for Student Behavior and Character . . .

Index of Figures for Student Behavior and Character . . .

Figure Number	Name	Description
2-1	First Class Steering Committee: Referral Form	Providing the opportunity for people in the school to acknowledge First Class behavior
2-2	Congratulations for Being First Class!	The actual form sent to the person being referred
2-3	Congratulations for Being First Class! (Sample)	A sample of how the form should be written
2-4	Mission/Vision/Beliefs	Mundelein High School's mission statement and expectations of student behavior

Activity 2-1: First Impressions

PURPOSE: To help students understand that their behavior and attitudes reflect not only upon themselves, but also upon their families, their school, and even their community. We live in an interdependent world today made smaller by telecommunication. Our actions affect those around us, and we must help students feel the responsibility that goes along with membership in a family, a school, and a community as well as the need to contribute to those groups in a positive way.

MATERIALS: Worksheets 2-1A, 2-1B, and 2-1C; a plain sheet of white paper for each student; pencils

PROCEDURE:

- Set the scene for the members of the class. Hand out Worksheets 2-1A and 2-1B. Have students imagine they are members of the Foreign Press visiting various American high schools in order to get an impression of the basic social principles of American teenagers for an article they are writing.

- Read one situation at a time from Worksheet 2-1A and allow students enough time to react to each on Worksheet 2-1B.

- Go over the worksheets with the class to see what their reactions were to the situations.

- Follow up with the discussion questions on Worksheet 2-1C. Give students time to jot down their responses to questions 1–7. Encourage students to share aloud their responses to the questions.

- Allow the class to work individually, in pairs, or in triads to complete #8 on Worksheet 2-1C. Have a "show and tell" for the students to explain their designs and then display them for all to see.

- Finish the lesson with the following quote from Australian Olympic swimmer 17-year-old Ian Thorpe:

    "I don't get a chance to rest because I'm always Ian Thorpe. No matter whether I go shopping or anything else, I always have to present myself as well as I would in an interview. It's because people see the Ian Thorpe on television and want to have that kind of relationship with him as well."

DISPLAY THIS THOUGHT FOR THE DAY:

No matter where we are, what we do, whom we interact with, we only get one chance to make a first impression. The ripples of first impressions touch our families, our school, and our community locally, and perhaps even globally.

First Impressions Situations

Imagine you are a member of the Foreign Press visiting various American high schools in order to get an impression of the basic social principles of American teenagers. Using Worksheet 2-1B, react to the following actual situations.

1. A group of senior girls, upholding an eight-year tradition, lifted their tops and bared their breasts as they drove by the high school campus.

2. Seniors caused an uproar by throwing thousands of rubber balls down the hallways and releasing dozens of mice, crickets, and other creatures.

3. Students streaked naked through the school, threatening to dunk freshmen's heads in a flushing toilet and burning letters into the campus lawn.

4. A high school was barred from conducting its graduation ceremonies in a local outdoor amphitheater after members of the graduating class cut flowers from the park's gardens, smoked cigars at the nonsmoking facility, and damaged property.

5. The members of the high school football team went out at 5:00 A.M. each morning all winter after snowstorms to shovel the driveways of senior citizens and disabled community members.

2-1B   # First Impressions Worksheet

Listen as your instructor reads the first impressions situations. Imagine you are a member of the Foreign Press visiting various American high schools in order to get an impression of the basic social principles of American teenagers for an article you are writing. Circle your reactions to these true incidents.

SITUATION 1 (Topless Tribute)

My first impressions are:	Positive	Negative
Based on my first impressions, I would tend to believe that practicing respect for self and others in this particular school is:	Taken seriously	A joke
School pride seems:	Important	Nonexistent
I would conclude that students in this school are generally:	Responsible	Irresponsible

SITUATION 2 (Creepy Critters)

My first impressions are:	Positive	Negative
Based on my first impressions, I would tend to believe that practicing respect for self and others in this particular school is:	Taken seriously	A joke
School pride seems:	Important	Nonexistent
I would conclude that students in this school are generally:	Responsible	Irresponsible

2-1B *(continued)*

SITUATION 3 (Student Streakers)

My first impressions are:	Positive	Negative
Based on my first impressions, I would tend to believe that practicing respect for self and others in this particular school is:	Taken seriously	A joke
School pride seems:	Important	Nonexistent
I would conclude that students in this school are generally:	Responsible	Irresponsible

SITUATION 4 (Egregious Graduation)

My first impressions are:	Positive	Negative
Based on my first impressions, I would tend to believe that practicing respect for self and others in this particular school is:	Taken seriously	A joke
School pride seems:	Important	Nonexistent
I would conclude that students in this school are generally:	Responsible	Irresponsible

SITUATION 5 (Team Triumph)

My first impressions are:	Positive	Negatvie
Based on my first impressions, I would tend to believe that practicing respect for self and others in this particular school is:	Taken seriously	A joke
School pride seems:	Important	Nonexistent
I would conclude that students in this school are generally:	Responsible	Irresponsible

2-1C   # First Impressions: Discussion Questions

Jot down your answers to the following questions.

1. In each situation, were the students right or wrong to do the things they did? Why?

    _____

    _____

    _____

    _____

2. Each situation was reported in a newspaper story. If you were a member of one of those high schools, how would you feel when you read the newspaper article? Why?

    _____

    _____

    _____

    _____

3. How do the ways we behave outside of school reflect upon our families, our school, and our community?

    _____

    _____

    _____

    _____

4. What is school pride?

    _____

    _____

    _____

    _____

Students' Names _____

Date _____

2-2C

Adult/Student Relationships: Discussion Questions

How do these roles affect the relationships between adults and students in this building?

1. _____

2. _____

3. _____

4. _____

5. _____

6. _____

How can teachers/adults in this building improve their relationships with students?

1. _____

2. _____

3. _____

4. _____

5. _____

6. _____

How can students improve their relationships with teachers/other adults in the building?

1. _____

2. _____

3. _____

4. _____

5. _____

6. _____

Activity 2-3: Adult/Student Relationships: Action Plan

PURPOSE: To improve adult/student relationships. This lesson can be used with both students and staff in the building. Since relationships are a two-way street and a work in progress, it's a good idea for adults to participate in the lesson also.

MATERIALS: Worksheets 2-3A and 2-3B; completed in-class consensus from Activity 2-2, *Adult/Student Relationships*; pencils

PROCEDURE:

- Ask students to sit in a circle. Then read the letter to the editor concerning the removal of the high school football coach from his job (Worksheet 2-3A). A copy can be distributed to each student.

- Use the questions to prompt discussion. Here are possible conclusions:

    1. Walk your talk.

    2. He has a great deal of respect for him.

    3. The adults in charge are sending a mixed message.

    4. Better communication.

    5. Answers will vary.

- When the discussion has concluded, give a copy of the completed in-class consensus from Activity 2-2 (Worksheet 2-2C) to each student along with a copy of Worksheet 2-3B.

- Allow enough time for the students to complete their action plans.

- Collect the action plans and keep them for Activity 2-4.

2-3A   # Adult/Student Relationships:
Action Plan—Discussion Questions

The following letter to the editor, written by James Benton, was taken from a local newspaper and concerns the removal of the high school's head football coach from his job.

"I was privileged to have had Tom as a student in my biology class back in the mid-1960s. I have never known a person with a higher sense of morality than this young man. He manifested every character then that he still possesses decades later: honesty, humility, seriousness of purpose, dedication, and a high regard for others' feelings. If I had to define 'role model' for adolescents, I could do no better than to respond with his name. Tom is the exemplification of what leadership is all about.

"If the school district wants among its faculty a teacher and coach who represents high moral and ethical standards both on and off the field, then Tom is their man. But, on the other hand, if a 'win–loss' column, parental pressure, and preparing young men for college athletics rather than for life is important, then, perhaps, the district might consider reviewing its mission."

1. In a few words, what is Tom's philosophy of life?

   _____

2. How does the teacher writing the letter feel about Tom?

   _____

   _____

3. In the last paragraph of the letter, what is the author of the letter really saying?

   _____

   _____

4. How can Tom and those involved in the controversy improve their relationships with each other?

   _____

5. How does the situation relate to First Class?

   _____

   _____

(Use the other side of this paper if you need more space to write.)

2-3B   # Adult/Student Relationships: Action Plan

The adult in the school with whom I am going to work at improving and/or changing my relationship is:

_____

This is the action I plan to take in order to improve and/or change the relationship.

A. _____

_____

_____

_____

B. _____

_____

_____

_____

C. _____

_____

_____

_____

D. _____

_____

_____

_____

Activity 2-4: Adult/Student Relationships: Action Plan Evaluation

PURPOSE: To follow-up Activity 2-3, *Adult/Student Relationships: Action Plan*. Students need to practice evaluating their own efforts. This lesson is designed to do exactly that. It also provides an opportunity to focus on responsibility, a First-Class character trait. Students need to understand they are responsible for their plans and actions. The success and/or failure of their action plan is directly proportional to the amount of effort they put into it. It is character building to experience success. It is also character building to realize that truthful self-evaluation reveals where the responsibility lies for a lack of success.

MATERIALS: Worksheet 2-3B (from Activity 2-3) previously completed by each student; Worksheets 2-4A and 2-4B; pencils

PROCEDURE:

- Return to each student his or her previously completed action from Activity 2-3.
- Give each student a copy of Worksheet 2-4A and allow the students time to complete it.
- Divide the group into triads.
- Using the discussion questions on Worksheet 2-4B as a springboard, have the students share the successes and problems of their action plans with each other.
- Based on their small-group discussions, encourage students who were dissatisfied with the results of their action plans to add a new step to their plans for changing and/or improving their relationship with the adult they have chosen.

2-4A

Adult/Student Relationships:
Action Plan Evaluation

The adult in this school I chose to work at improving and/or changing my relationship with was _____.

Evaluation

Circle the number you think best describes your achievement.

1   I set a goal. I designed an action plan. I used all of my effort to achieve my goal and I did it! I changed my relationship with the adult I chose.

2   I set a goal. I designed an action plan, but I didn't put in quite enough effort to achieve my plan. As a result, I didn't quite achieve my goal. My relationship with the adult I chose is better, but it still has a way to go in order to be really good.

3   I set a goal. I designed an action plan, but there isn't any indication that I have made any progress in changing the relationship with the adult I chose.

4   I set a goal and I designed an action plan. I knew I wasn't following my action plan and I did nothing to change the course of my lack of effort.

Reflections

Match the number of your achievement with the number of the corresponding reflection.

1   Congratulations! Working together cooperatively, showing respect for one another in the process, and taking responsibility for your actions are the most important life lessons you can learn.

2   You've made a change and that's important. Now, go back and finish what you've started! Do it right!

3   Kahlil Gibran, author of *The Prophet*, said, "You give but little when you give of your possessions. It is when you give of yourself that you truly give." Go back to your action plan and see what happens when you truly give.

4   George Eliot said, "It is never too late to be what you might have been." Rethink your action plan and be a positive participant in life. Remember the words from the Rodgers and Hammerstein song, "Nothing comes from nothing. Nothing ever could."

2-4B

Adult/Student Relationships:
Action Plan Evaluation–Discussion Questions

1. What changes have you noticed as a result of your action plan for changing and/or improving your relationship with an adult in school?

   _____

   _____

   _____

   _____

2. If your plan worked, why do you think it worked?

   _____

   _____

   _____

   _____

3. If your plan didn't work, why do you think it didn't work?

   _____

   _____

   _____

   _____

4. If you are not satisfied with the results of your action plan, what is one more step you could add that would help change or improve your relationship with the adult you have chosen?

   _____

   _____

   _____

   _____

Activity 2-5: To Be or Not to Be

PURPOSE: To establish the expectations that students have for teachers and also to examine what students *think* are teacher expectations for students. This lesson promotes dialogue between students and faculty and encourages students to look realistically at themselves.

MATERIALS: Worksheets 2-5A and 2-5B; chalkboard or large sheets of paper; pencils

PROCEDURE:

- Divide the class into small groups of three or four students.
- Give each group copies of Worksheets 2-5A and 2-5B. Have the groups choose one person to serve as recorder for the group to write down their answers.
- Allow the groups enough time to discuss and complete the worksheet.
- Return as an entire class and list on the board or on large sheets of paper the characteristics of a good student and a good teacher as determined by the small groups.
- Have the small groups share their reactions to the discussion questions with the entire class. Modify the class-generated list of criteria for a good student and a good teacher if that need becomes apparent from the large-group discussion.

Students' Names _____ Date _____

2-5A   # To Be or Not to Be

Complete the following in your small group:

Task 1:   Write 10 things you *think* teachers would say make a good student.

_____

_____

_____

_____

_____

_____

_____

_____

_____

_____

Task 2:   Write 10 things you *think* students would say make a good teacher.

_____

_____

_____

_____

_____

_____

_____

_____

_____

_____

2-5B

To Be or Not to Be:
Discussion Questions

1. How did you determine what teachers would say make a good student?

   _____

   _____

   _____

   _____

2. How did you determine what makes a good teacher?

   _____

   _____

   _____

   _____

3. What criteria should be used by students to identify a good teacher?

   _____

   _____

   _____

   _____

   _____

4. What criteria should be used by teachers to identify a good student?

   _____

   _____

   _____

   _____

   _____

Activity 2-6: It's Cool to Be First Class

PURPOSE: To reward and celebrate First Class achievement. John Cherwa, associate managing editor/sports of the *Chicago Tribune*, said it this way, "It's OK to put the cynicism button on hold every once in a while. It's OK to celebrate accomplishments." This activity is an opportunity to openly pat kids on the back for being First Class and doing good. It is an all-school party, but it is also an opportunity to continue to break down the barriers (age, race, ethnic background, interests) that divide kids into cliques. The activity rewards their appropriate behavior and does it within the confines of the school day which becomes a huge, appreciated treat for them. It allows kids to showcase their individual talents, have fun, and feel a sense of pride in their school.

MATERIALS: Advance announcements; access to stereo equipment and expertise; prizes; people to organize; microphone, emcee volunteer, music, disc jockey volunteer; judges; food appropriate for the setting

PROCEDURE:

- A committee made up of students, faculty/staff, and parents needs to work out the details and arrangements of the celebration. Check with the principal to schedule and find an appropriate place to hold an in-school activity approximately 90 minutes in length. Use posters and announcements for advanced publicity. Work out the mechanics of the music and stereo systems. Line up prizes and judges for the contests. Arrange with the school or volunteer parents for refreshments.

- The celebration consists of three parts: the Lip-synch Contest, the Dance Contest, and the All-School Dance to music with unity themes (e.g., We Are Family).

- The Lip-synch Contest is open to all faculty, staff, and students. Judging is by audience applause with prizes awarded for first, second, and third places.

- Allow 10 minutes to set up for the Dance Contest after the lip-synch contestants have been awarded their prizes. Some kind of transition activity helps (e.g., a performance by the Juggling Club).

- The 30-minute Dance Contest is open to all students, faculty, and staff in three categories: Line Dance (groups only), Polka, Cumbia.

- All contestants have numbers pinned to their backs. The judges circulate and tap those who are eliminated. The last three remaining are the winners.

- Contestants for the Lip-synch and Dance contests apply in advance so that plans can be made according to the number of applicants.

- In the time remaining for the celebration, the disc jockey invites all students, faculty, and staff to come to the dance floor and dance to music with unity themes (e.g., Dancing in the Streets, We Are Family, Everyday People).

- Refreshments are available in a designated area and staffed by volunteer parents, faculty, and staff.

Activity 2-7: Guidelines for Appropriate Public Behavior

PURPOSE: To hold certain expectations for the behavior of the entire school community in public arenas. This lesson is designed to clarify those expectations for everyone.

MATERIALS: Worksheets 2-7A, 2-7B, and 2-7C; pencils

PROCEDURE:

- Have two students role-play the assembly scenario on Worksheet 2-7A.
- Divide the group into triads.
- Hand out one copy of Worksheet 2-7B to each triad and have each group complete it.
- Discuss the questions as a whole class and come up with a class-generated list of appropriate guidelines for public behavior.
- Give a copy of the guidelines for public behavior (Worksheet 2-7C) to each student.
- Go over the guidelines to reassure students about their good use of common sense as they compare their own generated list of guidelines with the school's list of guidelines for behavior.

The Assembly Scenario

SUSIE: Hey, Andy.

ANDY: Hey, Susie.

SUSIE: Look for me at the assembly. We can talk about making plans for the weekend.

ANDY: Well, I'm supposed to sit with my First Class advisory.

SUSIE: Yeah, but you can't hear what's going on anyway. Why can't we just hang out?

ANDY: Well, you can't hear 'cause you talk. And that's just rude.

SUSIE: It's not just me. Everyone else does, too.

ANDY: Oh, so just 'cause everyone else has bad manners, that gives you permission to be a jerk, too. You know that's why I get so frustrated when we sing at assemblies. We work so hard at rehearsal for weeks and then people can't even hear us 'cause people like you make it too difficult.

SUSIE: I don't talk during concerts!

ANDY: No, 'cause you know me so you pay attention. But you talk through every Prom assembly and every Homecoming assembly, not to mention when we have guest speakers!

SUSIE: SO? I don't care about that stuff!

ANDY: But some people do. You owe your attention to everyone who works hard at whatever activity they do, or at least your silence. Sometimes I think people think they're watching TV and the performers or speakers can't hear them talk. But we can!

SUSIE: Whatever, I just talk in a low voice.

ANDY: Yeah, but when you do that, so does the guy two rows in front of you. And then three seats to the left of him. And then pretty soon whispering doesn't work. You have to talk out loud to be heard. Then more people start talking. And pretty soon, everyone feels like they have permission to do their own thing.

SUSIE: I suppose you're right.

ANDY: Of course I am. So, I'll meet you at lunch to talk about the weekend and you pay attention at the assembly. O.K.?

SUSIE: That's cool.

2-7B   # Guidelines for Appropriate Public Behavior: Discussion Questions

1. What does Susie think is the purpose of assemblies? _____

_____

_____

2. What bothered Andy about Susie's attitude? _____

_____

_____

_____

_____

3. What do you think are the most appropriate guidelines for public behavior?

_____

_____

_____

_____

_____

_____

_____

_____

_____

_____

_____

_____

_____

Guidelines to Acceptable Public Behavior at Pep Rallies, Assemblies, and Sporting Events

Assemblies are created to promote a sense of unity; a sense of "we are the school . . . we are family." To ensure everyone's right to enjoy this experience to its fullest, we have certain guidelines of conduct.

1. Students should accompany their First Class Team (with the Leader and the Teacher) to the designated area of the assembly.

2. Act with class. Many parents and community people attend these events. How you behave sends the community a direct message about our school. We want them to know what a "First Class" school and student body we have.

3. Stand up for the Pledge of Allegiance, the national anthem, and the school song. Everyone should act with respect.

4. Just as with assemblies, refrain from throwing things from the bleachers or using obscene language. Remember, everyone has a right to have a positive experience at school events.

5. Be a First Class athlete and/or fan. Win or lose, act with class.

6. Clean up after yourself. There are plenty of trash cans around the area. Have enough pride in the school MHS not to litter.

7. When you are listening to a speaker or watching a performance, it is considered rude to speak or even whisper while they are performing. Be silent until it is appropriate to laugh or applaud. Even if you want to tell your neighbor how much you are enjoying yourself, wait until an appropriate moment.

8. When you are gathering for an assembly or a performance in either the gym or the auditorium, take your seats quickly and settle down immediately when you are asked so the event can begin promptly.

9. Have fun . . . be kids, but remember to act with "class." A good rule to follow is: If you have to think about something being appropriate or not . . . do not do it! Show our community and visiting school what a "First Class" operation our school is!

Activity 2-8: Student Evaluation of the Rules

PURPOSE: To identify some guidelines by which school rules are established and evaluated. It also gives students some insight into the process of changing rules that are no longer valid or could be reevaluated. When students feel they have some control over what happens to them, they are more likely to cooperate and respect the outcomes and the process.

Because we live in a changing world, rules that encourage us to live in a productive, cooperative society must also change. This lesson is also aimed at helping students make decisions wisely in voting for rules both now and in the future by knowing what constitutes a well-designed rule.

MATERIALS: Worksheets 2-8A and 2-8B; pencils

PROCEDURE:

- Start with a couple of questions:
    1. Why do we have rules?
    2. How do you know when a rule is a good rule?
- Read the situation on Worksheet 2-8A.
- Arrange students randomly into groups of three.
- Give one Worksheet 2-8B to each group.
- Allow the groups enough time to complete the worksheet.
- Go over the worksheet and get input from each group on questions 1–4.
- Come to a consensus as a class on question 5.
- Resolve the issue in question 6. Let each group give input and allow discussion to follow.

The Rules Situation

Outerwear (multicolored jackets and caps, hooded and zippered sweatshirts) has in recent years become a way for gang members to identify each other. As a result, some schools have disallowed outerwear within the school building. In some schools, the rule states that all outerwear must immediately be removed upon entering the school building.

Styles change and fashion plays an important role at the high school level. Hooded and zippered sweatshirts have made a big fashion comeback for everyday indoor wear. In many schools, students making a fashion statement with the new trend have been asked to change clothes or have been sent home for wearing inappropriate clothing to school. Reactions from students and parents varied considerably.

Students' Names _____ Date _____

_____

2-8B   Student Evaluation of the Rules: Discussion Questions

Complete this worksheet in your small group. Select one person to serve as the recorder. Be prepared to share the answers with the entire class.

1. Is the rule from the situation well designed? Why or why not?

    _____

    _____

    _____

    _____

2. What is the reason for the rule?

    _____

    _____

    _____

    _____

3. What are the consequences of the rule?

    _____

    _____

    _____

    _____

4   Are there other ways to accomplish what this particular rule is focusing on?

    _____

    _____

    _____

    _____

5. Fill in the diagram with the most important criteria for designing a rule.

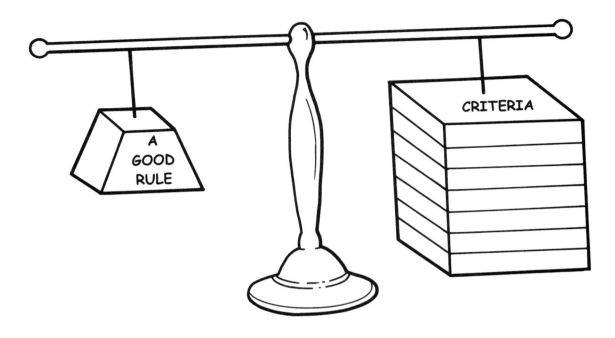

6. Based on your discussion, should the rule in question be maintained or eliminated? Why or why not?

_____

_____

_____

_____

_____

_____

_____

Activity 2-9: Feedback

PURPOSE: To keep a pulse on the First Class initiative and to give students an opportunity to supply the kind of valuable input necessary to customize the initiative to the needs and issues of the particular school community. This type of feedback also gives students a sense of ownership in the process.

MATERIALS: Worksheet 2-9

PROCEDURE:

- Give a copy of Worksheet 2-9 to each participating student.
- Allow enough time for the students to complete the worksheet individually.
- Go over the discussion questions with the entire class and come to a consensus on the main issues addressed in each question.
- Forward the class consensus to your First Class steering committee for use in developing new lessons and addressing pertinent issues in your school community.
- Here are examples of student reactions to question 1 at Mundelein High School. This particular feedback worksheet was used after First Class had been in effect for one semester.

Surroundings—the halls weren't trashed—been more clean.
Assembly—Behavior has been A LOT better, more respectful.
The year has been over-all running smoother.

I have seen less vulgar language by a larger percentage of the student population. Some people are starting to respect others better than in the past.

—assemblies—quieter, more respect.
—cleaner hallways, less garbage.
—better teacher/student relationship.
—language, small improvement.

The assemblies look a lot better. School spirit is a little better. More participation. Vandelism is less.

Better behavior at assemblies, Homecoming was a dramatic improvement. Less profanity & graffiti.

—Clean hallways
—Students' involvement

—Assemblies—behavior
—More respect between classes

The hallways, the language, and trash are better. Bathrooms are much better now.

—Assemblies
—Homecoming was positive, school spirit was good
—Profanity has decreased, but still has a way to go

I think the most improvement in our school can be seen in the assemblies. The overall attitude has improved. The students seem more cooperative and respectful to the leaders of the assembly.

Classes have been able to get along, Friendly—know each other

Student's Name _____ **Date** _____

2-9   **Feedback: Discussion Questions**

In order to help the First Class initiative continue to develop in a meaningful direction, please provide your thoughts and opinions on the following questions:

1. In what areas (surroundings, communication, etc.) have you seen the most improvements since the start of the First Class initiative?

_____

_____

_____

_____

2. What behaviors/issues next need to be addressed by First Class?

_____

_____

_____

_____

3. In your opinion, what would a visitor to our school think of it?

_____

_____

_____

_____

4. In what direction would you like to see First Class go?

_____

_____

_____

_____

(Continue on the other side of this sheet if you need more room to write.)

Figure 2-1

First Class Steering Committee:
Referral Form

Please recognize _____ for exhibiting the following
First Class behavior:

(To the referrer: Please describe the *specifics* of what actually happened.)

_____

_____

_____

_____

_____

_____

_____

Your Name: _____

Date of Referral: _____

Figure 2-2

Congratulations
for Being First Class!

_____ has notified the Steering Committee
that you are a First Class person! Congratulations! You are exactly the kind of person we
want to represent us at _____.

_____ told us what you did. We all want to
thank you for:

_____

_____

_____

_____

_____

_____

Without such generosity, consideration, and good example, our school will never
create the character we need to remain FIRST CLASS. Thanks for helping to lead the
way for the rest of us.

Figure 2-3

Congratulations
for Being First Class! (Sample)

_____ _Debby Taylor_ _____ has notified the Steering Committee that you are a First Class person! Congratulations! You are exactly the kind of person we want to represent us at _____ _Mundelein High School_ _____.

_____ _Debby_ _____ told us what you did. We all want to thank you for:

picking up her books the other day in B Hall. She told us that she

was afraid she was going to be late for class and, when she opened

her locker, all her books fell on the floor. You helped her pick them

up. It was a very thoughtful thing to do.

On behalf of Debbie and the school—thanks.

_____

_____

Without such generosity, consideration, and good example, our school will never create the character we need to remain FIRST CLASS. Thanks for helping to lead the way for the rest of us.

Figure 2-4

Section 1: Mission/Vision/Beliefs

1.01   Philosophy of MHS
The objective of Mundelein High School is to provide each student with the opportunity to secure knowledge and skills to the limits of his/her ability.

1.02   Education as a Shared Responsibility
Responsibility for education of the youth of the Mundelein community rests with all community members.

1.03   Objectives of MHS
Mundelein High School shall provide each student with many and varied experiences, both academic and nonacademic.

It is the objective of Mundelein High School to include students, staff, and community in the following goals:

1. To function effectively in society with a sound knowledge and understanding of the basic academic and nonacademic skills.
2. To work towards a mastery of English and the tools of communication, both written and oral.
3. To stimulate an awareness and appreciation of cultural heritages.
4. To help develop critical-thinking skills.
5. To develop a value system appropriate to and in promotion of a productive and responsible member of society.
6. To help understand and deal with reactions to environment and emotional development in a positive manner.
7. To help understand individual rights and restrictions of a citizen.
8. To become aware of various social, educational, and economic experiences.
9. To foster respect for individual differences and ways of providing for these differences.
10. To provide an environment that is conducive to instruction and is supportive of all individuals.

1.04   Role of Teachers, Administration, and Board of Education
The Board of Education believes that everyone who comes in contact with District 120 is an educator. The teacher is the key to quality instruction in our school. It is the responsibility of the teacher in District 120 to develop the full potential of each student.

It is the responsibility of the administration to assist the educational leaders of the community in the role as the educators of youth. It is the responsibility of the Board of Education to provide teaching materials necessary for the full realization of each student's potential.

1.05   Vision
Mundelein High School will perpetually seek and implement the most efficient and effective means to maximize student learning in an environment that promotes and celebrates the best qualities of humankind.

Figure 2-4 *(continued)*

1.06   Mission

Mundelein High School—"Committed to Excellence"—Where respect for academics, diversity, and social responsibility promotes active learning and self-worth in partnership with our community.

1.07   Beliefs

We believe that learners succeed in a community that:

- considers students first;
- embraces learner-centered principles;
- creates opportunities to insure and recognize individual student and staff success;
- promotes, respects, and celebrates acceptance, caring, communication, contributions, diversity, individuality, responsibility, self/others and our surroundings;
- fosters creativity, innovation, risk-taking, critical thinking, and life-long learning skills;
- maintains high expectations;
- makes ongoing personal, program, and school improvement decisions based on mission, vision, beliefs, research, data, and reflections;
- values all voices and embraces collaboration;
- practices servant/constructivist leadership; and
- maximizes opportunities and available resources.

1.08   Board of Education Statement Concerning Student Learning

The Board of Education of Mundelein Consolidated High School District 120 considers goal-setting a vital part of charting the course for the future of our school district. Goal-setting is the way in which the important social principles and beliefs are translated into every teacher's classroom. For that reason, goal-setting should be embraced by all members of the school community—teachers, parents, administrators, students, and members of the board of education.

As a Board of Education, we have determined goals for our school district predicated on a set of beliefs about the nature of effective organizations and our knowledge about student learning. We wish to share with you the goals and the important beliefs upon which these goals were formulated.

- We believe that effective schools hold high expectations for students and are staffed by highly motivated teachers in a warm and caring environment.
- We believe that student success is our goal and that schools control the conditions of success. Additionally, success must be recognized and celebrated whenever possible.
- We believe that creative, innovative teaching should be supported and that risk-taking is an important ingredient in successful student learning.
- We believe that teachers, students, and parents should have a strong voice in the work of the school.
- We believe that schools should offer a rich curriculum for all students in which student outcomes are paramount and in which student learning is assessed by many indicators.
- We believe that school should be a fun place for students and staff to work and learn.

Figure 2-4 *(continued)*

Section 2: Behavior

2.01 Behavior Expectations

Students by their very nature are guaranteed certain individual rights as members of the Mundelein High School student body. Implicit in these rights is a belief that every member of the school community, including the student, has the responsibility to promote regular attendance and maintain orderly conduct. All students are entitled to enjoy freedom from fear of insult or injury. Students will have maximum opportunities for learning.

Students have a voice in the governance of the educational system at Mundelein High School. They have substantial influence on the topics they study, the learning materials, the learning process, and the learning environment at our school. Thus, each student is expected to:

- Respect fellow students, teachers, rules, and regulations.
- Communicate with others to help unite the school.
- Eliminate the use of violence as an answer to problems.
- Demonstrate respect for the school campus.
- Support the school's activities and organizations.
- Display good sportsmanship and school spirit at all times.
- Refrain from slanderous remarks and obscenities.
- Refrain from behavior that disrupts the educational process.
- Dress in a manner that meets reasonable standards of health, cleanliness, and safety.
- Be punctual and present in the regular or assigned school program.

The success of the school year depends on all of us. The student body, teachers, administration, and parents must work together to develop the best educational program at Mundelein High School. Students attending any district-sponsored function either at home or away are covered by and shall abide by the school rules and regulations stated in *The Pathfinder*. In order to maintain and enforce the rules and regulations governing the student body, violations of the rules and regulations have been grouped into categories.

The Deans have discretionary powers in handling disciplinary violations.

SECTION 3

INTEGRATING SOCIAL PRINCIPLES

*"Morality is not really the doctrine of how
to make ourselves happy,
but of how we are* worthy *of happiness."*
IMMANUEL KANT

More of the Story:

The Steering Committee recognized from the start that character education misses the target if it fails to provide activities that promote social principles. This was a challenge for most of us. Morality is a touchy issue in some communities. It was no different in ours. We asked ourselves several important questions. What topics would we cover? How would we cover them? Would we even attempt to include sensitive issues? How would we handle such issues? How would we identify and select them? What levels of parent involvement would we seek?

Our struggles must have been evident to Superintendent Newbrough; he had gone through a similar situation a few years earlier when he helped implement a First Class program in his former school. He suggested that we invite several students and teachers from that school to discuss how they handled sensitive issues and to identify the materials and processes they used to implement them. Inevitably, we talked about their entire experience. The dialogue was very helpful.

We explored a range of issues and uncovered some disturbing but fascinating information. During a coffee break, Karen and Bill had a very revealing conversation with a visiting counselor. His comments were disturbing. He told them that he had met a couple weeks earlier with three students who represented many of his concerns. One boy was referred for cheating, another for fighting, the third, a girl, for passing a sexually explicit note in the library.

The parents of the first two students gave permission to the counselor to work with their children, but never seemed able to "break away" to meet with him. He said that he met each set of parents only once, although he had scheduled them for at least five meetings. The parents of the girl expressed genuine concern about their daughter's behavior and met regularly with him, but spent most of each meeting lamenting, "We just don't know what to do with her."

Said the counselor: "What the devil can I do when so many parents are clueless about their kids—or so unavailable to help me help them." Then he said something that renewed Karen and Bill's sense of urgency about the need for a character education program. "Do you know what's happening with a lot of kids today? Movies, TV, and God knows what else have pushed them beyond *im*morality to *a*morality."

The student who was referred for cheating, he said, was more concerned with being caught than with doing something wrong. The boy even mentioned a prominent athlete during the conversation with the counselor. The second boy failed to see any significance in others apart from his own needs. He was more concerned with a possible suspension than with the pain he inflicted on others. According to the counselor, the girl just didn't see any sense in saying no. "That's no fun," she said.

When Karen and Bill returned to the meeting, they mentioned the conversation and suggested that morality is a critical, if sensitive, issue and that the committee should consider it. Everyone agreed. One teacher even said to the counselor, "Right on, Fred, I was just saying to my husband last night that actors and actresses used to play parts; now they *reveal* them!"

One of the coaches in the group added: "Right! And look at pro sports. A lot of basketball players are teaching kids that it's good to be bad. Even news about upstanding athletes is taking a back seat to bar fighters, trash talkers, and cross dressers!"

The core of American principles is very uncomplicated. Our Steering Committee agreed immediately on several of them: basic consideration, honesty, respect for self, fairness, reverence for life, integrity, mutual cooperation, loyalty, respect for others, hard work. Such principles constitute the framework for all relationships: student/teacher, student/student, student/parent, even stranger/stranger. It is such character-building qualities that we decided to emphasize and that are highlighted in this section.

Index of Activities for Integrating Social Principles

Activity 3-1: Let's Talk Social Principles

PURPOSE: To introduce students to the subject of principles and to help them identify their own important principles.

MATERIALS: Worksheet 3-1; pencils

PROCEDURE

- Start the class by discussing the subject of social principles.

    1. What does the word "principle" suggest to you?

    2. What are principles and why are they important in our lives?

    3. How do they relate to our sense of success?

    4. Do you suppose they ever change?

- Distribute the worksheet and have students work on it individually. Tell them to take some time and think about their principles. This aspect of the whole question of principles will lay the foundation for future discussions.

- Depending on the amount of time it takes to complete this activity in class, think about using this activity in conjunction with Activity 3-2, *Hometalk*. That way, the kids will have something substantive to refer to.

3-1   # Let's Talk Social Principles

What Are Principles?

Principles are targets for our behavior, personal goals that give our lives a sense of direction. They are very important to us because they give us a sense of how successful we are. If we realize our principles, we feel successful; to the degree that we don't realize them, we feel less successful.

Can Principles Change?

Sure they can. In fact, they change all the time. As we mature and understand more of life, our goals and principles change. Sometimes, as we develop the ability to look deep inside ourselves, we discover that we have different interests and that we tend to look at people differently. At such times, our focus is less on ourselves and more on others. We frequently discover that self-improvement relates less to what we *have* and more to what we *are*. As these principles change, they remain very important to us.

What Are Some Examples?

Following is an incomplete list of several social principles. Look it over and use it as needed to identify your five most important principles. Use the list or add to it to determine what is important to you in life, then write your five most important principles on the spaces provided. Be honest. No one is going to judge you or criticize your choices. These five principles are yours and represent what you want to be in life.

Honesty	Power	Fame	Courtesy
Wealth	Possessions	Justice	Consideration
Family	Courage	Status	Wisdom
Freedom	Friendship	Competition	Helping others
Charity	Faith	Honor	Hospitality
Hard work	Morality	Respect for self	Respect for others

Think about it. There are others. What is important to you in life? Recognizing that the list can change as you mature, list your five most important principles as of now:

_____

_____

_____

_____

_____

Hang on to this sheet. You'll need it at home and later on in class. If you change your mind or think of others within the next day or two, feel free to change the sheet.

Activity 3-2: Hometalk

PURPOSE: To promote discussion at home about family principles.

MATERIALS: Worksheet 3-1 from previous activity; Worksheet 3-2; pencils

PROCEDURE:

- Instruct students to take their completed Worksheet 3-1 home to share with their parents.
- Tell them also to take home a copy of Worksheet 3-2 and to discuss them over dinner or at some other time, but before they resume their discussions of principles at school.
- Tell the students to have their parents sign Worksheet 3-2.
- Remind students to have the worksheet with them when the class is next scheduled to discuss principles. You might have them return it right away and store it in class until the next discussion.

3-2   # Hometalk

Dear Parents:

   Our class is discussing social principles. Your child has been asked to identify the principles that are currently most important in his or her life and to discuss with you the principles that are most important to your family. Please take a moment some time today (the dinner table is always a good place!) to discuss the questions on this sheet. Thanks for doing this. We're sure that you and your child will enjoy and benefit from the experience.

Suggestions:

- You might review the following list of principles. It is not exhaustive, but it will help to get you started. Select from the list or add to it to identify the five most important principles within your family.

Honesty	Power	Fame	Courtesy
Wealth	Possessions	Justice	Consideration
Family	Courage	Status	Wisdom
Freedom	Friendship	Competition	Helping others
Charity	Faith	Honor	Hospitality
Hard work	Morality	Respect for self	Respect for others

- What is important to your family and what principles do you try to promote within your child(ren)?
- It's fun and sometimes very revealing to make your own list, then have your child(ren) tell you what they think the family's principles are. Then compare the two lists.

Our family's principles are:

_____

_____

_____

_____

_____

Thanks for taking the time to do this. Please sign the form and be sure your child returns it to school. It will be important in class discussions.

                 Parent signature: _____

Activity 3-3: Principles to Build On

PURPOSE: To identify and discuss the principles that lead to character and to satisfying interpersonal relationships.

MATERIALS: Worksheet 3-3; pencils

PROCEDURE:

- Organize the class into groups of three or four.
- Distribute one worksheet to each group and tell them to work together to answer all the questions.
- Give groups enough time to discuss each item in detail.
- Identify a spokesperson for each group and have these students share their answers with the rest of the class.
- Discuss each question as a class and try to reach a consensus.
- Finally, discuss each general question found on the worksheet to summarize the activity.

3-3   Principles to Build On: Discussion Questions

Review the list of principles, then read each of the following questions and answer and discuss them in your groups.

Honesty	Power	Fame	Courtesy
Wealth	Possessions	Justice	Consideration
Family	Courage	Status	Wisdom
Freedom	Friendship	Competition	Helping others
Charity	Faith	Honor	Hospitality
Hard work	Morality	Respect for self	Respect for others

Specific Questions:

1. Consider one person who values honesty, another who values money.
   - Which of the two is more likely to drive a Lexus? Why?
   - Which of the two is more likely to steal? Why?
   - Might the person who values honesty ever drive a Lexus? Why?
   - Make a list of possible professions each might enter.

2. Consider one person who values consideration, another who values power.
   - Which of the two is more likely to cut you off while driving his or her car? Why?
   - Which of the two is more likely to be president of the senior class? Why?
   - Explain why both are important when being a parent.
   - Make a list of professions in which *both* are important.

3. Consider one person who values respect for self, another who values status.
   - Which of the two is likely to have a child out of wedlock? Why?
   - Which of the two is more likely to yield to peer pressure? Why?
   - Which of the two is more likely to try to cheat on the ACT? Why?

4. Consider one person who values wisdom, another who values status.
   - Which of the two is more likely to be interested in getting an A than in gaining understanding and knowledge? Why?
   - In what circumstances is valuing status better than valuing wisdom?
   - In what circumstances is valuing wisdom better than valuing status?

3-3 *(continued)*

General Questions: Take a few moments to answer each of the following general questions. We will discuss them as a class when each group is ready.

1. One set of principles may not be *better* than another, but are some more *important* than others for building personal and social relationships? Explain your answer.

   _____

   _____

   _____

   _____

2. We've indicated often that the realization of your principles helps determine how successful you feel in life. Exactly what does that mean?

   _____

   _____

   _____

   _____

3. In that regard, how do your principles relate to your self-concept, to how you feel about yourself as a person?

   _____

   _____

   _____

   _____

4. Similarly, how do your principles relate to how *others* feel about you as a person?

   _____

   _____

   _____

   _____

5. How do life's experiences and growing up relate to our principles?

   _____

   _____

   _____

   _____

Activity 3-4: Build a Foundation

PURPOSE: To explore foundational principles.

MATERIALS: Worksheets 3-4A and 3-4B; pencils

PROCEDURE:

- Set the stage by discussing principles generally:
  - In what ways are principles the same? In what ways are they different?
  - Politicians and others are talking a lot about "family values and principles." What are they?
  - Why are family principles so important to our society?
  - Do family principles require a "family" to promote them?
- Relate the concept of family principles to the idea of foundational principles, those principles that support us personally through life and that promote social harmony.
- Distribute Worksheet 3-4A that asks students to identify the four foundational principles that are most important to them individually.
- Next, put them into groups of three or four and have each group complete Worksheet 3-4B.
- After 15 to 20 minutes, ask each group to share its four principles and try to achieve consensus as a class. What four principles are most important to all of us? Can we agree on four?
- You may or may not be able to get agreement, but you and the class will identify several recurring principles. Discuss these by asking, "Why do you suppose this/these principle(s) are mentioned so often by each group?" "Exactly what is it about this principle that is so important to us individually and collectively?"
- The class may not achieve complete agreement on four principles. That's to be expected. What's important, however, is the thought process the students experience and their introduction to a different way of looking at principles.

3-4A   # Build a Foundation

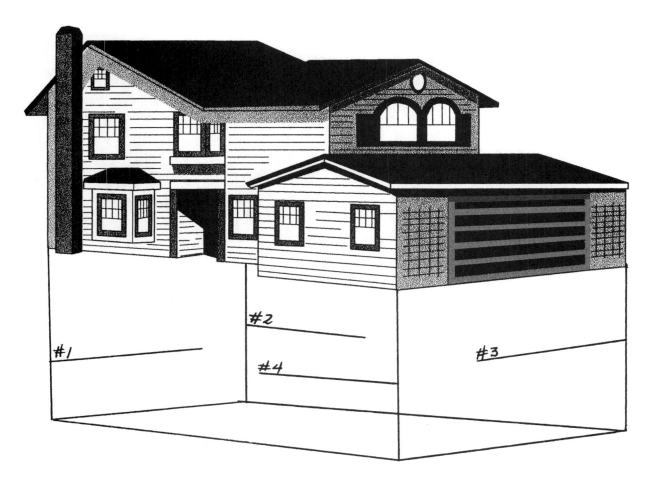

Think carefully about the four principles that are most important to you, the principles you will need to build a solid foundation for the rest of your life. Write those principles on the four spaces of the foundation. Remember, you already have the money to build your house. What you need is a solid foundation so the house will be strong and will meet your needs as you go through life.

Select your principles carefully. You will be asked to share your reasons for them in a group discussion. You might want to write your reasons on the other side of this sheet to be sure you remember them.

Students' Names _____   Date _____

_____

3-4B   **Build a Foundation**

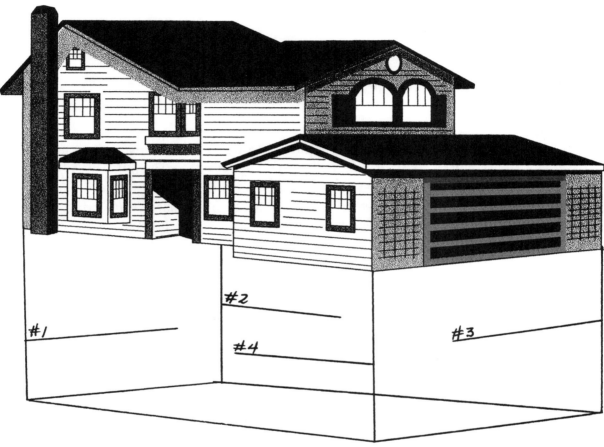

As a group, try to determine your four most important foundational principles. What are the four that will enable you to build a solid foundation for the rest of your life? Write them in the spaces provided on the foundation. Be sure to jot down the reasons for your choices. We will be discussing each group's selections in order to try to determine the four most important principles for the entire class.

Activity 3-5: When You Look at My Principles

PURPOSE: To explore how others perceive and react to our principles.

MATERIALS:
Worksheet 3-5; cut-up principle cards; pencils

PROCEDURE:

- Cut the sheets of principles into individual cards and place them face down on a table or desk. Have each student take one card. That tag will represent his or her principle during the activity.

- Introduce the activity by informing the class that certain principles are not received equally well by other people. Some people may like your principles; others may dislike them. Obviously, you express your principles through your behavior, and it's likely that some people will dislike you because of these behaviors.

- Continue the activity by having each student attach the card to his or her clothing. (Pin it to a shirt or paper clip it to a shirt pocket.)

- Then instruct everyone in class to get up and walk randomly around the room. Tell them to look at each other's principles and to respond to them nonverbally.

- Have them respond to a principle they dislike by frowning at it, showing a thumb down, or shaking their head. They can respond to principles they like by showing a thumb up, smiling, or nodding approvingly. They can smile mockingly at principles that seem silly or extreme. In fact, they can make faces or any appropriate gestures to any of the principles they see.

- After 5 to 10 minutes of circulating within the classroom, have them sit down. Distribute Worksheet 3-5 and have students complete the first half individually. Put them into groups of three or four to complete the second half.

- Give them 15 or 20 minutes to complete it, then discuss their answers as a class.

HONESTY	**WEALTH**
CHARITY	**POWER**
POWER	**POSSESSIONS**
FAME	**STATUS**
WISDOM	**HONOR**

HELPING OTHERS	**COMPETITION**
MORALITY	**HARD WORK**
CONSIDERATION	**COURAGE**
HONESTY	**WEALTH**
CHARITY	**POWER**

POSSESSIONS	**FAME**
STATUS	**WISDOM**
HONOR	**HELPING OTHERS**
COMPETITION	**MORALITY**
HARD WORK	**CONSIDERATION**

When You Look at My Principles

Individual Reflection

Directions: Answer this set of questions individually.

Your principle was: _____

1. How did most people react to your principle, positively or negatively?

   _____

   _____

2. Why do you suppose they reacted this way?

   _____

   _____

3. How did you feel when you observed their reactions?

   _____

   _____

4. Based on their reactions, what do you now think of that particular principle? Why do you think that?

   _____

   _____

Group Dialogue

Directions: Try for group consensus when answering these questions.

1. Are all principles equally acceptable? Defend your position.

   _____

   _____

   _____

2. Defend or attack the position that some principles are more effective than others when it comes to establishing positive relationships with others and/or helping society generally.

   _____

   _____

   _____

3. As parents, which principles will you emphasize with your children? Why?

   _____

   _____

Activity 3-6: To Know or Not to Know

PURPOSE: To help students understand that cheating is *not* a first-class character trait. This activity enables students to understand that while they get immediate help from cheating, they will be hurt in the long run and will regret the action. How we behave is directly linked to personal punishment and reward, the rules and perceptions of others, and a personal code of conduct. Therefore, the way we question behavior is directly proportional to the level of our moral development.

MATERIALS: Worksheets 3-6A and 3-6B; pencils

PROCEDURE:

- *Do not* tell the class about the lesson.
- Administer the quiz on Worksheet 3-6A for each student to take individually. It consists of academic questions. Watch to see if anyone cheats on it, but don't name names or identify the student(s).
- Collect the quizzes when the students have finished taking them.
- Explain that cheating is *not* a First Class character trait. Say the following to your students: "If you cheated on this quiz, I want you to take some time to reflect on this statement. Cheating may bring you immediate help, but in the long run it will hurt you."
- After an appropriate pause for reflection, explain that the quiz was not real. Its purpose was to discuss cheating and why people do it.
- Next, randomly divide the class into groups of three.
- Give one copy of Worksheet 3-6B to each group.
- Have each group choose a recorder to write his or her group's answers to the discussion questions.
- When the small groups have finished their discussions, ask a spokesperson from each group to share his or her group's answers with the whole class.
- Make a class list (on the board, on poster board, on big paper) of the long-term and short-term effects of cheating.

ANSWER KEY: Here are the answers to the quiz on Worksheet 3-6A.

1. Thomas Jefferson
2. The mathematical theorem credited to Pythagoras for having formulated the first geometrical proof that in any right-angled triangle, the square on the hypotenuse is equivalent to the sum of the squares on the other two sides.

3. Paris

4. Signatures on the Declaration of Independence include those of John Hancock, Josiah Bartlett, Matthew Thornton, William Whipple, Samuel Adams, John Adams, Robert Treat Paine, Elbridge Gerry, Stephen Hopkins, William Ellert, Roger Sherman, William Williams, Samuel Huntington, Oliver Wolcott, William Floyd, Phillip Livingston, Francis Lewis, Lewis Morris, Richard Stockton, Jonathan Witherspoon, Francis Hopkinson, John Hart, Abraham Clark, Robert Morris, Benjamin Rush, Benjamin Franklin, John Morton, George Clymer, James Smith, George Taylor, James Wilson, George Ross, Caesar Rodney, George Read, Thomas McKean, Samuel Chase, William Paca, Thomas Stone, Charles Carroll, George Wythe, Richard Henry Lee, Thomas Jefferson, Benjamin Harrison, Thomas Nelson, Jr., Francis Lightfoot Lee, Carter Braxton, William Hooper, Joseph Hewes, John Penn, Edward Rutledge, Thomas Heyward, Jr., Thomas Lynch, Jr., Arthur Middleton, Button Gwinnett, Lyman Hall, George Walton

5. Solid, liquid, gas

6. Jonathan Swift

7. District of Columbia

8. Monet, Renoir, Degas, Rodin

9. Leonardo da Vinci (1452–1519) was a Florentine artist and engineer. One of his most famous creations is the *Mona Lisa*, located in The Louvre in Paris.

10. Secretary of State during the Clinton administration

3-6A

To Know or Not to Know: Quiz

1. Who was the third president of the United States?

   _____

2. What is the Pythagorean Theorem?

   _____

   _____

3. What European city is known as the city of light?

   _____

4. Name three people who signed the Declaration of Independence.

   _____

   _____

5. Name three states of matter.

   _____

6. Who wrote *Gulliver's Travels*?

   _____

7. What does D.C. stand for in Washington, D.C.?

   _____

8. Name three artists from the Impressionist period.

   _____

9. Why is Leonardo da Vinci famous?

   _____

10. Who is Madeleine Albright?

    _____

3-6B   # To Know or Not to Know: Discussion Questions

Complete the following discussion questions in your group. Choose one person who will serve as the recorder to write your group's answers. Be prepared to share your answers with the other groups.

1. What's wrong with cheating?

_____

_____

_____

2. Is it unfair?

_____

_____

_____

3. Is anyone hurt by it?

_____

_____

_____

4. Does it make a difference if you know that you won't get caught? Why or why not?

_____

_____

_____

_____

5. Is it wrong if someone cheats off of you?

_____

_____

_____

6. What is the relationship between cheating and who you are as a person?

_____

_____

_____

_____

_____

_____

7. What do you think are the short-term effects of cheating?

_____

_____

_____

_____

_____

_____

8. What do you think are the long-term effects of cheating?

_____

_____

_____

_____

_____

_____

Activity 3-7: We're in This Together: A Look at Love and Marriage

PURPOSE: To explore the essential qualities needed in a marriage partner.

MATERIALS: Worksheets 3-7A and 3-7B; pencils; paper

Note: If you think students might be embarrassed by standing in front of the class for this activity, simply mention each decision point consecutively and tell the class to think about each and to write their reactions. Follow the rest of the activity as indicated.

PROCEDURE:

- Set the stage by indicating to the students that principles influence our qualities as persons. What we value is what we *are*—and what we *are* is evident in our *behavior*. Discuss this concept as needed.

- Distribute Worksheet 3-7A.

- Select a boy and a girl from the class, and tell them to stand on one side of the room in the back. Tell them: "You are about to be the audio-visual part of this activity."

- Tell the two students and everyone else in class to identify from the list of qualities the five most important things they look for in someone to date. "You're going out this weekend, and you want the perfect date. What are you looking for?" Tell them to add to the list as needed.

- Give everyone time to write down their five qualities, then tell the two students to start walking toward the front of the room.

- After they take two or three steps, tell them to STOP! Now say, "The date was wonderful! In fact, the next couple of years were great! Or maybe they weren't so great and you found someone else, but now you're planning to get married. Look at the list of qualities and identify the five most important things you want in a marriage partner. List them on a sheet of paper."

- Give everyone time to write down the qualities, then tell the two students to resume their walk toward the front of the room. After two or three steps, again say, "STOP! You're married and you just discovered that you're about to have a baby. List the qualities you'll want in your marriage partner."

- Again, give everyone time to write. Then tell the students to resume their walk.

- After two or three steps, say, "STOP! Now you want to buy a house, one of those big beauties in a nice suburb. List the qualities you now want in your marriage partner."

- Again, have them walk, stop, and this time respond to "The two of you are now raising teenagers—and I think you know what teenagers can be like! List the five most important things you'll want in your marriage partner."

- Finally, after they take two or three steps and stop the last time, tell them, "Now, one of you has to care for an elderly parent. What qualities do you want in your marriage partner?"

- Next, distribute Worksheet 3-7B.

  - Tell the class, "Review your responses to each situation and take several minutes to answer the questions. Think about them carefully. We're going to discuss them as a class."

  - Finally, discuss the questions. As you identify disparities in the qualities they seek in a date and in a marriage partner, discuss them. Ask students to elaborate on their answers, seeking further insights in what they look for. Probe their answers for deeper meanings. Conclude the activity by asking, "What is it about marriage that makes it different from dating, that makes it more important than dating?"

We're in This Together: Personal Qualities

Loyal

Hard-working

Sexy

Patient

Fun-loving

Intelligent, educated

Physically attractive

Good sense of humor

Considerate, caring

Wealthy

Level-headed

Popular

Sensitive

Athletic

Communicative

Lots of interests

Any others you can think of

Student's Name _____   **Date** _____

3-7B   # We're in This Together: General Questions

1. What were the five most important qualities you needed throughout all the situations to guarantee a good marriage?

_____

_____

_____

_____

_____

2. Based on these qualities, how would you define "a good marriage"?

_____

_____

_____

_____

3. Defend and/or attack the statement: "The qualities you looked for in a dating partner were less important in a marriage partner."

_____

_____

_____

_____

_____

Activity 3-8: Love and Marriage

PURPOSE: To help students understand that love and marriage are not Hollywood productions, but are extensions of the tenets of First-Class, respect for self and others, and respect for how we communicate. The ingredients for a successful marriage—love, respect, pervasive caring, and commitment—are principles that don't just happen. They need to be nourished with thoughtful reflection and concentrated effort if they are to survive and thrive.

MATERIALS: Worksheets 3-8A and 3-8B; pencils

PROCEDURE:

- Divide the class into groups of three.
- Read (or have someone read) aloud the passage on Worksheet 3-8A.
- Give one copy Worksheet 3-8B to each group.
- Instruct each group to select a recorder who will write the group's answers to the questions on the worksheet.
- Allow the groups enough time to complete Worksheet 3-8B.
- Use the worksheet questions to prompt a discussion by asking each group to share their answers.
- As a class, come to a consensus on the most important qualities in a successful marriage (question 4 on Worksheet 3-8B) and rank them in order of importance.

I Do

Pat and her family moved into the neighborhood when she was in high school. She wasn't sure she was going to like this new town and neighborhood. Walking to school that very first day she met the boy down the street who winked at her and said, "Hi, I'm Gayle. I know you're new here. Come on, I'll introduce you around." Pat couldn't help immediately liking his friendly and outgoing personality. And that was the beginning.

They dated in high school, but went to different colleges. She was an art major and he, a chemistry major. They wrote often and saw each other during vacations. People couldn't help noticing how in-tune they were with each other and how much fun they always seemed to have together. They married soon after college. Gayle worked as a chemist for a large corporation and Pat took a job in the city. Life was good. Life became even better after their first daughter was born, followed four years later by their second daughter. Time flew by as they raised their family, worked, and enjoyed their time together with their children, families, and friends.

Pat and Gayle were amazed when they realized that they had worked long enough and hard enough to be able to retire to their dream retreat. Their daughters were grown and married and had provided Pat and Gayle with adored and adoring grandchildren. The retirement home on the bay surrounded by an entirely new group of friends attracted by their warm, generous, and outgoing personalities was a dream come true.

Rheumatoid arthritis was a disease that ran in Pat's family, and although she had known for years that she had it, she never allowed it to impinge on her active life filled with friends and family. As Pat and Gayle approached their 45th wedding anniversary, it became evident that the arthritis would no longer stay at bay and knee replacements would be necessary. Pat came through without a complaint and worked hard at rehabilitation. Gayle was always there, encouraging, helping with the rehab, teasing in his endearing way, and telling her how proud he was of her effort and courage.

Two years later, elbow replacement was necessary. Again the rehab, but it took longer. Gayle was ever present and supportive. He laughed about learning to cook at age 77. He explained that Pat and he were a formidable team in the kitchen. She gave the cooking instructions and he carried them out. They impressed everyone with the wonderful dinners they whipped up to entertain their friends. Their home was and continued to be the social center of their very happy and loving universe.

Next, one of Pat's artificial elbows became infected, and before the doctors realized what was happening, Pat became very seriously ill and spent weeks in the hospital fighting for her life. She lived, but she lost the use of her arms and legs. She also lost the ability to put words together to form thoughts and sentences.

Gayle couldn't wait to bring her home where he could take care of her himself. Even though he is 83 now, he feeds her, bathes her, dresses her, and takes her for walks in her wheelchair daily, while he tells her how fortunate he feels to be able to continue his life with her. They communicate now as beautifully as they always have. Gayle uses words and actions while Pat communicates with her eyes, and every once in a while, the three words "I love you" come as if by magic. Gayle and Pat's mutual love, respect, caring, and commitment continue to sustain and support them after 55 years of marriage, serving as an inspiration to all those whose lives they have touched.

3-8B   # Love and Marriage

Select one member of your group to serve as the recorder to write your group's answers to the following questions.

1. What is the difference between being "in love" and being "in lust"?

    _____

    _____

    _____

    _____

    _____

2. Ralph Fiennes, esteemed actor known for his roles in *The English Patient* and *Schindler's List*, stated in a newspaper interview that he believes success in marriage is about being able to extend love. Not, he said, in the big capital-letter sense of the word, but in an everyday way. Little by little, task by task, gesture by gesture, word by word. Do you agree or disagree with his point of view? Why or why not?

    _____

    _____

    _____

    _____

    _____

3. In the book *The Little Prince* by Antoine de Saint Exupery, the fox reveals an important secret to the Little Prince. He says that we only see well with our hearts because what is essential is invisible to the eyes. (a.) How does his statement relate to love and marriage? (b.) Do you agree or disagree with this opinion? Briefly explain your answer.

    _____

    _____

    _____

    _____

    _____

4. In your group, come to a consensus on the most important qualities in a successful marriage and rank them in order of importance.

    _____

    _____

    _____

    _____

    _____

    _____

    _____

    _____

Activity 3-9: Playing Nice

PURPOSE: To identify and discuss destructive behaviors in a marriage and to explore important values.

MATERIALS: Worksheets 3-9A and 3-9B; pencils

PROCEDURE:

- Start the class by reminding students of when their parents told them to "play nice" with their friends. What did they mean by "play nice"? They probably meant don't hit others on the head with your sand bucket; don't step on their hands; do share your toys; and say nice things.

  The same principles apply to married couples. Half the marriages in this country end in divorce, primarily because many couples forgot how to PLAY NICE. They may not be hitting each other on the head with their sand buckets, but they're doing the equivalent of stepping on each other's hands. Let's look at one couple.

- Select a boy and a girl from the class to act out the dialogue on Worksheet 3-9A. The two students should be spontaneous and capable of bringing the episode to life.

- Give the class copies of the episode so they can follow along while the two students act it out.

- When the episode has been read, distribute Worksheet 3-9B and ask the class to respond to the particulars of the episode. You lead this discussion. Be sure to probe and ask them to elaborate on some of their answers.

- When this initial discussion is completed, divide the class into groups of four or five and have them discuss and write down their answers to the general questions. Then discuss these answers as a class to see if you can achieve consensus.

- Conclude the activity with a discussion of the hard work that goes into a marriage, the consideration and the compromise that must take place almost on a daily basis to maintain the relationship. Ask the class: "In what ways is maintaining a relationship with your marriage partner like keeping a good friend?" Summarize with the idea that your marriage partner should be your *best* friend.

Ed and Cathy

ED (*just coming home from work*): That traffic is driving me nuts! This seems to be the worst time of day for it.

CATHY: Yeah, it's getting bad. Why don't you come home earlier?

ED: Here we go again! I've told you a million times! I have to stick around until the last driver goes out. Somebody has to watch what they put in the trucks—and I guess that's what I was hired to do.

CATHY: I know, I know. But 12 hours a day? You leave before anyone is up, and you come home every day after the kids are in bed. Do you even remember what they look like?

ED: Yeah—little round faces, runny noses, and smelly diapers. How could I forget that?

CATHY: Then you sleep all day on the weekends, and I take the kids to the park.

ED: I'm tired! You understand "tired," don't you?

CATHY: Who do you think changes those diapers all day? And fixes meals and keeps this place clean—and shops, irons, does dishes, changes beds, does the laundry, and tries to keep in touch with the rest of the family?

ED: Wait a minute! This long-suffering attitude of yours is driving me nuts. You don't know what work is, sweetheart. I've got 45 minutes of travel both ways to work, then I've got at least a 10-hour day in the warehouse. Without it, you wouldn't be able to do all your shopping and meal fixing, so get off my back.

CATHY: Fine. Just save yourself for your precious job and forget everyone else in the house. That's probably what you want anyway. Fine (*sarcastically*), we'll just try to stay out of your way.

ED: What a wonderful place to come home to. Can't you say *anything* nice? You've got the attitude of a pit bull. Maybe that's why I stay at work.

CATHY: Oh, I'm so sorry, Mr. Father of the Year. Maybe you'd better take a few hours off work to treat that thin-skin condition of yours.

ED: (*leaving the room and heading for the kitchen*): I'm getting a beer. Did you buy any of that at your precious store?

CATHY (*muttering to herself*): Good riddance.

3-9B   **Playing Nice**

Regarding the Episode:

1. *Ask the two students who did the reading*: How did you feel about each other while you were reading these parts?

2. *Then, ask everyone else:* What were a few of the destructive things you heard in this episode?

3. Based on the behaviors and the things said, what do you think Cathy's and Ed's principles are? At least in this one episode, what seems to be most important to them?

4. How did their behaviors relate to these principles?

5. What are the real issues here? What is it that seems to be bothering each of them the most?

6. Did they get into personal issues that really didn't have much to do with the real issues? How? Specifically what did they say or do?

7. Identify some specifics of how they failed to "play nice."

8. Can Ed and Cathy love each other and still talk to each other this way? Explain your answer.

9. Give another example of how our principles and our behavior can be inconsistent.

General Discussion Questions

1. How do mutual *respect* and *responsibility* enable couples to "play nice" in a marriage?

   _____

   _____

   _____

2. Write down your group's opinion of the real issue(s) in this episode. Then suggest how respect and responsibility might have enabled Ed and Cathy to behave differently to resolve those issues.

   _____

   _____

   _____

3. Discuss the relationship of behavior to principles. In what different ways does behavior *reveal* or *hide* our principles?

   _____

   _____

   _____

Activity 3-10: Think Tank

PURPOSE: To identify and emphasize with students the principles that are important for the successful operation of the school.

MATERIALS: Worksheets 3-10A and 3-10B; pencils

PROCEDURE:

- Begin the session by discussing with the class how principles relate to the goals of any school system. It isn't necessary to discuss all the goals of education, just to emphasize that our focus is on student learning—learning positive self-concepts, adult behaviors, subject matter, etc.

- Next, mention that schools in the twenty-first century will face new and sometimes unpredictable challenges. For example, knowledge is increasing at a rate that was unheard of only 20 years ago. Knowledge that may be important to us today may be irrelevant or obsolete in months, even weeks! Jobs in new industries are being created every day. Many American citizens may have to change jobs, even careers, six or seven times during their lifetimes. Their *lifetimes* may last 100 to 125 years!

- Divide the class into four or five groups and distribute Worksheet 3-10A. Have them identify and list their five most important principles for schools of the twenty-first century. Tell them they can borrow from the list of principles on their worksheet or create one or more of their own.

- Go from group to group to discuss their selections. Try to get the entire class to reach consensus about their four or five most important principles.

- Next, have each group identify the three or four *behaviors* that are necessary to assure each principle. In essence, how will students have to *behave* to make sure the principles are realized in the school? Cooperation, for example, may require spontaneous interactions, friendliness, consideration, empathy, etc.

  If students identify honesty as a principle, ask them, "How do you behave when you're being honest?" This is not an easy question, so give the class enough time to think about and discuss these issues. Behaviors when being honest might include good eye contact, forthright answers to questions, acknowledgment of wrongdoing, a willingness to rely only on your own knowledge and understanding when taking tests or quizzes, and telling the truth.

  Identifying the behaviors that bring principles to life can be so difficult for kids that you may want to devote more than one session to this activity. Students must have the time to reflect on these behaviors. Without them, the principles that are important to all of us remain only so many words.

- Next, ask the class to identify four or five ways that schools can promote these important behaviors. Be sure your students don't focus only on punishment. Tell them to think about rewards and positive learning experiences. Indicate that you plan to share their ideas with the school's administration.

- Finally, ask the class to reach consensus on the five or six behaviors that are most important in the school and on the best ways for the school to promote these behaviors. Have the groups share their thinking, then write their reactions on Worksheet 3-10B and forward it to the principal's office.

- The activity should conclude a few days later with a reaction to the school or to each individual class from the principal.

3-10A   **Think Tank**

Your group is a think tank responsible for identifying the four or five principles that will be most important to schools in the twenty-first century. We already have discussed some of the changes that will confront us within the next 100 years. We will experience even more, most of which are unpredictable. Given these changes and the need for students to learn how to learn, what principles will be important to us?

Look at the following list and borrow from it, or identify one or two of your own to indicate the principles that your group thinks are important.

Honesty	Power	Fame	Courtesy
Wealth	Possessions	Justice	Consideration
Family	Courage	Status	Wisdom
Freedom	Friendship	Competition	Helping others
Charity	Faith	Honor	Hospitality
Hard work	Morality	Respect for self	Respect for others

Our Group's Four or Five Principles (List them next to the numbers below.)

1. _____   2. _____   3. _____
   a. _____   a. _____   a. _____
   b. _____   b. _____   b. _____
   c. _____   c. _____   c. _____
   d. _____   d. _____   d. _____

                   4. _____   5. _____
                      a. _____   a. _____
                      b. _____   b. _____
                      c. _____   c. _____
                      d. _____   d. _____

What behaviors will assure these principles? The principles are only words unless we behave in ways that bring them to life. If wisdom is one of your important principles, for example, how must people in the school behave to promote wisdom? They might seek knowledge, study hard, relate one learning situation to another, look beyond surface meanings in the facts they study, encourage friends to study, discuss classroom activities and knowledge outside the classroom, and constantly seek knowledge and understanding beyond the classroom.

List your group's three or four important behaviors under each principle you listed. Take time to do this. You'll discover that this is a tough question. How do I behave when I'm being honest? How do I behave when I'm being fair? How do I behave when I'm being cooperative? These are tough questions. Give them a lot of thought.

Finally, on the back of this sheet, identify the best four or five ways for schools to promote all these behaviors. What will your school of the twenty-first century do to get students to behave in ways that guarantee its important principles? Don't think only of disciplinary codes or punishments. Think of learning experiences, programs, rewards, etc., that will help students behave positively.

Come up with some good ones. We will share your thinking with the principal. This is your chance to affect our school in a very positive way.

3-10B

TO: the Principal

FR: _____

Listed below are the four or five important principles our class identified for our school. We have also listed our four or more suggestions for promoting positive behavior in our school.

Our Principles:

1. _____

2. _____

3. _____

4. _____

5. _____

Our Suggestions for Promoting Positive Behavior

1. _____

    _____

2. _____

    _____

3. _____

    _____

4. _____

    _____

5. _____

    _____

Thanks for looking at this material. We hope to hear from you.

Activity 3-11: Name Your Poison!

PURPOSE: To explore the world of drugs and to emphasize their harmful effects.

MATERIALS: Worksheets 3-11A and 3-11B.

PROCEDURE:

- Set the stage for this activity by informing the class that drugs are poisons and, as such, can kill people, especially if abused.

- Even beneficial drugs like the popular blood thinner and "stroke preventer" Coumadin can be dangerous. Coumadin is a rat poison—and people who use it must have their blood levels monitored, usually monthly, to keep the drug at a safe level.

- Ask the students how much they know about individual drugs. Let them respond randomly.

- Next, put students into groups of three or four and distribute Worksheet 3-11A.

- Give them ten to fifteen minutes to make the matches. Encourage them to look carefully at the descriptions and to discuss them before making their choices. We want students to interact with the information as long as possible to make sure it sinks in!

- Answers to the matching items are: 1. alcohol (A); 2. marijuana (P); 3. cocaine (C); 4. heroin (H); 5. PCP (PCP); 6. methamphetamine (M).

- Use Worksheet 3-11B to stimulate more class discussion and to share important facts about drug use.

- Conclude the activity with a statement such as, "Decades ago, bartenders started using the phrase 'name your poison' to ask people what kind of drink they wanted. Even then, people knew that alcohol had poisonous qualities. So, folks, if you want to do drugs—name your poison!"

3-11A **Name Your Poison**

Directions: Select the name of the drug listed in the box below that best fits the description and place the abbreviation in the circle. Discuss these descriptions with other members of your group to be sure you understand them.

1. 25% of hospital admissions are related to this drug. Damages brain, pancreas, and kidneys. Can cause cancer. Causes ulcers, colitis, and colon problems. Elevates blood pressure and causes strokes.

2. Causes premature aging and lung diseases. Can cause birth defects. Causes apathy and problems concentrating. Signs include diminished capacity and hunger.

3. Carries risk of HIV. Can cause seizures, stroke, and cardiac arrest. Can cause paranoia and depression. Extremely addictive. Signs include restlessness and increased excitement.

4. Causes nausea and panic. Is also extremely addictive. Use of needles causes hepatitis and AIDS. Causes euphoria followed by depression. Signs include clammy skin and shallow breathing.

5. Is used as an anesthetic for animals. Causes profound departures from reality. Causes bizarre and violent behavior. Can cause permanent changes in thinking and memory.

6. Several different street names. Causes nausea, hot flashes, hypertension, and dryness of mouth. Signs include severe anxiety and aggressiveness. Very addictive.

Heroin (H)	Methamphetamine (M)
PCP (PCP)	Marijuana (P)
Cocaine (C)	Alcohol (A)

Name Your Poison:
Additional Information

Use this additional information about drugs for continued discussion of the descriptions and matching items on Worksheet 3-11A. Know the potentially devastating effects of drug use.

ALCOHOL

- Most states set the drinking age at 21 for good reason. The human liver is not completely mature until that age. What that means is this: Adults who abuse alcohol can become addicted in 5 to 15 years. Teenagers who drink excessively can become alcoholics in 6 to 18 *months*! Pre-teenagers who drink excessively can become alcoholics in only *3* months!

- Over half the people killed in drunk-driving accidents are teenagers, even though they account for only 20% of licensed drivers.

- Alcohol abuse can lead to impotence and infertility, birth defects, and diminished immunity to disease.

MARIJUANA

- The poisonous qualities of marijuana today is 10 to 20 times more pronounced than it was in the 1960s and 1970s.

- One joint contains as many as 421 chemicals. When lit, it contains as many as 2,000!

- Alcohol is water-soluble. That means it is removed from the body in approximately 24 hours. Marijuana is *fat*-soluble. It isn't removed from the body for up to three weeks. If used daily, therefore, its poisonous effects stay in the body and continue to increase, causing brain damage and heart problems.

- Children who start using marijuana at an early age inevitably end up in drug-treatment programs.

COCAINE

- "Freebased" cocaine—cocaine that is smoked—is called "crack." Crack can be immediately addictive. Use it just once, and you might be hooked!

- No one who uses cocaine can be sure that the next dose will not cause addiction or even death!

- The manufacture and distribution of cocaine has strong ties to gangs, which can lead to a whole new set of problems for users.

- Cocaine does provoke momentary happiness, but it's often followed by sudden and severe depression, which sometimes involves a need for psychiatrists.

- A problem with crack cocaine is that it is relatively inexpensive, so it is used by the young and the relatively poor. It is inexpensive because it is made in basements, unsanitary labs that care little for the unhealthy effects on users.

- When injected, cocaine also carries the risk of infection with HIV and AIDS.

HEROIN

- Addiction causes the need for persistent use of the drug. Attempts to stop using it are physically very painful.

- Users of heroin report nausea, insomnia, and panic attacks.

- Heroin is taken primarily by injection, which increases the possibility of infection. HIV and AIDS often result.

- Uncertain dosage of the drug, contamination of the drug with cutting agents, and unsterile equipment can result in hepatitis, cardiac disease, overdose, and death.

- Signs include euphoria followed by depression, restricted breathing, nausea, clammy skin, and sometimes coma.

PCP

- PCP is a hallucinogenic drug. It alters consciousness, hearing, and visual sensation.

- When used by humans, it provokes profound departures from reality.

- Its effects often lead to serious injury and death because behavior becomes bizarre and violent.

- Chronic users suffer from decreased brain function and fine-motor function.

- It can also cause terrifying flashbacks well after the first use.

METHAMPHETAMINE

- On the street it is often referred to as "speed," "crystal," "crank," or "ice."

- When its chemical structure is modified—commonly called analog—it results in a drug commonly referred to as "ecstasy."

- Ecstasy is a drug made in underground labs with no regard for cleanliness or quality.

- Side effects of all these drugs are irritability, sweating, palpitations, nausea, and elevated blood pressure.

- Excessive doses can lead to severe anxiety, and continued use can lead to addiction and even death.

Now you know why they call it DOPE!
Don't even call them drugs!
Just name your poison!

SECTION 4

DEALING WITH EMOTIONAL ISSUES

"It is only with the heart that one can see rightly;
What is essential is invisible to the eye."
ANTOINE DE SAINT-EXUPERY

More of the Story:

Students struggle with their emotions for all kinds of reasons, most of which are predictable. Our Steering Committee understood that the ego and social needs of all students, as discussed in Section Two of this book, are critical to their development. When students enter school—whether elementary, junior high, or secondary—they seek acceptance, even popularity. They want to be successful in the classroom and/or in a variety of co-curricular and extracurricular activities. They fear rejection. If rejected, for any of several reasons, they become anxious, even angry.

We knew, even before Paducah, Columbine, and Santee, that such anxiety and anger can express itself in senseless violence, some of which is even self-inflicted. School violence and youth suicide have been problems in our society for a long time. We wanted to develop a program that sensitized the entire school to students' needs to be accepted and successful, that reached out to students and worked with them, and that made such violence unnecessary by actively promoting character and a solid sense of self in every one of our students.

Some of the issues affecting student emotions, however, are less predictable and every bit as complicated. One such issue challenged our school—and thousands across the nation—long before Bill and his friends were angered by their Homecoming queen's humiliation. This issue involved the toughened admissions requirements in many of the country's colleges and universities. Certainly, this was not the only issue that provoked stress in our students, but it was one that is unique to education and that demanded a response from all of us at Mundelein High School.

Officials in some schools simply communicated the toughened standards to students and parents and informed them of the need to improve the quality as well as the quantity of their academic courses. Apparently, college and university authorities had become concerned about the declining academic achievement of applicants and decided to require a greater academic emphasis in high school. Their concerns probably were well-founded, but their demands provoked reactions from students and parents that heightened anxiety everywhere, certainly in our school.

When our students enter Mundelein High School, they invariably find themselves in competition for grades, acceptance to accelerated and advanced placement courses, ACT and SAT scores, selection to the National Honor Society, and college admission. Such competition seems inevitable in school, and Mundelein High School, like every other high school in the country, accepted the demands of the colleges and universities and informed students of the need to add more academic courses to their programs.

But we went a step further. About the time Bill and his friends were questioning the behaviors of their classmates, our counselors and many of our teachers were questioning the decisions of some of our parents. Some of them had reacted to the increased admissions demands of colleges and universities by doing everything necessary to get their children scheduled for as many accelerated and advanced placement courses as possible.

Certainly, our school was not unique in this regard. Our Steering Committee couldn't help but consider the chain of events that was confronting our school as well as others across the nation. All parents of college-bound students want their children to be accepted to the best possible college or university. Some of them realized that if they wanted their children to attend an Ivy League school, the children would have to be enrolled in as many advanced placement courses as possible in high school or as many honors courses as possible in elementary school or junior high.

A result is that some schools across the country now have honors *kindergarten* courses! If this isn't extreme enough, many parents are getting their children tutored in readiness and achievement tests in early elementary grades, even in preschool, to assure their acceptance into these honors programs, reasoning that if the child doesn't start now, he or she won't qualify for advanced placement courses in high school.

Even if the circumstance is not this extreme in all schools—fortunately it wasn't in ours—we wanted to acknowledge that the toughened standards of colleges and universities were provoking understandable stress in our kids. While we agreed that students must be as well-grounded educationally as possible when they graduate from high school, we also acknowledged that such new demands were causing stress in our students and that such stress must be accommodated. We knew that if it wasn't, it would express itself in destructive ways.

CONSIDERING THE EFFECTS ON NON-COLLEGE-BOUND STUDENTS

While these increased standards were provoking stress in college-bound students, what was happening to our non–college-bound population? They, too, were stressed and angered. They found themselves further removed educationally from their college-bound classmates. Many felt that their acceptance in the growing academic environment of our school was suffering. As a result, their self-worth suffered, and their willingness to interact with college-bound classmates declined.

The requirements of colleges and universities—which were intended to improve the academic performance of students everywhere—were also driving a wedge between these two educational groups in our schools. Enrollment in vocational education programs was waning, and parents of students with learning disabilities were questioning if special education courses were satisfying the academic expectations of colleges and universities.

Anxiety and stress and the anger they provoke are growing realities in our society. Competition for admission to the best colleges is only one part of the problem. Competition for jobs, the prettiest and biggest house on the block, the most accomplished kids, the shiniest car, and the most elegant clothes have provoked struggles that have alienated many of us from one another and that often result in senseless conflict.

Much of this is our own problem. We cause it by being unable to distinguish our needs from our wants or by allowing self-indulgence to leave little room for anyone else in our lives. Our Steering Committee wanted to do something about this, even if some of these issues weren't so pronounced in our own community. We knew that unrelieved tension sometimes causes kids to abandon reality or to distort their perceptions about the forces behind the tension, a fact that can provoke a range of irrational behaviors.

Our guiding principle throughout the development of the following activities is to reward students every time they handle stress in a reasonable way. We know we are unable to remove stress from the lives of our students. In a society such as ours, it is almost as inevitable as death and taxes. But we can help them manage stress, cope with their own anger, and devise ways to learn from their failures.

Index of Activities for Dealing with Emotional Issues

Activity Number	Name	Description
4-1	Attitude	Understanding that attitude shapes who we are as people
4-2	Attitude Follow-up	Evaluating situations involving attitude
4-3	Stepping Up	Understanding how to handle adversity
4-4	It's Your Call: If I Weren't Afraid!	Understanding fear and risk-taking
4-5	Failure Is My Friend	Understanding how to learn from failure
4-6	Rejecting Rejection	Learning how to handle rejection
4-7	Stress	Understanding and handling stress
4-8	Handling Anger	Learning how to deal with anger
4-9	Take Your Pick	Emphasizing reflection of right and wrong
4-10	Leadership	Understanding the concept of leadership

Activity 4-1: Attitude

PURPOSE: To help students understand that attitude is more important than winning, fame, money, or other "things" the media leads people to believe are important. Attitude plays a vital role in shaping who we are as people and is reflected in what happens to us in life.

MATERIALS: Worksheets 4-1A and 4-1B; small plastic chips or paper clips to use as tokens; pencils

PROCEDURE:

- Divide the group into small groups of three or four students.
- Give one copy of Worksheets 4-1A and 4-1B, and one token to each group.
- Explain the circumstances and the rules of the game.
    a. The students are to imagine that they are the people in each of the situations.
    b. The students discuss the possibilities within their small groups for each situation and come to a consensus on the best choice.
    c. Next, they check the consequence of their choice and move their token accordingly on the game sheet.
    d. The object of the game is to see who will be the first group to get to P.M.A. (Positive Mental Attitude).

Attitude: It's Your Call

Imagine you are the people in each of the following situations. In your small groups, discuss the possibilities for each situation. Come to a consensus on the best choice and check the consequence of your choice below. Move your token on the Attitude Game Sheet as indicated in the corresponding consequence. The object of the game is to see who will be the first group to get to P.M.A. (Positive Mental Attitude).

SITUATION 1

You're the quarterback of a professional football team meeting the press after playing poorly in four consecutive games resulting in team losses. The disgruntled fans booed you as you left the field.

What Is Your Response?

A.   You tell the press you're not motivated by fans who come to boo at you.
B.   You tell the press the fans are taking it out on you and you don't want to whine about it.
C.   You tell the press the way you played you would have booed yourself, too, and you intend to turn things around starting now.

Consequences

A.   Now doubts of your leadership ability loom as great as those of your playing ability. *You lose a turn.*
B.   You didn't completely blame others for your mistakes, but you didn't show a positive attitude either. *Move ahead 3 spaces.*
C.   You accepted some of the blame and showed a positive attitude. That's how you begin to win. *Move ahead 5 spaces.*

SITUATION 2

You are an Olympic wrestler competing for the U.S.A. in the gold-medal round. You lose your match to the Russian athlete competing against you.

What Is Your Response?

A.   You say, "I can only say I was truly happy that I could fight him, but he was the better warrior."
B.   You throw your mouthpiece and refuse to shake the referee's hand.
C.   You threaten to protest against the Olympic scoring rules.

Consequences

A.   You have taken part in the competition with the right attitude. Attitude is even more important than winning. *Move ahead 6 spaces.*
B.   Your attitude and tantrum behavior are appropriate for a two-year-old, not a winner. *You lose a turn.*
C.   Rules are rules and they apply to everyone. It's good to challenge rules if they don't apply. But think about your method. *Move ahead 3 spaces.*

SITUATION 3

You are the U.S. tae kwon do fighter who made it to the Olympics because your best friend and training partner forfeited her slot on the team so that you could go to represent the United States. In the first round of the Olympic competition, you crashed out.

What Is Your Response?

A. You say, "I'm a loser. My friend should have come instead of me."
B. You say, "I lost. It happens to the best of athletes."
C. You shout "Get lost!" to the members of the press who try to interview you after the match.

Consequences

A. That defeatist attitude might make you feel better, but it won't help the team or your friend who gave up her spot on the team for you. *Move ahead 2 spaces.*
B. Your attitude is positive and healthy. Life goes on and so will you. *Move ahead 6 spaces.*
C. Your attitude is an embarrassment to everyone around you. *You lose a turn.*

SITUATION 4

You're a young American woman coming from an average athletic career to soundly win the inaugural women's pole vault in the Olympics. When interviewed afterward, you talk about why you won.

What Is Your Response?

A. You say, "I think that anyone, if they put their heart and soul into it, can accomplish anything. It's a great feeling."
B. You say, "I won because I deserved it."
C. You say, "Your dreams don't always come true when you want them to. This time I was lucky because they did."

Consequences

A. According to Tommy Lasorda, coach of the 2000 Olympic American baseball team, "It's not always the best or the fastest that wins. It's the athlete that wants it the most." A positive mental attitude brings about amazing results. *Move ahead 6 spaces.*
B. Having self-confidence is important, but there is a very distinct line between self-confidence and arrogance. *Go back 2 spaces.*
C. If you think success is determined by luck, your mental attitude needs perspective. *You lose a turn.*

Attitude Game Sheet

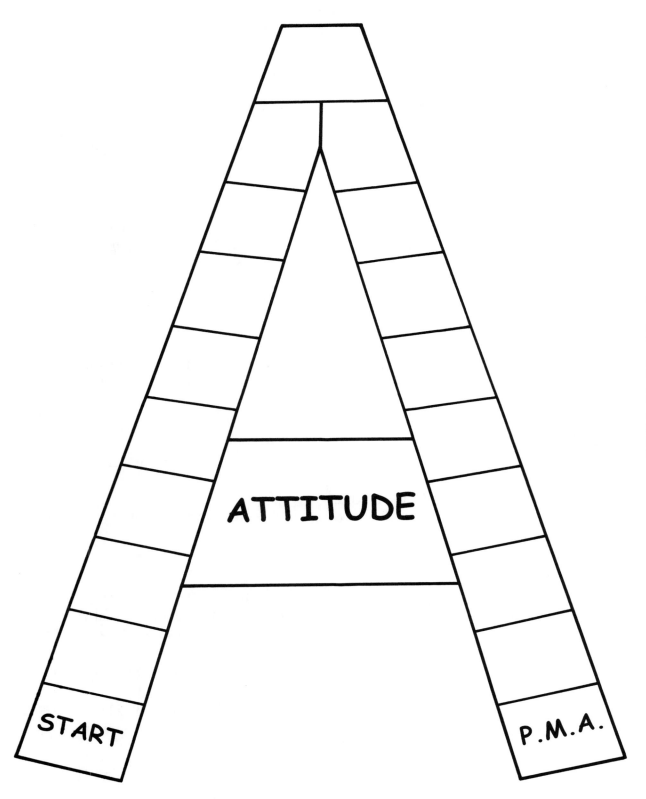

ATTITUDE

START

P.M.A.

Activity 4-2: Attitude Follow-Up

PURPOSE: To enable students to analyze and evaluate situations involving attitude. To allow students to discuss and support or disagree with the consequences of the Attitude Game Sheet from Activity 4-1. The situations and consequences provided in the previous activity might be interpreted differently by different students. This lesson allows them to express their own ideas on situations they didn't agree with or perhaps supported when the rest of the group disagreed. Analysis and evaluation are important cognitive skills to hone.

MATERIALS: Worksheet 4-2; copies of Worksheet 4-1A from Activity 4-1 to use as the springboard for discussion; pencils

PROCEDURE:

- Have the students get into the same small groups they were in for Activity 4-1.

- Give each student a copy of Worksheet 4-1A to use as a springboard for thought.

- Give each group a copy of Worksheet 4-2 and allow them time to discuss it together. Tell students to choose one person in the group to write down their answers in order to share them later with the entire class.

- After they have had enough time to discuss the situations and answer each question, have the groups share their answers with the entire class. After each group shares its answers, ask the entire class for a reaction.

- Tell the class to choose the best from each group and establish a consensus opinion for the entire class on each of the four situations from Activity 4-1.

4-2   # Attitude Follow-Up: Discussion Questions

Complete the following discussion questions in your small groups. Choose one person to serve as the recorder who will write down your group's answers. Be ready to share your answers with the entire class.

1. Choose two of the four situations from Worksheet 4-1A to revisit because you had another way of looking at the situation.

     A. _____   B. _____

2. Which of the consequences in those situations concerned you? Why?

Situation   **Consequence**   **My Concern**

_____

_____

_____

_____

_____

_____

_____

_____

_____

_____

_____

_____

_____

_____

_____

_____

_____

_____

_____

3. Based on your attitude, what would you have done in each situation you chose to revisit? It's your call.

Situation A:

I/We would have

Situation B:

I/We would have

_____

_____

_____

_____

_____

_____

_____

_____

_____

_____

_____

_____

_____

_____

_____

_____

_____

_____

_____

_____

_____

_____

_____

_____

Activity 4-3: Stepping Up

PURPOSE: To help students realize that if they face their problems by shaking off fear and stepping up, they will most likely succeed. It's important to understand that the way they handle adversity is what matters.

MATERIALS: Worksheets 4-3A and 4-3B; pencils

PROCEDURE:

- Invite all the students to sit in a circle.
- Read aloud "The Parable of the Mule" on Worksheet 4-3A.
- Give each student a copy of Worksheet 4-3B.
- Allow the students time to complete it.
- Discuss their answers to the questions. Allow the discussion to flow.
- List on the board the students' responses to question 2.
- Generate a class list for question 6.

The Parable of the Mule

There once was a farmer who owned an old mule. One day the mule fell into the farmer's well and the farmer heard the mule braying. After carefully assessing the situation, the farmer sympathized with the mule, but decided that it wasn't worth saving either the mule or the well. As a result, he called his neighbors together, told them what had happened, and asked them to help haul dirt to bury the old mule in the well and put him out of his misery.

At first the old mule was hysterical, but as the farmer and his neighbors continued shoveling and the dirt hit his back, a thought struck him. It occurred to him that every time a shovel load of dirt landed on his back, he could shake it off and step up. And so he did! Blow after blow he repeated to himself, "Shake it off and step up . . . shake it off and step up . . . shake it off and step up."

No matter how painful the blows or how distressing the situation seemed, the old mule fought panic and just kept right on shaking it off and stepping up. It wasn't long before the old mule, battered and exhausted, stepped triumphantly over the wall of the well. What seemed like it would bury him actually helped him just because of the way he handled his adversity.

*For the complete parable, see 2nd International Cyber Pow-Wow events, Ranger Net Home, Official Royal Rangers web site, www.rangernet.org

4-3B   **Stepping Up: Discussion Questions**

1. How does the parable of the mule relate to life?

    _____

    _____

    _____

    _____

2. Give examples of people you know personally or people you have read or heard about who have shaken off adversity and stepped up.

    _____

    _____

    _____

    _____

3. What happened to the people you cited as examples who shook off adversity and stepped up?

    _____

    _____

    _____

    _____

4. Why is shaking it off and stepping up an admirable way to face adversity?

_____

_____

_____

_____

5. Think of one thing you need to shake off and step up to this week. Share it with the class if you feel comfortable doing so. If you don't feel comfortable sharing it, you don't have to.

_____

_____

_____

_____

6. With a partner, make a list of five ways you can make "shaking it off and stepping up" to adversity a habit.

_____

_____

_____

_____

_____

_____

_____

_____

Activity 4-4: It's Your Call:
If I Weren't Afraid!

PURPOSE: To enable students to analyze and evaluate a situation involving a fear of risk-taking.

MATERIALS: Worksheets 4-4A and 4-4B; pencils

PROCEDURE:

- Distribute worksheet 4-4A and give the class enough time to read it. Then arrange them in groups of three or four to discuss it. Tell them to discuss the questions, then seek consensus among themselves for answers. Tell them to write down their answers in order to share them later with the entire class. Challenge students during this phase of the activity to determine individually "What would you do if you *weren't* afraid?" In essence, "How might fear interfere with your ability to do the right thing?"

- After they have had enough time to discuss the situation and answer each question, have students share their answers with the entire class. After each group shares its answers, ask the entire class for a reaction.

- After every group has shared its answers, tell the students to choose the best from each group and establish a consensus opinion for the entire class.

- If enough time remains, keep the students in their groups and have them discuss and answer the discussion questions on Worksheet 4-4B. Then discuss them as a class.

- Conclude the activity by sharing the following statement with the class: "To grow, let go!" Determine what the saying means to them and how it relates to risk-taking. Then remind them of the principle: "What would I do if I *weren't* afraid?" Sometimes this is a question we have to ask ourselves quite often in order to do the right thing!

The Situation: "If I Weren't Afraid!"

You and a group of friends are planning a big party for the weekend. Tom tells you that his parents are out of town for a week, and he assures you that his basement is the perfect place for a "really good one!" Everyone agrees to go for it. Bill says he'll arrange for the beer; his big brother always handles it for him. Jim says he can get some pot. He even says that he can get his hands on some crack cocaine.

Suddenly, you feel that things are getting out of hand. You've been involved in similar parties in the past but have always refrained from drinking. It's not that you're some kind of a saint. You just don't like it, and you've never said anything when your friends drank. You've been careful to make sure they don't drink and drive, but that has been the extent of your intervention.

Your problem now is that you've learned in your health class that the combination of beer and pot, especially when overused, can cause serious problems. Your teacher indicated that the two simply don't mix. You also learned that crack cocaine can be immediately addictive. These kinds of problems just don't seem worth it to you. You are bothered enough by the idea of using Tom's house without his parents' knowledge.

But now a couple of your friends are talking about taking this party to a whole new level. It doesn't sound worth it to you, but—at this point—you're afraid to say anything.

IT'S YOUR CALL!

What will you do?

- Will you find some reason to avoid the party yourself, maybe just pass on it and avoid the whole issue? Explain your answer. Why did you say "yes" or "no"?

- Will you fabricate some unrelated reason(s) why the party might not be a good idea after all? Explain your answer. Why did you say "yes" or "no"?

- Will you decide to go to the party but only to be sure friends don't drink and drive or do anything stupid? Explain your answer.

- Will you speak up right now? Will you tell your friends to stop talking about something so potentially dangerous? Explain your answer.

- Will you still encourage them to have the party, but to forget about bringing pot and crack cocaine? Explain your answer.

- If your friends tell you to back off, will you continue trying to convince them or will you just decide against the party? Explain your answer.

- Finally, if it's evident they plan to continue with the party as planned, will you tell an adult? Explain your answer.

- If you tell an adult, will that person be one or both of your parents, a teacher, the dean of students for your school, a counselor, or the local police? Explain your decision.

4-4B   # It's Your Call: Discussion Questions

1. What is it about peer pressure that makes it such a powerful influence in the lives of students?

    _____

    _____

    _____

2. Why is risk-taking so difficult for some of us?

    _____

    _____

    _____

3. Think about the question: "What would you do if you *weren't* afraid?" How do answers to this question relate to risk-taking and character?

    _____

    _____

    _____

    _____

    _____

    _____

Activity 4-5: Failure Is My Friend

PURPOSE: To emphasize to students that failure is not the demon many of them think it is. Rarely does the world come to an end when we fail, and, if used thoughtfully, the failure invariably leads to learning and improvement. It is important for students to learn that when they fail, they have failed only at a task—*not* as human beings.

MATERIALS: Cutouts of the nose and mouth for the drawing on the chalkboard; Worksheet 4-5; pencils; blindfold; adhesive tape

PROCEDURE:

- Prior to the start of class, draw a face on the chalkboard with only the eyes included. As you will see, one of your students—blindfolded—will be expected to attach the nose and mouth. Write the word HOMES across the top of the board. Finally, apply adhesive tape to the back of the nose and the mouth so they will stick to the board.

- Select a student and engage him or her in this kind of dialogue: "Tom, the survival of the world depends on your answer! In ten seconds, name—in order— the first seven Presidents of the United States. GO!"

- When Tom doesn't do it, ask him first: "Now, did the world come to an end? It usually doesn't!" Second, ask him: "Did you fail the task of naming them, or did you fail as a person?" "Of course, you failed only the task. You're still a great person!"

- Next, ask the class if someone knows the answer or can find it. If no one can, provide the answer (George Washington, John Adams, Thomas Jefferson, James Madison, James Monroe, John Quincy Adams, Andrew Jackson). "OK, Tom, learn the names and practice saying them in ten seconds."

- Then call on another student and say, "Cindy, the survival of the world depends on your answer! In five seconds, name the Great Lakes! GO!"

- When she doesn't name them, say, "Now, did the world come to an end? We're all still here, aren't we? Did you fail a task, or did you fail as a person? Absolutely, just a task. You're still a great person!"

- Next, underneath the word HOMES, write Huron, Ontario, Michigan, Erie, and Superior.

- Tell Cindy to memorize HOMES and be able to recite the names of the Great Lakes in 5 seconds.

- Finally, call another student and say, "Joe, the survival of the world depends on you!" (Blindfold him.) Then tell him, "Take this nose and mouth and attach them to the drawing on the board so that you make a relatively normal face."

- The result should be funny. Maybe have two or three more students try it. The results, like "Pin the Tail on the Donkey," are humorous. When they don't attach them correctly, distribute Worksheet 4-5 and lead the class through it.

- Regarding self-evaluation and other-evaluation, they know that the nose and mouth weren't attached correctly, so have them determine what was wrong with the approach. Joe might stand in front of the face with his hands in the proper position, then take five steps backward, stop, go forward with his hands still in the proper position, and reattach the nose and mouth.

- To emphasize another approach, have Joe go back to his original five steps away from the board and have one member of the class give him verbal directions: "Right, left, a little higher, a little lower, etc." Emphasize to him and the class that to learn from failure, we must determine what we did wrong, work hard on corrective action, and, as needed, get some help!

- Finally, have the students answer the questions on the worksheet. The obvious answer to the first student's problem is knowing the right answer, then studying it!

- The answer to the second student's problem is finding the structure in the material, even if structure must be applied artificially.

- Toward the end of the period, have the first student recite the names of the first seven Presidents in order, then have the second student name the Great Lakes. Congratulate them and reaffirm how easy it was when they learned from their failures.

- Conclude the activity by summarizing the key elements:

    —When we fail, we fail only a task, not as human beings.

    —Rarely does the survival of the world depend on our completion of the task.

    —Failure can be our friend, especially if we make sure we learn from it.

    —If we don't fail once in a while, we don't learn!

    —Therefore, the only way we truly learn is to take an occasional risk!

    —Remember, you're a failure only if you quit, if you give up.

    —We can all lose, sometimes quite often, but—if we keep trying—we'll never fail!

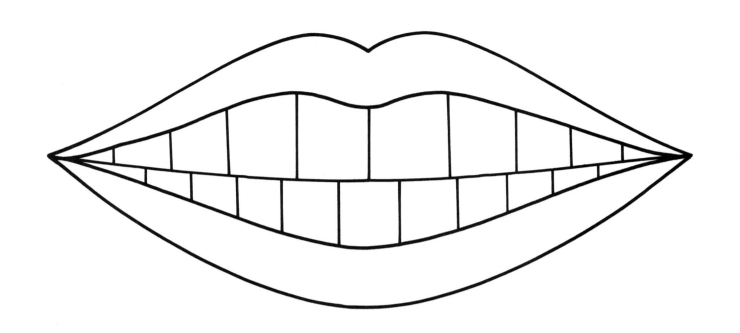
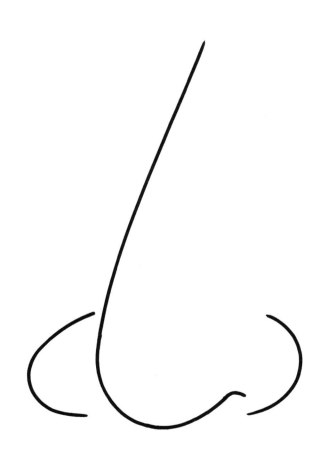

4-5   # Failure Is My Friend

1. Consider the following steps to correct a failure:

   • Self-evaluate to determine what you did wrong.
   • If self-evaluation doesn't work, get advice from trusted others.
   • Determine corrective action and work hard at it.
   • Try again. If you fail again, determine if the corrective action was the right action. If not, find another way to improve your performance and work hard at it!

2. Why did the first student fail to name the first seven Presidents? What was needed to resolve the problem?

   _____

   _____

   _____

3. Why did the second student fail to name the Great Lakes? How did HOMES help to memorize them?

   _____

   _____

   _____

4. What's the difference between being a failure and being a loser?

   _____

   _____

   _____

5. Why was this activity named "Failure Is My Friend"? When is failure your friend?

   _____

   _____

   _____

   _____

Activity 4-6: Rejecting Rejection

PURPOSE: To explore rejection and to emphasize that the person who does the rejecting is often the loser.

MATERIALS: Worksheets 4-6A and 4-6B; pencils.

PROCEDURE:

- Divide the class into five groups. The size of each group doesn't matter. Tell them that they're going to be involved in a competition, so they better put on their thinking caps.

- Tell the groups: "As soon as you know the name of the person being described, shout it out. A correct answer gives your group four points; an incorrect answer takes away one point!" (Research tells us that impulsivity is not a sign of intelligent behavior! The point taken away is designed to reduce impulsivity.) Keep a tally of the scores on the board.

- Read the descriptions given below of people who were rejected. Insert as much drama and suspense as you can. (You might play theme songs from TV game shows.) Distribute Worksheet 4-6A when you read the description of Thomas Edison.

- He was born in Milan, Ohio. His mother was a teacher.
- At age 12, he was selling fruit and candy on a railroad line.
- He was rejected as a student because of a severe learning disability. (*Distribute Worksheet 4-6A.*)
- He joined Western Union Telegraph in 1868.
- He built his own factory a short time later in Newark, New Jersey.
- He went on to invent the phonograph, the light bulb, the movies, and thousands of other inventions.

(Thomas Edison)

- He was born in 1887 in Prague, Oklahoma.

- His mother died when he was only 14.

- Rejected by his father, he was sent to a boarding school. He was orphaned only months later when his father died.

- When he entered the boarding school at age 16, he was 5 feet 5 inches tall and weighed only 115 pounds.

- A few short years later, he was named to the third-team All-American football team.

- A few years after that, he went on to win two gold medals in the 1912 Olympics and, later, to play professional football and professional baseball.

- He has been named by many as the Greatest Athlete in American history.

(Jim Thorpe)

- She was born in New York City and raised in a housing project.

- Rejected by her father, who abandoned the family, she was raised by her mother.

- She was later rejected by the academic teachers in her school because of a severe learning disability.

- She dropped out of school at age 17.

- She struggled with rejection for nine years in California as an actress.

- Five years later, she got a starring role in the movie *The Color Purple* and won a Golden Globe Award.

- She starred in *Ghost*, *Sister Act*, and hosted the Academy Award show three times.

- You'll find her in the center square on the "Hollywood Squares."

(Whoopi Goldberg)

- He was born in Ulm, Germany and was rejected by many teachers who claimed they were unable to deal with such a poor student.

- He moved to Milan, Italy and applied to the Swiss Federal Institute of Technology.

- He was rejected because of poor test scores on the entrance exam.

- He eventually got in and went on to get a Ph.D. from the University of Zurich.

- He helped introduce the quantum sciences.

- He gave the world the theory of relativity.

(Albert Einstein)

- He was born in Brooklyn, New York, and is now married with three children.
- He was rejected from his high school basketball team. He was cut because they thought he wasn't good enough.
- He attended college in North Carolina.
- He helped his college win a national Championship in basketball.
- He went on to play for the Chicago Bulls.
- He enjoys the reputation of being the greatest basketball player ever.

(Michael Jordan)

- He was born in Syracuse, New York, and was rejected by the academic community in high school because of his dyslexia.
- When his parents divorced, he moved to Kentucky with his mother.
- Because of poor academic performance, he quit high school and moved to New York City.
- Trying to be an actor, he was rejected at one audition after another.
- Finally, he was given bit parts in *Endless Love* and *Taps*.
- Ultimately, he went on to star in *Risky Business*, *Top Gun*, and *Born on the Fourth of July* for which he received a Golden Globe award.
- Then he made *Mission Impossible*, *Jerry McGuire*, and many other movies.

(Tom Cruise)

- He was born in Shrewsbury, England. His mother was the daughter of Josiah Wedgewood, the founder of the famous pottery firm.
- His mother died when he was 8, and he was rejected by many of his teachers because he was a poor student.
- He went to Edinburgh to study, but was rejected by most professors because of a poor academic record.
- He floundered with the study of theology at Cambridge and eventually majored in geology.
- He spent five years aboard the *Beagle*, an English ship, studying fossils.
- His study resulted in his theory of evolution.
- He wrote *The Origin of the Species*, in which he shared his ideas about natural selection.

(Charles Darwin)

- She was born in Clarksville, Tennessee, and became virtually crippled at an early age.
- She had to wear a leg brace for three years as a child.
- She was rejected by sports teams as a child because even walking was difficult.
- Eventually she played basketball in high school. She set state records in scoring.
- She went on to run track in college.
- She was the first black woman to win three gold medals in the Olympics: the 100 meters, the 200 meters, and the 4 by 100-meter relay.
- She is regarded as one of the greatest sprinters in Olympic history.

(Wilma Rudolph)

- He was born in Oak Park, Illinois, and graduated from high school in 1917.
- He never attended college.
- He was rejected from the army because of a bad eye. Eventually he entered the war anyway as an ambulance driver for the Red Cross.
- He so feared rejection and so loved to write that he would often rewrite his short stories 20 or 25 times to perfect them.
- He wrote *The Sun Also Rises* and *A Farewell to Arms*.
- He suffered severe depression and eventually killed himself.

(Ernest Hemingway)

- He was born in Chicago, Illinois, and eventually moved to a farm in Kansas.
- He decided to study art but could only do it through a correspondence school.
- He dropped out of high school in 1917 to serve in World War I.
- He set up his own studio in 1922, but failed because his work was rejected by so many national companies.
- He decided to go to Hollywood in 1923, where he took up cartoon production.
- His first success was with the cartoon *Steamboat Willie*, starring Mortimer Mouse—who later became—Mickey Mouse.

(Walt Disney)

- Assign the appropriate points for each group. Maybe even reward the winners with extra credit or something equally appropriate.

- Next, distribute Worksheet 4-6B and have students answer each question as a group.

- Finally, have each group read its answers and try to achieve consensus as a class.

- Conclude the activity by emphasizing the importance of perseverance!

Who Wrote This?

Dear Mother—

    I started the store several weks. I have growed considerably
I don't lik much like a Boy now-hows all the folk did you receive
a Box of Books from Memphis that he promised to send them—
Languages.

                    Your son Tom

4-6B   **Rejecting Rejection**

Please answer the following questions in your groups. We'll discuss them as a class when you have finished.

1. What is it that all these people have/had in common?

    _____

    _____

2. Identify two or three qualities that helped each of them overcome the adversity of rejection.

    _____

    _____

    _____

3. In what ways does rejection hurt the ones who do the rejecting?

    _____

    _____

    _____

4. Jot down a reaction to the statement: "Rejection hurts us only if we allow it to."

    _____

    _____

    _____

5. Argue *for* or *against* the statement: "If you never quit, you'll never fail. You may lose, but you'll never fail."

    _____

    _____

    _____

    _____

Activity 4-7: Stress

PURPOSE: To discuss openly the causes and effects of stress and to realize that stress is found in the daily lives of everyone. It is necessary to help students understand that stress never goes away, and that the way to combat stress is to learn good ways of handling it. This lesson is important for each of them now and in the future.

MATERIALS: Worksheet 4-7; paper; pencils

PROCEDURE:

- Divide the class into small groups of three or four students.
- Ask each group to select a person from the group to serve as the group's recorder, who will write down the group's answers and share them with the rest of the class.
- Give each group one copy of Worksheet 4-7.
- Allow the groups sufficient time to complete the worksheet.
- Go over the questions on the worksheet one at a time, asking each group to share its answers to the questions with the entire class.
- List the objects on the board that the students suggest represent stress (question 1).
- List on the board the main stressers in a teenager's life as the groups provide them (question 3).
- As an entire class, come to a consensus on the ten best ways to combat stress. Write them on the board. Ask each student to write this list on a sheet of paper to keep where he or she can refer to it regularly.

4-7   **Stress: Discussion Questions**

In your small groups, respond to the following items. Choose one person from your group to serve as the recorder, who will write down your group's answers on this sheet.

1. When you hear the word **STRESS**, what object comes to mind? Explain briefly why you chose this particular object to represent stress.

   The object our group thinks best represents **STRESS** is _____

   _____

   because _____

   _____

   _____

   _____

2. How do you know when you're stressed out? What are your symptoms?

   _____

   _____

   _____

   _____

   _____

   _____

   _____

   _____

3. What are the main stressers (sources of stress) in a teenager's life? List three main stressers and, under each broad category, write three specific examples for each. For instance, academic pressure is a stresser, and examples include (a) preparing for exams, (b) maintaining a certain grade point average, (c) doing well on placement exams.

Stresser: _____

    a. _____

    b. _____

    c. _____

Stresser: _____

    a. _____

    b. _____

    c. _____

Stresser: _____

    a. _____

    b. _____

    c. _____

4. As a group, come to a consensus on the five best ways to combat stress. (Examples: Plan ahead. Talk to a supportive friend.)

1. _____

2. _____

3. _____

4. _____

5. _____

Activity 4-8: Handling Anger

PURPOSE: To help students learn about dealing with anger. Students who learn to deal with their own anger and the anger of others gain strength of character and become more successful both in and out of school. Handling anger is an important step toward *living* the 3R's of First Class: RESPECT for self and others, RESPECT for how we communicate, RESPECT for our surroundings.

MATERIALS: Worksheets 4-8A, 4-8B, 4-8C, and 4-8D; pencils

PROCEDURE:

- Have each student fill out Worksheet 4-8A.
- Ask for volunteers from the class to role-play as many of the role-play situations on Worksheet 4-8B as possible in the time allotted.
- Divide the class into small groups of three to four students.
- Give each group one copy of the discussion questions on Worksheet 4-8C. Ask each group to select a recorder from the group to write down the answers to the discussion questions.
- Allow the groups enough time to complete the discussion questions.
- Reconvene as a large group. Ask the spokesperson from each small group to share the group's responses to questions 1–5 of the discussion questions.
- As a whole group, come up with a class-generated list of six good things we can do when we feel angry (question 6 of the discussion questions). Write the list on the board or butcher paper.
- Ask the students to copy the list onto their copy of Worksheet 4-8A, and keep it where they can refer to it regularly.
- Finish by having the students move into their small groups again.
- Give each group a copy of Worksheet 4-8D.
- Allow the groups enough time to come to a consensus on the best solutions to the role-play situations.
- Have each group share its best solutions with the entire class.

4-8A   # Handling Anger

Answer the following questions about yourself.

1. How do you know when you're angry?

     _____

     _____

     _____

2. What kinds of words or actions trigger your anger?

     _____

     _____

     _____

3. Do you think it takes a lot to make you angry or do you get angry quickly?

     _____

     _____

     _____

4. What do you do when you're angry?

     _____

     _____

     _____

5. Does what you do when you get angry help solve the problem? Why or why not?

     _____

     _____

     _____

(If you need more room to write, use the back of this worksheet.)

Handling Anger:
Role-Play Situations

- You and your friend Chris plan to spend a weekend visiting another friend who is a freshman at the university. You've made all the arrangements to stay with your college friend in his dorm. You even bought tickets for the football game on Saturday afternoon and your college friend got you dates for Saturday night. At the last minute Chris, who was going to drive you there, says he has changed his mind and decides he doesn't want to go. What do you do? What do you say?

- One rainy morning you are walking down the hall in school as two kids playing with a Frisbee™ throw it and hit you in the back of the head. As you whirl around to find out what's going on, you step on a wet spot on the floor, twist your ankle, and fall down—while your books and papers fly all over the place. Everyone starts laughing at you. What do you do? What do you say?

- You're working on a joint project for History with one of your friends who is also in the class. You've finished your part of the project and your friend decides to take it home and finish up her part of the project. The next day you wait for your friend to come into the classroom with the finished product, but when she arrives she has nothing. She explains that she woke up late, rushed to school, and forgot the project at home. You are furious at yourself for not checking up on her. You explain the situation to the teacher who refuses to give you an extension because he feels you had adequate time to prepare the project. Now you'e not only mad at your friend, but you're mad at your History teacher, too. What do you do? What do you say?

- Some friends invite you to go to a movie on Friday night. You all agree to meet at the theater at 7:30. You arrive at 7:15 and wait until 7:30, but no one shows up. Finally, you decide maybe they already went in, so you buy a ticket and go in. They are not inside either. You sit down to watch the movie, thinking that maybe they got caught in traffic and are late. You watch the entire movie, but your friends never show up. You go home and call them. They laugh and say they decided at the last minute to rent a movie and stay home. You are angry. What do you do? What do you say?

Students' Names _____ Date _____

4-8C   **Handling Anger: Discussion Questions**

In your small group, answer the following questions about the role-play situations you observed. Choose one person in your group to record your group's answers.

1. What kinds of behaviors did you see and hear?

   _____

   _____

   _____

2. How do you think the "victim" in each of these situations felt?

   _____

   _____

   _____

3. How did you feel as an observer of the behavior? Why?

   _____

   _____

   _____

4. Did the behavior of the people in the role-play situations help solve the issues? Why or why not?

   _____

   _____

   _____

5. How does handling anger tie to the 3 R's of First Class (RESPECT for self and others, RESPECT for how we communicate, RESPECT for our surroundings)?

   _____

   _____

   _____

6. Come up with a list of six good things you can do when you are feeling angry.

- _____

  _____

- _____

  _____

- _____

  _____

- _____

  _____

- _____

  _____

- _____

  _____

Students' Names _____   **Date** _____

_____

4-8D

Let's Resolve It

In your small groups, using the class-generated list of six good things to do when you feel angry (question 6 of Worksheet 4-8C), find the best solutions to each role-play situation. Write your best solutions on the following continuums between the two overused solutions (fight or flight).

SITUATION 1 (a college visitation weekend)

_____
fight   **flight**

SITUATION 2 (a bad morning)

_____
fight   **flight**

SITUATION 3 (the history project disaster)

_____
fight   **flight**

SITUATION 4 (Friday night at the movies)

_____
fight   **flight**

Activity 4-9: Take Your Pick

PURPOSE: To promote reflection of right and wrong, and critical-thinking skills. One of the purposes of the activities in this book is to enable students to reflect on issues of principles and to make enlightened decisions about their own behavior as well as their relationships with others. The situation provided in this activity provokes serious reflection and involves students in a possible real-life experience that challenges their ability to react reasonably.

MATERIALS: Worksheets 4-9A, 4-9B, 4-9C, and 4-9D; pencils

PROCEDURE:

- Distribute Worksheet 4-9A to the students and have them respond to it individually. Then distribute Worksheet 4-9B and have them respond. Finally, Worksheet 4-9C. They should respond to each situation one at a time.

- Then organize the class into groups of three or four and have them discuss the situations as a group to try to reach group consensus.

- After they have achieved or approximated consensus, have a spokesperson for each group read the answers for each situation to the rest of the class. Discuss all the alternatives and consequences as a class and try to determine the "best" thing to do in each situation. Promote as much discussion as possible. Be sure to remind the students that this discussion is not a win–lose situation. We're not trying to determine if one student's idea is better than everyone else's. We're trying to build on each other's ideas in order to determine the "best" alternative(s) available to Tom.

- If time permits, have the groups answer the questions on Worksheet 4-9D. Discuss them as a class. Depending on the involvement of the class, this activity may require more than a single session. Make that determination as the activity progresses.

4-9A   # The Situation—Tom's Decision

You are Tom. You're a fullback on the sophomore football team and well-liked in school. You're walking down B Hall on your way to Sophomore English and suddenly someone bumps you from the side and you find yourself slammed into a locker. You look quickly to see who did it and find yourself confronted by a junior on the varsity football team. He is expressionless. What do you do?

The Search for Alternatives:

In the space provided, write each alternative available to you. Underneath each alternative, write at least two consequences of that decision.

ALTERNATIVE 1: _____

_____

    CONSEQUENCE: _____

    _____

    CONSEQUENCE: _____

    _____

ALTERNATIVE 2: _____

_____

    CONSEQUENCE _____

    _____

    CONSEQUENCE _____

    _____

ALTERNATIVE 3: _____

_____

    CONSEQUENCE: _____

    _____

    CONSEQUENCE: _____

    _____

Which of the above alternatives would likely reflect your behavior in this situation? Why?

4-9B   # More of the Situation—Tom's Decision

Phil, the junior on the varsity football team, suddenly reaches out to grab you and says, "Tom, I'm so sorry! Some kid ran into me and knocked me into you! I'm really sorry!" Now what do you do?

The Search for Alternatives:

1. Identify two alternatives still available to you.

ALTERNATIVE 1: _____
_____

    CONSEQUENCE: _____
_____

    CONSEQUENCE: _____
_____

ALTERNATIVE 2: _____
_____

    CONSEQUENCE: _____
_____

    CONSEQUENCE: _____
_____

2. Which of the two alternatives is the most desirable to you? Why?

_____
_____
_____

3. How did this new set of circumstances reflect on your earlier decision? Based on these circumstances, was your decision on Worksheet 4-9A appropriate? Explain your answer.

_____
_____
_____

4-9C

A Possible Alternative Circumstance—
Tom's Decision

What if it had not been Phil? What if it had been a senior soccer player who called you a football wimp and had been threatening you since the beginning of the school year because of your decision to play football instead of soccer? He is smiling threateningly when he says, "This is just the start, little boy. You better watch your back or you're gonna meet a lot of lockers!" What do you do?

The Search for Alternatives:

In the space provided, write each alternative available to you. Underneath each alternative, write at least two consequences of that decision.

ALTERNATIVE 1: _____

_____

    CONSEQUENCE: _____

    _____

    CONSEQUENCE: _____

    _____

ALTERNATIVE 2: _____

_____

    CONSEQUENCE: _____

    _____

    CONSEQUENCE: _____

    _____

ALTERNATIVE 3: _____

_____

    CONSEQUENCE: _____

    _____

    CONSEQUENCE: _____

    _____

MORE ALTERNATIVES AND CONSEQUENCES? Write them here.

_____

_____

_____

4-9D

Take Your Pick!

Discuss the following questions in your group:

1. What does the advice "Count to ten" mean? How does it apply in this situation? What advantage does it have over immediate, thoughtless reaction?

_____

_____

_____

_____

2. What have you learned from this activity? Identify some principles you will use to guide your behavior if you are suddenly confronted by a situation that angers you.

   Example: I'll hesitate before I act; I'll try to react thoughtfully instead of thoughtlessly!

   What else will you do?

   • _____

   _____

   • _____

   _____

   • _____

   _____

   • _____

   _____

   • _____

   _____

Activity 4-10: Leadership

PURPOSE: To give students the opportunity to explore and reflect upon the concept of leadership. Leaders are different in how they view their purpose in guiding others. Leadership comes in all shapes and forms, and while the end product is the same, the means of getting there might be very different. This activity also encourages students to use their artistic and creative skills.

MATERIALS: Worksheets 4-10A, 4-10B, and 4-10C; colored pencils, crayons, or markers

PROCEDURE:

- Divide the students into small groups of three or four.
- Give each group one copy of the discussion questions on Worksheet 4-10A. Have each group choose a recorder to write down the group's ideas on the worksheet.
- Next, give the groups one copy each of Worksheets 4-10B and 4-10C. Allow the groups enough time to complete each sheet.
- Have each group share and explain their comparisons with the entire class.
- Display students' drawings and explanations where they can be seen regularly.

4-10A   **Leadership: Discussion Questions**

Complete the following items. Choose one member of the group to serve as the recorder to jot down your group's ideas.

1. What are the characteristics of a good leader?

_____

_____

_____

_____

2. Make a comparison between a leader and some other concept or idea. For example, a leader is like a gardener who is responsible for the growth and well being of what he or she is caring for. Or, a leader could be compared to headlights, which guide others in times of darkness or fog.

A leader is like_____

_____

because _____

_____

_____

_____

_____

_____

_____

_____

4-10B   **Leaders Are Like . . .**

Draw a picture of the item your group compared to a leader.

Students' Names _____   Date _____

_____

4-10C   # Because They . . .

Complete this diagram by writing seven words or sentences, each beginning with one of the letters in the word LEADERS, to describe your group's concept of leaders.

L _____

_____

E _____

_____

A _____

_____

D _____

_____

E _____

_____

R _____

_____

S _____

_____

SECTION 5

DEALING WITH SOCIAL ISSUES

*"Tell me what company you keep, and I'll
tell you what you are."*
MIGUEL DE CERVANTES

More of the Story:

Character is not only knowing the right thing to do, but *doing* it. Our Steering Committee reasoned early in the planning of the program that behavior is the truest expression of character. We agreed with philosopher John Locke that ". . . the actions of men [are] the best interpreters of their thoughts." One of the committee members indicated that American essayist and philosopher Ralph Waldo Emerson expressed a similar sentiment when he said, "What you do speaks so loud that I cannot hear what you say."

In other words, what teachers and students say about character is one thing; their behavior is quite another. The school's mission statement and philosophy were well-conceived, and the cooperation and good intentions of student leaders were noteworthy. But the Steering Committee was convinced that our behavior as a school was the most obvious and accurate expression of our character. We decided to take a look at it from several different perspectives.

Frankly, we didn't like some of what we saw. Swearing everywhere in the building was troubling many of us. A student raised this issue initially, but everyone on the committee agreed with it. Custodians were complaining about general sloppiness, not only in the cafeteria and halls but in the teachers' offices. In addition, open displays of affection among some students were rivaling the silver screen for shock value.

Some of us were also insensitive to the needs and feelings of our growing Mexican-American population. This issue is discussed from a different perspective in the next section of this book. For now, the social implications of this insensitivity warrant consideration. The issue was brought home to all of us on the committee when we read one student's response to our earlier questionnaire about behavior and relationships in our school.

He shared a recent experience. During a class discussion (it was still early in the school year), he answered a teacher's question and was told by the teacher, "Hey, pretty good answer for a Mexican." The student indicated that he was so surprised by the teacher's comment that he could think of nothing to say until he got home and mentioned the incident to his parents.

Needless to say, his father contacted the superintendent. He felt that no matter what the context or intent of the teacher, the comment was inappropriate. He even mentioned something his son said during dinner, "Why did he call me a Mexican student? I thought I was American." Dr. Newbrough agreed, in part because of the insensitivity of the comment and in part—much to the teacher's future surprise—because the father was a member of the board of education.

Other Mexican-American students in our school were experiencing similar insensitivity; unfortunately, their parents were not members of the board of education. The problem wasn't restricted to ethnic issues, either. One student reported on the same questionnaire that he's a good kid and that he resented being treated by some teachers as a "problem about to happen." He felt that many teachers were constantly "on guard," treating all students as potential troublemakers. He resented such an expectation.

We agreed with him, and we decided to emphasize the need to "catch them being good." We admitted as a faculty that rewarding good behavior is more important to a positive organizational atmosphere than punishing bad behavior. Moreover, we realized that painting all students with such a broad stroke is unfair to the majority who play by the rules and who need to identify with the school as a social group that accepts and values them as individuals.

Famed psychologist Abraham Maslow is well-known among educators and psychologists for his belief that each of us is motivated to belong to *some kind* of social group. In fact, according to Maslow, we are unable to develop any ego strength until our social needs are satisfied. The need to belong, to feel wanted by others, is a pronounced need within all of us.

Superintendent Newbrough mentions often in faculty and small-group meetings that an accepting atmosphere does much to cultivate the soil of positive change within the school community. He emphasizes often that students and faculty members who feel a sense of belonging within the school identify with it and, in a sense, *own* it. He indicates that it is this ownership that promotes their involvement and concern for the appearance as well as the success of the school.

This is, perhaps, one reason why gang activity, a growing concern in some parts of the community, was yet to become a problem at Mundelein High School. Our Steering Committee was sensitive to this issue. We reasoned that when the ego and social needs of students are satisfied and when they feel a sense of belonging, they are able to work on their self-concepts and to learn to discipline themselves. At that point, gangs become unnecessary.

We became convinced that this is not pie-in-the-sky unreality. Student self-discipline results when motivational needs are satisfied, even in schools battling community disregard. Consider once again the example of gangs. What are some of the factors in the home, community, and school that foster their growth? If we accept the assumption that kids join gangs because they don't feel accepted or respected anywhere else, then it's critical for schools to accept and respect their students. It's that simple.

Young people don't respect the institutions that don't respect them. Our Steering Committee knew that some schools spend more money on the effects of vandalism than on textbooks. Some of this vandalism, maybe most of it, is gang-related. This was all the more reason why our committee dedicated itself to the development of the character education program. We knew we had to seriously reevaluate relationships with and among students.

DEVELOPING A CARING SCHOOL

We realized that in the caring school, there is genuine affection for students, shared openly and spontaneously. We know that such a school praises and encourages a lot, reasons with students, and relies on punishment only as a last resort. During our discussions, we contrasted such a school with one that regards students as so many annoyances and that confuses control with punishment. We took a serious look at ourselves to determine where we were in relationship to these two kinds of schools.

The activities in this section reflect that introspection. We knew that to promote a sense of belonging in our school, a variety of issues must be explored. We decided to look at hate, gossip, bullying, violence, peer pressure, cooperation vs. competition, even etiquette and the influence of the media. These are important issues for students, not just to avoid further senseless violence in our schools but to encourage consideration and mutual caring in a society that purports to thrive on it.

Index of Activities for Dealing with Social Issues

Activity 5-1: Family Roles

PURPOSE: To explore and understand family roles.

MATERIALS: Worksheets 5-1A, 5-1B, and 5-1C; pencils

PROCEDURE:

- Set the stage for the activity by telling the students to imagine they are working in a personnel office and have the responsibility of developing job descriptions for vacancies to be filled within a family.

- They must find persons to fill three jobs: Father, Mother, and Child.

- Read the sample job description on Worksheet 5-1A to give students an idea of how to write their own.

- Individually, write job descriptions for the three jobs. Tell students to make sure they include on Worksheet 5-1B all the essential characteristics for each role.

- Next, divide the class into five groups and have the members of each group share its job descriptions with each other.

- Then instruct the groups to develop three job descriptions that represent the best thinking of the group.

- Have each group share its job descriptions with the rest of the class. Ask the class to react to elements of each description.

- Don't worry about achieving consensus. Just be sure to have everyone in the class build on each other's thinking. This is a cooperative effort, *not* a competition.

- Finally, have the groups discuss the questions on Worksheet 5-1C. Again, have them share their opinions with the rest of the class.

- The fundamental purpose of this activity is to get everyone thinking! The actual roles will vary according to ethnic group, socioeconomic conditions, etc. It's important that students realize that as well.

- Conclude with: "George Santayana once said that a good family is one of nature's masterpieces." Remember, no masterpiece was ever made without hard work.

VARIATION:

As time permits, allow the students to take the descriptions home to get input from their parents and siblings, then return them the next day for their group work.

5-1A

Sample Job Description:
School Coach

DUTIES AND RESPONSIBILITIES

1. Instructs athletes in fundamental skills, training, and strategies necessary to achieve success.
2. Understands the rules of the game and implements them consistently.
3. Respects and dignifies each athlete as an individual.
4. Promotes the conditions and the circumstances that encourage each athlete to realize his or her full potential.
5. Assures the safety of each athlete and asks no more in practice or competition than each is capable of delivering.
6. Is responsible for the conduct of his or her athletes.

KNOWLEDGE, SKILLS, AND ABILITIES

1. Understands and consistently applies sound motivational principles.
2. Understands how to promote self-discipline in athletes.
3. Uses external punishment as a last resort and applies it fairly and consistently.
4. Exhibits responsible conduct in and out of the competitive arena.
5. Serves as a model of appropriate language, behavior, and values.
6. Imposes time demands that acknowledge the primary importance of each athlete's academic and family responsibilities.
7. Promotes among athletes and coaches a sense of team membership.

CREDENTIALS AND EXPERIENCE

1. Must be appropriately certified by the state.
2. Head coaches must have had at least two years' prior experience as an assistant coach.

SPECIAL REQUIREMENTS

1. Is available to parents at times that are mutually convenient.
2. Works with other school personnel to guarantee the best interests of each athlete.
3. Assigns specific duties, and supervises and evaluates performance of colleagues.
4. Consistently releases positive information to the media as appropriate.
5. Is responsible for equipment inventory and replacement.
6. Consistently monitors playing area and locker rooms.
7. Develops in each athlete a respect for school property.
8. Is responsible for annual budget.

Student's Name _____ **Date** _____

5-1B   # Family Roles

Use the sample job description for a coach to give you an idea of the format for this activity. Remember, the roles in a family may have additional responsibilities. With that thought in mind, develop a job description for:

FATHER

Duties and Responsibilities

1. _____

2. _____

3. _____

4. _____

Knowledge, Skills, and Abilities

1. _____

2. _____

3. _____

4. _____

Credentials and Experience

1. _____

2. _____

3. _____

4. _____

Special Requirements

1. _____

2. _____

3. _____

4. _____

MOTHER

Duties and Responsibilities

1._____

2._____

3._____

4._____

Knowledge, Skills, and Abilities

1._____

2._____

3._____

4._____

Credentials and Experience

1._____

2._____

3._____

4._____

Special Requirements

1._____

2._____

3._____

4._____

CHILD

Duties and Responsibilities

1._____

2._____

3._____

4._____

Knowledge, Skills, and Abilities

1._____

2._____

3._____

4._____

Credentials and Experience

1._____

2._____

3._____

4._____

Special Requirements

1._____

2._____

3._____

4._____

Students' Names _____ Date _____

5-1C

Family Roles:
Discussion Questions

1. What does a business do if no one is available to fill a certain position? What must other workers do to satisfy those additional responsibilities? Who satisfies them?

_____

_____

_____

_____

2. How do things like cultural expectations and family finances influence each role? For example, what if both parents must work? How does this affect their at-home duties?

_____

_____

_____

_____

3. What happens to the family if the person in one of these roles refuses or is unable to perform the responsibilities? How does the role of one member depend on the role of another member?

_____

_____

_____

_____

4. What must happen within the family if one member feels overburdened? How are the roles changed as circumstances require?

_____

_____

_____

_____

Activity 5-2: Get It Right

PURPOSE: To help students understand that etiquette is not just a set of arbitrary rules handed down by adults for the purpose of annoying kids. Etiquette, although seemingly arbitrary, helps to form the norms that allow us as a community to function. Rules of etiquette are based on respect for self and others.

MATERIALS: Worksheets 5-2A and 5-2B; pencils

PROCEDURE:

- Hand out the quiz on Worksheet 5-2A to each member of the class.
- Allow students enough time to complete the quiz.
- Go over the quiz, allowing for comments/discussion as you go.
- Divide the class into small groups of three.
- Hand out one copy of Worksheet 5-2B to each group of three students.
- Give the groups time to complete the worksheet. Have each group choose one student to serve as the recorder for the group.
- Go over the worksheets one question at a time. Have the groups share their response to each question with the entire class.
- Come to a consensus as an entire class on the answers to the questions.

5-2A   # Get It Right: Quiz

1. You're at your locker before school starts. The principal walks by. You:

   A. Say, "Hey, s'up dude."
   B. Pretend you don't see him and keep shuffling stuff in your locker.
   C. Say, "Good morning, Dr. Jones."

2. A very personal note meant for someone else ends up in your locker by mistake. You:

   A. Photocopy it and hand it out to all your friends.
   B. Read it, laugh, and toss it in the trash.
   C. Quietly give it to the person it was intended for, explaining that it was left in your locker by mistake.

3. Mrs. Smith, one of the older faculty members, is struggling to open the door to the school while hanging on to all her books. You say:

   A. "You ought to work out, Smith. You're losing it."
   B. "Let me help you, Mrs. Smith."
   C. You're in a bad mood so you scowl and walk on by.

4. Your teacher is out for the day and you have a sub. You:

   A. Switch seats so he calls everyone by the wrong names.
   B. Climb out the window when he turns his back to write on the board.
   C. Make a special effort to be helpful and cooperative.

5. You are supposed to sit with your advisory group in an assembly. You:

   A. Walk with the group and sit in the designated area at the assembly.
   B. Lag behind the group, then duck around the corner into the washroom for a smoke.
   C. Ditch the group once you get to the gym and go sit with your friends.

6. At the assembly the president of the Student Council asks everyone to rise for the Pledge of Allegiance. You:

   A. Say, "Whatever, dude" and lounge back.
   B. Stand and repeat the Pledge.
   C. Claim that you're not American by birth; therefore, you don't have to take part.

7. You're in the cafeteria having lunch and would like to get the attention of the cool new girl from your math class who is sitting at the next table. You:

   A. Throw an ice cube from your drink and hit her in the head.
   B. Notice your friend sitting next to her, so you shout, "Hey, Ron, who's the dork sitting next to you?"
   C. Go over to where she's sitting and start a conversation by asking some open-ended questions.

5-2B   **Get It Right**

In your groups, choose one student to write down the group's answers to the following discussion questions:

1. Why do we have rules of etiquette?

    _____

    _____

    _____

    _____

2. Why do we use titles here at school for teachers, administrators, and other staff members (Mr., Ms., Mrs., Dr.), but not for students?

    _____

    _____

    _____

    _____

3. How do the titles help us understand how our school community works?

    _____

    _____

    _____

    _____

4. How would eliminating titles for teachers, administrators, and staff change the school climate?

    _____

    _____

    _____

    _____

5. Are there some rules of etiquette you think should be changed? Example: Is it okay not to stand up for the Pledge of Allegiance?

_____

_____

_____

_____

6. What are the basic principles behind rules of etiquette?

_____

_____

_____

_____

Activity 5-3: Gossip

PURPOSE: To establish the concept that gossip is *not* a First Class character trait. It is most often harmful and contributes to the problem rather than the solution. First Class individuals work at contributing to the solution of problems, *not* to the continuation or augmentation of them. Putting students together in small groups in this activity allows them to consider and discuss the responses of their peers in a safe and secure setting where they can have an immediate response or reaction to a question. Often this type of environment helps to change the direction of their thinking on an issue.

MATERIALS: Worksheet 5-3; paper; pencils

PROCEDURE

- First, arrange students in rows.
- Give a sheet of paper and a pencil to the first person in each row.
- Have the first person in each row write the name of a person in the class (Mary, Jim, Teresa, Wyatt) on the first line of the paper. Having completed this task, the student folds the paper over just to cover what was written and passes it, along with the pencil, to the person seated behind him or her.
- The next person writes what happened over the weekend (played basketball, went to a party, danced up a storm), folds the paper over to cover up the writing, and passes the paper and pencil to the next student in the row.
- The next student completes the phrase "with_____," filling in the blank with the name of another student in the class. The student folds the paper over to cover the writing and passes the paper and pencil to the next student seated behind.
- This student writes a place where the activity took place (in the park, at the dance, during math class), folds the paper over, and passes the paper and pencil to the next student behind.
- The next student writes at what time the event took place (at midnight, at noon, at 2:00 P.M., at 6:00 A.M.), folds the paper over, and passes the paper and pencil to the last student in the row.
- The last student writes the result of the activity. (The car broke down. The police arrived. The roof caved in.)
- The last student in each row returns the "gossip" to the person at the beginning of the row who started it.
- The students at the beginning of each row read each bit of "gossip" aloud to the class.
- Now, divide the students into groups of three and give each student Worksheet 5-3.
- Have the students complete and discuss the worksheet together.
- Ask students to share their small group's feelings about the questions with the whole class.
- Come up with a class-generated list of ways to eliminate gossip (question 8 on the worksheet).

5-3 **Gossip: Discussion Questions**

Respond to the following questions individually and then discuss your answers with the other students in your small group.

1. On a scale of 1–10, where would you rank gossip as a student issue in our school?

    _____

    _____

    _____

2. Have you ever discovered that untrue rumors were circulating about you? How did you feel?

    _____

    _____

    _____

    _____

3. How have you taken part unwittingly in spreading a false rumor? Explain, if you can.

    _____

    _____

    _____

4. What's wrong with gossiping?

    _____

    _____

    _____

5. Is gossiping unfair?

    _____

    _____

    _____

6. Is anyone hurt by it? Explain.

    _____

    _____

    _____

    _____

7. How is gossip like the activity we just did?

    _____

    _____

    _____

8. How can we eliminate gossip?

    _____

    _____

    _____

    _____

    _____

    _____

(Use the back of this paper for more ideas.)

Activity 5-4: Peer Pressure

PURPOSE: To help students realize they are subjected to peer pressure every day. This activity helps students see how they bow to peer pressure on a regular basis and what alternatives they have for handling it.

MATERIALS: Worksheets 5-4A and 5-4B; pencils

PROCEDURE:

- Have the students take the quiz on Worksheet 5-4A individually.

- When students have finished the quiz, give the number of points earned for each answer so that students can compute their scores. An **a** answer is worth 1 point, a **b** answer is worth 2 points, and a **c** answer is worth 3 points.

- Have those who scored 10–16 points stand in one area of the room. Have those who scored 17–23 points stand in another area of the room. Finally, have those who scored 24–30 points stand in a third area of the room.

- Form new groups of three by putting one student from each of the three point-scoring groups together. That is, place one student who scored 10–16, one who scored 17–23 points, and one who scored 24–30 points together in one group.

- Follow up with the discussion questions on Worksheet 5-4B.

- Give one copy of Worksheet 5-4B to each small group.

- Have each group choose a recorder to write on the worksheet the group's responses to the discussion questions.

- Have a spokesperson from each group share the group's answers to the discussion questions.

- Come up with a class-generated list of ways to handle peer pressure.

5-4A   **Peer Pressure: Quiz**

Complete each situation with the solution you would choose. Circle the letter of your answer.

1. You and your two best friends are supposed to do something Friday night. They decide to get a video and invite their girl- or boyfriends over. You're not seeing anyone currently, so you:
    a. Feel bummed, go home, and sulk.
    b. Invite your little cousin over to watch a Disney video with you.
    c. Invite your new crush to join you and your friends.

2. You go to a party that everyone's going to. When you arrive, you find out there are no adult chaperons and someone brought alcohol. You feel uncomfortable, so you:
    a. Join the party and start drinking so you forget you are uncomfortable.
    b. Join the party, but refuse the offer of alcohol and drink soda.
    c. Leave the party.

3. On the night of your grandparents' 50th-wedding anniversary party, your best friend is having the biggest party of the year. You:
    a. Build a very strong case with your parents for going to your friend's party (you'd be the social failure of the year and never have any friends again) and go to the party.
    b. Go to the family anniversary party, but leave right after dinner to get to your friend's party.
    c. Go to the anniversary party and enjoy it. (They are your grandparents and you're lucky to have them.)

4. You change the color of your hair just because you want a new look. Your friends start making rude comments about how it looks. You:
    a. Have it dyed back to your own color.
    b. Wear a baseball cap as often as possible.
    c. Laugh and tell your friends to get a life.

5. Your best friends are in French class with you. You do pretty well because you study it every night and do your homework. They think homework is a waste of time and energy. The night before a big unit test, your friends want you to go to a movie with them. You:
    a. Figure your grades are pretty good and you can wing it for one test, so you go with them.
    b. Tell them your parents won't let you go out the night before a test.
    c. Tell them you really want to do well on the test and that you'll go to the movies with them on Friday night.

6. You're at the mall with a group of friends. One of your teachers walks by. You:
   a. Make rude comments about teachers in general and laugh at the one walking by.
   b. Get involved in animated conversation with your friends and pretend you don't see the teacher.
   c. Greet the teacher by name as he or she walks by.

7. It's Saturday and your parents ask if you'd like to go to the beach for the afternoon. It's really hot and you'd love an afternoon of swimming and sunning. You:
   a. Know you'd be mortified if any of your friends saw you at the beach with your parents, so you decline the invitation.
   b. Agree to go if you can invite several of your friends to go also.
   c. Accept their invitation and even offer to help pack a picnic lunch.

8. Two of your friends who are thinner than you are complaining about how fat they are while watching you polish off a hefty, but healthy after-school snack. You:
   a. Find the nearest mirror and decide you really have to go on a strict diet.
   b. Feel embarrassed at the size of your snack compared to their glasses of water, immediately throw your snack away, and get a glass of water.
   c. Laugh and tell them if they played a sport like you do, they could eat anything they wanted and not gain a pound.

9. On a typical school night, you:
   a. Eat dinner, watch TV, talk on the phone, listen to music and e-mail your friends, read magazines, get to bed by midnight.
   b. Eat dinner, watch one hour of your favorite TV program, do your homework while listening to your favorite music, talk on the phone with friends, get to bed by 11:00.
   c. Eat dinner, do your homework while listening to your favorite music, receive a couple of phone calls, get to bed by 10:30.

10. You have a new crush. Your crush is in one of your classes, but doesn't hang with the same group you do. When you mention your crush casually to some of your friends, they react negatively. You:
    a. Forget the whole idea. (There are a lot of fish in the sea.)
    b. Continue to pursue your crush, but stop talking about it with your friends.
    c. Tell your friends you really like this person and if they were really your friends, they'd give your crush a chance before reacting so negatively.

11. Your parents have imposed a weekend curfew for you that none of your friends have. You're embarrassed and humiliated as well as annoyed with your parents. Your friends don't want to hang with you because they always have to stop what they're doing to drop you off at home. You:
    a. Argue with and get angry with your parents, generally making their lives—and yours—miserable.
    b. Accept their curfew resentfully, knowing there's not much you can do about it.
    c. Sit down with your parents and work out a curfew that is more reasonable and not so restrictive.

5-4B   **Peer Pressure: Discussion Questions**

In your groups, answer the following discussion questions. Choose one person in the group to serve as the recorder.

1. What does peer pressure mean to you?

   _____

   _____

   _____

   _____

2. Where do you see, use, or feel peer pressure?

   _____

   _____

   _____

   _____

3. What happens when someone is experiencing peer pressure? How does peer pressure affect others in that person's life?

   _____

   _____

   _____

   _____

4. What are some effective ways of dealing with peer pressure?

   _____

   _____

   _____

(Use the back of this sheet if you need more space for your answer.)

Activity 5-5: Positive Interdependence

PURPOSE: To demonstrate the social as well as the practical outcomes of cooperative work. There is a huge difference between working in groups and working cooperatively. Cooperative group work is structured so that there is positive interdependence. In other words, everyone in the group has a stake in the success of everyone else in the group.

MATERIALS: Worksheets 5-5A and 5-5B; pencils; enough edible prizes (mini candy bars, pieces of candy, etc.) for everyone in the class

PROCEDURE:

- Randomly divide the group into small groups of three students. You might use assorted flavors of hard candies, pieces of colored paper, birthdays, heights (tallest to shortest), etc.

- Give one copy of Worksheet 5-5A to each group.

- Allow the groups enough time to practice and complete their tasks.

- Pair two groups together. Have one group perform the tasks on the task list for the other group. The observing group awards 1 point per person for each task performed correctly by the performing group. Then the two groups switch roles. The observing group now becomes the performing group and the performing group is the observing group. A perfect score for the performing group results in a prize for everyone in that group.

- The group must have a perfect score in order to be eligible for a prize. If all groups have perfect scores, everyone in the class gets a prize. (Edible prizes are the most popular among teens.)

- Follow-up with the discussion questions on Worksheet 5-5B. Give each group a copy of the discussion questions and allow students enough time to complete it. Then have each group share its answers to the questions with the entire class.

- The following are student reactions to the concept of cooperative learning. Feel free to share these with your students during the discussion.

Every one has to put forth the effort and you have to be able to open up & communicate with everyone.

It still helps you understand, but you meet new people also.

I think that cooperative learning is better than learning alone and it helps to know people better and to work with them.

Cooperative learning is helping me personally to get more organized and learn how to work w/different people besides just my friends.

It's more than just working together. You have to understand each other, give out ideas, be able to work & get along with others.

You have to be able to get along with others really well. You have to be able to talk to them, and share your ideas with them.

We have learned social skills such as listening, participating and working with other people. Working well with others is the hardest of all the skills we use, but having the help of others is great.

Also, it makes me feel good when I help other people understand things.

I know that it's not as easy as it sounded at first, because to help other people, you have to have patience and sometimes that's hard.

You must give and take, like you need to help others and let them help you. And participate.

We have to all contribute our ideas and say our opinion or ask questions if you have one so everyone can do good.

To have it work I have to pay attention. It has helped me by having me understand something, by just asking someone, when I didn't know.

The social skill I have learned is communication, to express any feelings in more detail. I don't think I have mastered any skills, and I could work on all of them.

I have used these social skills in communicating with my friends. Mostly when I'm playing in my band, and I have ideas for something.

Students' Names _____   Date _____
_____

5-5A   ## Task List

Each student in your group must complete and perform the following tasks individually in order for your group to be eligible for a prize. You will be given time now to confer and help each other practice for the performance.

Task 1:   Say the following in a language other than English.

"Hello. My name is _____. How are you?"

Task 2:   Come to a consensus on a special handshake. Learn how to do it and be prepared to teach it to someone else.

Task 3:   Name the 3 R's of First Class and explain what they mean.

5-5B   # Positive Interdependence:
                              ## Discussion Questions

Discuss the following questions in your cooperative groups. Be prepared to share your answers with the entire class.

1. This activity was designed as a cooperative group activity. What is the difference between working in a group and working in a cooperative group?

   _____

   _____

   _____

   _____

2. What are the benefits of working in a cooperative group? How is this similar to real-life situations?

   _____

   _____

   _____

   _____

   _____

3. What are the disadvantages of working in a cooperative group? How are these similar to real-life situations?

   _____

   _____

   _____

   _____

   _____

4. If someone in a cooperative group is not pulling his or her fair share of the load, how do you handle it?

Best Solutions: _____

_____

_____

_____

_____

_____

Last Resort: _____

_____

5. In addition to accomplishing given tasks quickly and creatively, what are the First Class social skills you learn when working in cooperative groups?

_____

_____

_____

_____

_____

_____

Activity 5-6: Competition vs. Cooperation

PURPOSE: To explore the concept of cooperation. Students should have a stake in each other's success, not in each other's failure. In life, from conception on, little can be accomplished without the cooperation of others. It's difficult to think of a life situation where we sit in long rows and complete worksheets while someone says, "Don't talk! Don't share your answers! Keep your eyes on your own paper!" Let's consider the overused practice of competitive education. If everyone else in a class does poorly, the easier it is for me to do well. In a competitive classroom, how then can educational levels be raised when the philosophy is founded in negative thinking? In fostering competitive education, we are denying students access to the interpersonal skills they will need in life. Proficiency in listening, interacting, group problem solving, confrontation, and negotiation skills are all cooperative skills and necessary in order to lead productive and satisfying lives. Those skills can't be well-developed in competitive situations.

MATERIALS: Worksheet 5-6; pencils; copies of any kind of word game (an example of "Wacky Wordies" is included as a sample); a bag of assorted hard candies

PROCEDURE:

- Before the students arrive, divide the number of students in your group by three. Cooperative groups work well with three people. Two are not enough for a good discussion and four sometimes lose focus.

- Next, put three hard candies of the same flavor in a bag for each group you have in the class. For example, if you have 27 students in the class (27 divided by 3 equals 9 groups), you would put nine different flavors of candy with three pieces per flavor into the bag. Shake the bag to mix the candy and save it until after the quiz.

- Tell the students you are going to give them a timed quiz. Hand out a copy (quiz-side down) of the word game to each student, seated in traditional rows in the classroom set-up.

- Instruct the students to keep the quizzes face down until you give the signal to begin.

- Inform the students that they will have 5 minutes to complete the quiz. Instruct them to begin.

- After 5 minutes have elapsed, instruct the students to stop and mark the number of items they have completed in the upper right-hand corner of the quiz.

- Now go around the classroom and have each student choose a hard candy from your bag of assorted candies.

- Tell the students to group themselves according to the flavor of the piece of candy they selected from the bag. **No trading of candy.** In life we don't often get to work with our friends or people who are the same age or have the same intellectual capacity we do. This is a life lesson.

- Have the students sit or arrange their desks so they can face each other. Eye-to-eye contact is an important part of learning to become a good listener.
- Now have the students continue to work on their quizzes in their new cooperative groups. Allow them another 5 minutes to work together.
- When the time has elapsed, ask the groups to mark down the number of items they have completed in the upper left corner of the quiz.
- Follow up with the discussion questions on Worksheet 5-6.
- Finish the lesson by reading aloud the passage entitled "Lessons from the Geese" by Angeles Arrien.

ANSWERS: Here are the answers to the sample "Wacky Wordies."

1a	Just between you and me	5a	World without end
1b	Hitting below the belt	5b	Way behind the times
1c	Head over heels in love	5c	Word to the wise
1d	Shrinking violets	5d	Search high and low
1e	Bermuda Triangle	5e	Go off half-cocked
1f	A mixed bag	5f	No two ways about it
2a	Cry over spilt milk	6a	Hole-in-one
2b	Lying in wait	6b	Down-to-earth
2c	*Unfinished Symphony*	6c	Three-ring circus
2d	Pineapple upside-down cake	6d	One at a time
2e	You're under arrest	6e	Better late than never
2f	Split-second timing	6f	Get a word in edgewise
3a	Nothing on TV	7a	Let bygones be bygones
3b	Fly-by-night	7b	An outside chance
3c	Raise a big stink	7c	Three degrees below zero
3d	Add insult to injury	7d	A terrible spell of weather
3e	Railroad crossing	7e	World Series
3f	A person after my own heart	7f	Cut loose
4a	At the point of no return	8a	Reading between the lines
4b	The inside dope	8b	Chicken Little
4c	Long underwear	8c	Fourth of July fireworks
4d	Ostrich with its head in the ground	8d	London Bridge
4e	Lucky break	8e	Change of pace
4f	Corner the market	8f	Square dance contest

Wacky Wordies

The object in solving is to discern a familiar phrase, saying, cliché, or name from each arrangement of letters and/or symbols. For example, box 1a depicts the phrase "just between you and me." Box 1b shows "hitting below the belt." The puzzles get more diabolical as you go.

	a	b	c	d	e	f
1	you just me	belt hitting	lo head ve heels	V I O L E Tₛ	A B E DUMR	agb
2	cry m i l k	—⊏ ⵿⊐ᴔ—⊢	Symphon	ǝlddɐǝuᴉd cake	arrest you're	timing tim ing
3	O TV	night fly	S T I N K	injury + insult	r o rail d	my own heart a person
4	at the · of on	dothepe	wear long	strich groound	lu cky	the market
5	worl	the x way	word YYY	search and	go off coc	no ways it ways
6	oholene	t o e a r t h	ooo circus	1 at 3:46	late nₑᵥₑr	get a word in
7	let gone gone be gone gone	a chance n	O MD BA PhD	wheather	world world world world	lo ose
8	lines reading lines	chicken	y fireworks	L D Bridge	pace k̶	danc c t e s c etno

"Lessons From the Geese"

As each goose flaps its wings, it creates an "uplift" for the bird following. By flying in a V formation, the whole flock adds 71% more flying range than if each bird flew alone.

LESSON: People who share a common direction and sense of community can get where they are going quicker and easier because they are traveling on the thrust of one another.

Whenever a goose falls out of formation, it suddenly feels the drag and resistance of trying to fly alone and quickly gets back into formation to take advantage of the lifting power of the birds immediately in front.

LESSON: If we have as much sense as a goose, we will join in formations with those who are headed where we want to go.

When the lead goose gets tired, it rotates back into the formation and another goose flies at the point position.

LESSON: It pays to take turns doing the hard tasks and sharing leadership with people, as with geese, interdependent with one another.

The geese in formation honk from behind to encourage those up front to keep up their speed.

LESSON: We need to make sure our honking from behind is encouraging—not something less helpful.

When a goose gets sick or wounded or shot down, two geese drop out of formation and follow their fellow member down to help and provide protection. They stay with this member of the flock until he or she either is able to fly again or dies. They then launch out on their own, with another formation or to catch up with their own flock.

LESSON: If we have as much sense as the geese do, we'll stand by one another like they do.

by Angeles Arrien
for Outward Bound, 1991

5-6   # Competition vs. Cooperation: Discussion Questions

1. In which situation (working alone or working in the cooperative group) did you figure out more answers? Why?

   _____

   _____

   _____

   _____

2. Which situation was more fun—working alone or working in a group? Why?

   _____

   _____

   _____

   _____

3. Why do you think working together cooperatively is an important life skill to develop?

   _____

   _____

   _____

   _____

4. What are the advantages of cooperation vs. competition?

   _____

   _____

   _____

   _____

5. What are the disadvantages of cooperation vs. competition? How can we turn any disadvantages into advantages?

   _____

   _____

   _____

   _____

   _____

   _____

   _____

Activity 5-7: Handling Bullying

PURPOSE: To promote reflection on principles and critical-thinking skills. A published report by the U.S. Secret Service on the prevention of violence in schools states that bullying played a major role in a number of the recent school shootings. It follows, then, that combating bullying in our schools is a topic requiring attention and work. The situation provided in this activity provokes serious reflection and involves students in a real-life experience that examines their core principles.

MATERIALS: Worksheets 5-7A, 5-7B, and 5-7C; pencils

PROCEDURE:

- Read the situation on Worksheet 5-7A aloud to the class (or give each student a copy).

- Hand out a copy of the discussion questions on Worksheet 5-7B to each member of the class.

- Allow students time to complete the questions and then ask them to share their responses with the entire class.

- Divide the class into small groups of three or four.

- Give each group a copy of Worksheet 5-7C. Tell each group to select a recorder to write down the group's answers on the worksheet.

- When the groups have completed the worksheet, have a spokesperson from each group share its responses to questions 2 and 3 on Worksheet 5-7C with the entire class.

- Come up with a class-generated list for ways of combating bullying (question 4 on Worksheet 5-7C).

- Here are sample answers to questions 1 and 3 of Worksheet 5-7C.

    1. **Alternative 1**   Explain the situation to the coach.

        Consequence: The bullying would get worse.

        Consequence: The coach would think I was a wimp.

    Alternative 2   Get a gun and shoot them all.

        Consequence: Innocent people would get hurt.

        Consequence: I'd spend the rest of my life in prison.

    3. BULLYING→ REACTIONS→ANGER→REVENGE→VIOLENCE

Situation: Handling Bullying

Jay goes out for the football team against his parents' wishes. He isn't very big, nor is he very coordinated, but he is willing to work hard and he loves football. His parents feel he would be better off getting involved with the stage crew for theatrical performances at school where he has shown some talent and has been recruited by the director. But Jay, who also stutters a bit, tells his parents emphatically that he has made up his m . . . m . . . m . . . mind and he will play f . . . f . . . football.

After much hard work and weeks of sore muscles, Jay is pleased when he makes the practice squad. He has a football jersey and he's an official member of the varsity team. However, the members of the first string don't see it that way. They tease him relentlessly about his stuttering, mimicking what he says. This makes his stuttering get even worse and he becomes afraid to open his mouth around any of the members of the football team when off the field.

The members of the first string who are much bigger than Jay love to hit him hard during practices and then push his head into the dirt as they get up off of him. In the locker room Jay often finds his equipment on top of a locker where he can't reach it or in the shower all wet. Because of this, he couldn't find his equipment on more than one occasion and was reprimanded by the coach for arriving late for practice. Jay becomes angry, but doesn't want the humiliation of quitting. He goes to his parents and tells them he'd like to begin taking shooting instruction at the gun club's rifle range.

5-7B

Handling Bullying:
Discussion Questions

Answer the following questions. Be prepared to share your answers with the entire class.

1. As Jay, how did you feel in this situation?

   _____

   _____

   _____

   _____

2. What's wrong with bullying?

   _____

   _____

   _____

   _____

3. Consider the 3R's of First Class, the core of who we are as a school and as a community. What belief or principle is most affected in this situation? Why?

   _____

   _____

   _____

   _____

   _____

_____

5-7C   # Handling Bullying

Complete the following worksheet in your small groups. Select one person from your group to serve as the recorder to write your group's answers.

1. In the space provided, write each alternative available to you if you were Jay. Underneath each alternative, write at least two consequences of that decision.

ALTERNATIVE 1: _____

     CONSEQUENCE: _____

     CONSEQUENCE: _____

ALTERNATIVE 2: _____

     CONSEQUENCE _____

     CONSEQUENCE _____

ALTERNATIVE 3: _____

     CONSEQUENCE: _____

     CONSEQUENCE: _____

2. Based on your First Class principles and beliefs, what is the best solution to this situation? Explain.

_____

_____

_____

_____

_____

_____

_____

3. What is the typical pattern of behavior that bullying promotes?

    BULLYING→_____→_____→_____→**VIOLENCE**

4. List five ways to combat bullying.

    _____

    _____

    _____

    _____

    _____

    _____

    _____

    _____

    _____

    _____

    _____

Activity 5-8: Violence

PURPOSE: To examine violence and all those who are affected. Some states have tried to enact Good Samaritan Laws, but it is very difficult to legislate social principles. It often doesn't do a good job of changing conduct. The way we change conduct, then, is to rekindle forgotten principles so that we don't end up with a "bankrupt" society. This lesson asks young people to think beyond *what's best for me* to *what's the right thing to do*.

MATERIALS: Worksheets 5-8A, 5-8B, 5-8C, 5-8D, and 5-8E; pencils

PROCEDURE:

- Have the students sit in a large circle.
- Give each student the survey on Worksheet 5-8A to complete. Teachers should complete their own survey on Worksheet 5-8B. Use the results of these surveys as a diagnostic tool.
- Read aloud Worksheet 5-8C (or give a copy to each student).
- Give each student a copy of the discussion questions on Worksheet 5-8D. Ask students to write their answers to the questions.
- Have the students share their responses. Allow every member of the group to express an opinion on the subject.
- Divide the large group into small groups of three or four students.
- Give each member of the group a copy of the reflection questions on Worksheet 5-8E. Allow the groups time to discuss the questions and then have each group share its thoughts and feelings with the class as a whole.
- Allow for mature disagreement and for differences of opinion, but try to focus on the ethics of actions. The lesson is intended to create some feelings toward responsibility to do the right thing.
- After the discussion has concluded, finish by asking students to think of ways they could make better bad situations they have witnessed.

Relationships and Dating Violence in High School:
Student Survey

Grade: (*circle one*)   (1) Freshman   (2) Sophomore   (3) Junior   (4) Senior

Sex: (*circle one*)   (1) Male   (2) Female

1. In your opinion, is violence a problem in your school?
   - ❐ yes
   - ❐ no
   - ❐ don't know

2. In your opinion, is abuse in dating relationships a problem in your school?
   - ❐ yes
   - ❐ no
   - ❐ don't know

3. I know someone in a dating relationship in which one person: (*check all that apply*)
   - A. ❐ was emotionally abused
   - B. ❐ was afraid of his or her partner
   - C. ❐ was threatened physically
   - D. ❐ was physically harmed
   - E. ❐ was pressured into having sex

4. Have you ever felt afraid that your parents' fighting got out of control?
   - ❐ yes
   - ❐ no
   - ❐ don't know

5. I have dated or am currently dating someone who: (*check all that apply*)
   - A. ❐ threatened me with physical harm
   - B. ❐ punched, kicked, shoved, or physically harmed me
   - C. ❐ pressured me for sex
   - D. ❐ was forceful or frightening during sex
   - E. ❐ threatened to harm me if I ever left
   - F. ❐ threatened suicide if I left
   - G. ❐ chose my clothes, friends, and/or activities
   - H. ❐ was jealous and possessive toward me
   - I. ❐ wouldn't let me have friends
   - J. ❐ needed to know where I was all the time
   - K. ❐ tried to control me by being very bossy, giving orders, making all decisions
   - L. ❐ pressured me into using drugs or alcohol
   - M. ❐ caused my family or friends to worry about my safety
   - N. ❐ criticized the way I looked or acted
   - O. ❐ embarrassed me in front of friends

5-8A *(continued)*

Questions 6–16, True or False (*please check your answer next to each question*)

6. It is okay to insult or make fun of someone. ❏ True ❏ False

7. If your partner shows remorse after hurting you, it really isn't abuse. ❏ True ❏ False

8. If you don't leave an abusive relationship, then you deserve what you get. ❏ True ❏ False

9. You have the right to say no to sex even if you've been dating a long time. ❏ True ❏ False

10. Abusers come from all races, religions, and income levels. ❏ True ❏ False

11. Victims come from all races, religions, and income levels. ❏ True ❏ False

12. Sometimes people are abusive because they've been pushed too far by their partner. ❏ True ❏ False

13. Staying with a partner who slapped you only a few times is better than being alone. ❏ True ❏ False

14. People can't help being abusive when they have been drinking. ❏ True ❏ False

15. Jealousy is a sign of love. ❏ True ❏ False

16. If your partner is under a lot of stress and lashes out at you, it's really not his or her fault. ❏ True ❏ False

17. Would you talk to someone if you were concerned about an abusive relationship?
   - ❏ yes
   - ❏ no
   - ❏ undecided

   If yes, to whom would you speak? (check all that apply)

FAMILY	**SCHOOL**	**COMMUNITY**
❏ mother	❏ social worker	❏ friend/neighbor
❏ father	❏ teacher	❏ pastor/rabbi/priest
❏ sibling	❏ counselor	❏ police
❏ other relative	❏ nurse	❏ doctor
		❏ crisis hot line

   Please list any other types of people to whom you would speak: _____

18. If you were concerned about an abusive relationship in your life, would you go to a support group if one were offered at your school?
   - ❏ yes
   - ❏ no
   - ❏ undecided

19. Please check which of the following topics you would like to learn more about:
   - ❏ family violence   ❏ managing anger
   - ❏ gender differences   ❏ relationship violence
   - ❏ stalking   ❏ healthy relationships

20. Comments _____

_____

Relationships and Dating Violence in High School:
Teacher Survey

Sex (*circle one*): (1) Male (2) Female

Please write in the number(s) of your department(s): _____/_____/_____

  (1) Math/Sciences; (2) English/Social Sciences; (3) Physical Ed/Health Ed;

  (4) Business Ed/Vocational; (5) Administrative; (6) Support Staff; (7) Other

1. In your opinion, is violence a problem in your school?
   ❏ yes
   ❏ no
   ❏ don't know

2. In your opinion, is abuse in dating relationships a problem in your school?
   ❏ yes
   ❏ no
   ❏ don't know

3. I personally or professionally know someone in a relationship in which one person: (*check all that apply*)
   ❏ was emotionally abused
   ❏ was afraid of his or her partner
   ❏ was threatened physically
   ❏ was physically harmed
   ❏ was pressured into having sex

4. Have any of the following experiences helped to promote your interest in violence prevention? (*check all that apply*)
   ❏ Discussions with staff about violence
   ❏ One of your students having had a personal experience with violence
   ❏ A personal experience with violence as a child
   ❏ A personal experience with violence as an adult
   ❏ Having heard about violence through the media
   ❏ Participating in a school-based violence-prevention week

5. Check any of the following reasons why you would *not* support a dating violence-prevention program in your school.
   ❏ Discussion with staff about violence
   ❏ Other student needs have greater priority
   ❏ There is no clear mandate for this issue in our school
   ❏ Not comfortable in talking to students about this issue
   ❏ Unfamiliar with the topic
   ❏ A personal experience with violence
   ❏ Other

6. Is violence prevention taught in your school?
   ❏ yes
   ❏ no
   ❏ don't know

   If yes, what topics are covered and by whom? _____

   _____

7. Have there ever been guest speakers at your school who discuss violence prevention?
   ❏ yes
   ❏ no
   ❏ don't know

   If yes, what topics did they cover and by whom? _____

   _____

8. To whom would you talk if you were concerned about a student witnessing or experiencing a violent relationship? (*check all that apply*)

   ❏ the student   ❏ principal   ❏ school nurse
   ❏ student's parent or ❏ teacher   ❏ crisis hot-line worker
     legal guardian   ❏ school counselor/ ❏ other _____
                            social worker

9. Does your school offer support groups for children experiencing violence in their homes?
   ❏ yes
   ❏ no
   ❏ don't know

10. Please check which of the following topics you would like your school to learn more about:
    ❏ family violence   ❏ managing anger
    ❏ gender roles   ❏ relationship violence
    ❏ stalking   ❏ healthy relationships

11. Who is responsible for arranging speakers in your school?

    _____

12. Comments_____

    _____

Violence: The Crime

In the summer of 1998 before he entered Berkeley as a Nuclear Engineering student, David Cash and his best friend Jeremy Stromeyer, accompanied by David Cash's father, went to a casino in Las Vagas to have some fun. At 3:00 A.M., as recorded by the casino video cameras, Jeremy Stromeyer followed 7-year-old Sherise Iverson, whose father was gambling nearby, into the washroom. Stromeyer was followed into the washroom by his best friend David Cash. In the washroom, David Cash saw Stromeyer grab the 7-year-old girl, restrain her physically, and rape her. He said nothing to stop Stromeyer. When questioned by the TV show "60 Minutes," Cash said he tapped his friend Stromeyer on the head as a signal that he was going too far. However, he also said he never actually told his friend Stromeyer to stop, nor did he attempt to get help from any of the security people at the casino. What he did do was leave the washroom where his friend was sexually assaulting a 7-year-old girl and go back to gambling. Twenty-five minutes later Jeremy Stromeyer emerged from the washroom and came back to gamble with David Cash. When Cash asked what happened, Stromeyer confessed to Cash that the little girl would never come out of the washroom because he had strangled her. The boys then left to do some more gambling at another casino. David Cash never reported the crime to anyone else.

As soon as the videotapes at the casino were reviewed, Jeremy Stromeyer was arrested and charged with murder. He is now serving life in prison with no parole.

David Cash was not charged in the crime. When interviewed on "60 Minutes," he said, "How much am I supposed to cry about this. I do not know this little girl. I do not know starving children in Panama. I do not know people that die of disease in Egypt." He showed no remorse that the girl had been murdered. The prosecuting attorney called David Cash "morally bankrupt," but explained that watching and failing to report is not legally considered a crime. However, David Cash is the one person who could have stopped the crime from happening. When asked if he could relive that night at the casino what he would have done differently, Cash responded, "I don't feel there's much I could have done differently."

5-8D   # Violence: Discussion Questions

1. The way David Cash figures, he is just protecting his best friend. What do you think of this way of looking at the situation?

   _____

   _____

   _____

2. Is David Cash guilty of anything?

   _____

   _____

   _____

3. Do you think you would have done what he did? Why?

   _____

   _____

   _____

4. If not, what would you have done?

   _____

   _____

   _____

5-8E

Violence:
Reflection Questions

Discuss these questions in your small group. Be prepared to share your group's thoughts and feelings with the rest of the class.

1. What obligations do we have in our society, community, or school to look out for the best interest of other people?

    _____

    _____

    _____

    _____

    _____

2. How much does the degree of damage done in a situation determine our responsibility to intervene? (Is stopping others from teasing as important as stopping others from doing bodily harm? Is stealing money from a fast-food store worse than getting free food from a friend's employee?)

    _____

    _____

    _____

    _____

    _____

3. What percentage of people/students do you think maintain an attitude similar to David Cash's? ("If I didn't directly commit the offense, it's none of my business.")

    _____

    _____

    _____

4. How might the "If I didn't directly commit the offense, it's none of my business" attitude change society?

    _____

    _____

    _____

    _____

    _____

5. Are students wronged here at school whom others witness and choose to ignore? In what kinds of situations would students be wronged? Why do you think people ignore this?

    _____

    _____

    _____

    _____

    _____

*Thanks to Katie Lacio and Kate Dumich for this activity.

Activity 5-9: "Gift" Giving

PURPOSE: To determine personal ways we can make situations better for others by our commitment to making positive choices. This activity, a follow-up to Activity 5-8, is designed to encourage students to reflect on the great differences they can make in the lives of others with just a little effort. It should not be done to receive recognition. Understand that these commitments may be quite personal and only each student can evaluate for him-/herself the good that others may receive.

MATERIALS: Worksheets 5-9A, 5-9B, and 5-9C; pencils; brown paper cut into a tree shape

PROCEDURE:

- Before the activity begins, cut the piece of brown paper into the shape of a tree and display it somewhere in the classroom.

- Read Worksheet 5-9A aloud to the class (or give a copy to each student).

- Ask the students to think about a simple act of kindness/consideration they performed recently. Encourage them to share their act of kindness with the class. To encourage participation, you should begin with your own example.

- Give each student copies of Worksheets 5-9B and 5-9C.

- Challenge the students to think of a personal situation in their own lives that they can make better with a little effort to treat someone as they themselves would like to be treated. For example, they might make a difference in the lives of others by:

    volunteering for charity work

    helping peers study for exams

    visiting with students who are often alone after school

    picking up trash in the hallways, cafeteria, or on campus

    spending quality time with family members

- Each student should reflect on the "gift" he or she could give to others and then write the idea on both leaves.

- Have the students keep one leaf as a reminder to themselves of what they plan to do. Have them give the other leaf to their faculty facilitator who will keep them until each student completes his or her act of giving kindness/consideration.

- When the student reports that he or she has accomplished the designated "gift" of giving kindness/consideration, he or she should glue or tape the leaf to the paper tree displayed in the classroom.

- Now each classroom taking part in the activity has visible proof that teenagers know how to "walk their talk."

Frances

Frances lives in the house in Euclid, Ohio in which she was born 79 years ago. People marvel at this attractive, energetic, and selfless mother of 14, mother-in-law of 13 (who proudly call themselves the Outlaws and elect an international president every year), and grandmother of 39. There is only an 8-year age difference between the youngest child and the oldest grandchild. After cooking, cleaning, baking, doing mountains of laundry, and attending every kind of sporting event imaginable from elementary school through college level for her own children, she began all over again by taking on the role of main babysitter for many of her grandchildren while their parents worked. Needless to say, the family can't exist without her and she can't seem to get enough of her family.

I know Fran well, for she is my mother-in-law. Very soon after I was married, I lost both of my parents. I was devastated and angry. Why me? Without a moment's hesitation, Fran gathered me into her warm and loving circle. She encouraged me to keep the memories of my parents close in my heart while she quietly and gently did for me all the things that my mother could no longer do. She let me know that if I wanted it, she would like to be my mother on Earth. I found it amazing that someone who loved and had the responsibility for so many still had room in her heart to reach out and embrace yet another.

That was just the beginning of my admiration for my mother-in-law. I have watched her over the years finish her housekeeping chores and then go to the home of an invalid friend and voluntarily clean her house on a weekly basis. Baking 350 cookies a week for the hunger center has been as normal over the years as the changing seasons. Dinner at home always amazed me. When I'd ask her how many places to set, she would invariably say, "Start with 25. We can always add or subtract." Usually, we added, as unexpected "guests" arrived for dinner. Volunteering in church and in the children's and grandchildren's schools was and is a regular occurrence.

Fran won't receive any Academy Awards or huge sums of money for all the good she has done and still continues to do on a daily basis. Her reward comes from the simple "thank you" of her invalid friend, from the genuine hugs and squeals of delight she gets from her grandchildren, and from the enormous pleasure the folks who come for their weekly meal at the hunger center receive from her chocolate chip and oatmeal cookies. She is truly a person who lives her life so that she can be a source of life for others, knowing that the greatest gift is giving of herself, her time, and her talent.

Interpretations of the Golden Rule

Christianity

Do unto others, as you would have others do unto you.

Judaism

What you hate, do not do to anyone.

Confucius

What you do not want done to yourself, do not do to others.

Islam

No one of you is a believer unless he loves for his brother
what he loves for himself.

Aristotle

We should behave toward others as we wish others
to behave toward us.

"Gift" Giving Leaves

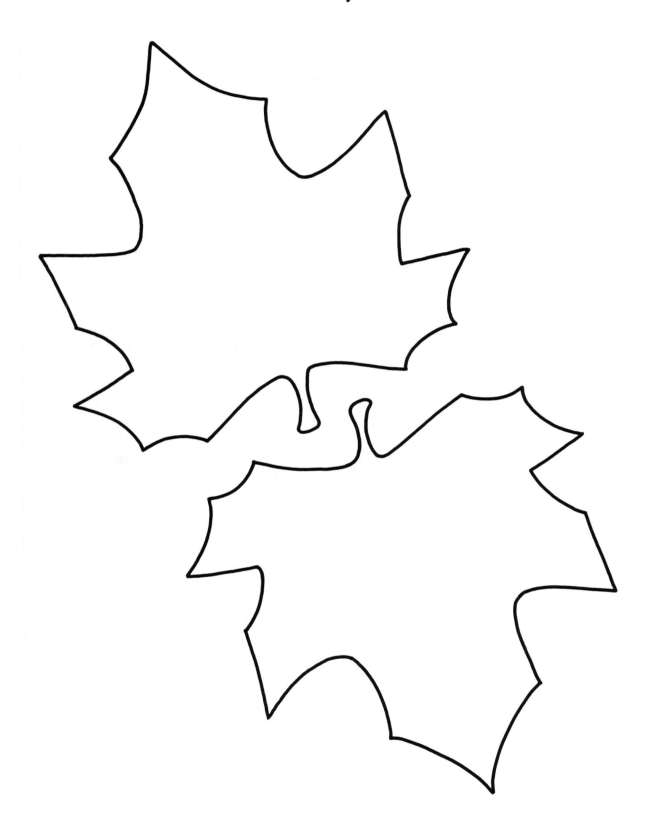

Activity 5-10: Hate

PURPOSE: To enable students to reflect upon the reality of "hate" and to identify our roles in reducing the possibility for hateful situations to arise.

MATERIALS: Worksheets 5-10A and 5-10B; pencils

PROCEDURE:

- Divide the students into small groups of three or four.
- Give each group a copy of Worksheet 5-10A. Ask each group to select a recorder to write the group's answers on the worksheet.
- Allow the groups enough time to complete their worksheets and then have each group read their similes aloud to the entire class.
- Write the characteristics and effects of hate on the board as the groups reveal them while sharing their similes.
- Give each group one copy of questions on Worksheet 5-10B and have the recorder in each group write the group's answers on the sheet.
- Facilitate a discussion of the questions. Encourage each group to contribute to the discussion.
- Come to a consensus as an entire class on the best ways to stop hate (question on Worksheet 5-10B. Write them on the board.

Students' Names _____   **Date** _____

_____

5-10A   **Hate**

In your small groups, complete the following items. Choose one person from your group to serve as the recorder to write your group's answers on this sheet.

1. What does **HATE** look like and sound like? (Brainstorm the words that come to mind.)

    LOOKS LIKE   SOUNDS LIKE

    _____

    _____

    _____

    _____

    _____

    _____

    _____

    _____

2. **HATE** is like what animal? Why?

    HATE is like _____

    because _____

    _____

    _____

    _____

5-10B   # Hate: Reflection Questions

Discuss the following questions in your small groups. Jot down your answers and be prepared to share your answers with the entire class.

1. Hate is usually the result of fear and ignorance. What do human beings fear that causes them to hate?

   _____

   _____

   _____

   _____

2. What kinds of expressions of hate do you see in school?

   _____

   _____

   _____

3. What groups are the most targeted?

   _____

   _____

   _____

4. How do you think hate affects the targeted students in their performance and in how they feel about school?

   _____

   _____

   _____

   _____

5. Who is responsible for stopping expressions of hatred in school? Why?

     _____

     _____

     _____

     _____

6. How can schools have rules that protect students from verbal expressions of hate
    and still allow for freedom of ideas and intellectual expression?

     _____

     _____

     _____

     _____

7. How do the 3R's of First Class tie in with stopping hate?

     _____

     _____

     _____

     _____

8. List five actions that you can take starting today to stop hate.

     Action _____

     Action _____

     Action _____

     Action _____

     Action _____

Activity 5-11: Let's Take a Closer Look at Television

PURPOSE: To determine how television influences the way kids behave and the values they think are important. The people of the television industry maintain that the behavior and principles of kids are not influenced by what they see on TV. They insist that kids are able to tell the difference between what is real and what is fiction. Yet it is evident in the behavior and attitudes of many young people today that "me first" and "respect nothing and no one" are recurring television themes they have been internalized. This activity attempts to look at the influence television has on shaping the principles of young people and to determine the difference between worthwhile and worthless principles.

MATERIALS: Worksheet 5-11

PROCEDURE:

- Divide the class into four small groups.

- Ask each group to make up a 10-question quiz about several favorite TV programs that they will use in competition with another group. The questions they write should *not* have "yes" or "no" answers. The questions must address the behavior and attitudes of the main characters in the TV productions. For example, "In what TV series is the main character married to one man and sleeping with his sons?" Or, "In what cartoon series is the main character funny because he disrespects everyone who is of a different race or nationality?"

- Allow the groups enough time to complete their task. Circulate to offer help if needed.

- When the quizzes are ready, have two groups "face off" in order to compete with each other. Tell them to arrange their chairs so that they are sitting in two lines facing each other. Have the other two groups do the same so that both competitions are occurring simultaneously. The starting group will ask its first question to the group it is competing against. The competing group has 15 seconds to confer with each other and then must answer the question. If the group asking the question believes the answer is correct, they will award 1 point to the competing group. Then they reverse the process so that each group alternately asks and answers a question until all ten questions are asked and answered by each group. The winner is the group that has earned the most points.

- Hand out one copy of Worksheet 5-11 to each group.

- Allow each group enough time to complete the worksheet.

- Use the worksheet questions as a springboard for discussion.

- Encourage everyone to participate in the discussion.

5-11   # Let's Take a Closer Look at Television

In your groups, answer the following questions. Be prepared to share your answers with the entire class.

For many people, it is impossible to hear the "William Tell Overture" without thinking about the Lone Ranger. In another era, a hero to generations of children around the world came to life when Butch Cavendish and his gang ambushed the six Texas Rangers who were chasing them. They killed all but one of the lawmen. The sole survivor of the ambush, John Reid, became known as the Lone Ranger. The Lone Ranger, played on television by Clayton Moore, was an outstanding example both on television and in real life, of a man who *lived* his principles—fairness, justice, courage, and loyalty.

1. Robert J. Thompson, professor of TV, film, and popular culture at Syracuse University, said, "That creed might seem out of date today, but the Lone Ranger and his [principles] live on." Give some examples of TV characters who fight for justice and fairness while exhibiting courage and loyalty.

   _____
   _____
   _____
   _____
   _____

2. Explain why the characters you have chosen fit into the Lone Ranger's creed.

   _____
   _____
   _____
   _____

3. Why is the Lone Ranger's unwavering creed one that we know deep down is right?

   _____
   _____
   _____
   _____

4. From the TV shows you talked about in your quizzes, what are some alternative creeds that different characters in the shows make us aware of?

_____

_____

_____

_____

5. How do their creeds for conducting their lives measure up against the Lone Ranger's creed?

_____

_____

_____

_____

6. Tyne Daly stars as the mother of the title character on "Judging Amy." According to her co-star, Amy Brenneman, Ms. Daly is very good at keeping "vanity on the back burner." With that in mind, what do you think is the creed that guides her as a person?

_____

_____

_____

_____

7. In your opinion, what are some of the worthless principles that TV shows advocate?

_____

_____

_____

_____

8. In your opinion, what are some of the worthwhile principles advocated by TV shows?

_____

_____

_____

_____

9. How do you decide which principles exhibited on TV are worthwhile and which ones are worthless?

_____

_____

_____

_____

10. Suppose your younger brother, sister, or cousin thinks that what counts is not necessarily what is right, but instead, what you can get away with. It is a creed he or she has learned by watching a number of TV programs. What do you say to your younger brother, sister, or cousin?

_____

_____

_____

_____

SECTION 6

UNDERSTANDING AND CELEBRATING DIFFERENCES IN OTHERS

*"Love everyone. Love as one human being to
another, who just happens to be white or black,
rich or poor, enemy or friend."*
VINCE LOMBARDI

More of the Story:

Prior to the development of First Class, Mundelein High School had enjoyed a program every year that celebrated differences in others. They called it Jubilee and enjoyed an annual feast of colorful ethnic costumes and cultural cuisine that lit up the cafeteria and commons for three days and became the standard bearer for several area schools that observed and eventually copied it—and it worked. Students openly discussed their ethnic differences, relished the traditions as well as the tastes of other cultures, even took pride in recently discovered facts about themselves and their families. (Several of this section's activities deal with the Jubilee program.)

Jubilee was so successful that we found we were able to include "An Understanding and Celebration of Differences in Others" in the First Class program by simply revisiting the three days of—as the kids called it—"gnawing and jawing." A few called it "grazing and praising." We liked that better. It got at the heart of what we were trying to accomplish. We enjoyed the vision of lederhosen, breechclouts, saris, and almost every representation of ethnic costume imaginable. We joined the kids sampling couscous, schnitzel, kielbasa, and saganaki. Even more, we enjoyed their reactions to each other: "Hey, neat" and "Cool!"

But other problems persisted in the community. Gang activity was on the rise in one end of town. Bill knew that weekend parties had become battlegrounds for rival gangs who were quickly changing the kids' drug preferences from beer and pot to crack cocaine and heroine. Paradoxically, vandalism and delinquency were increasing in a community that was fast becoming a showcase of upper middle-class success. The other end of town was transfigured by sprawling developments of half-million-dollar homes. Even the students realized that the distance separating the "haves" and the "have nots" was growing almost daily.

Separated by less than two miles in the community, the socioeconomic barrier dividing the north and south ends of town was growing. Like all isolated cultures, both parts of town were failing to exchange the influences and perspectives that enrich and expand our appreciation of the world around us. Our students were bound by static cultures that ritualized their belief system, the south end by a misunderstanding of white culture, the north by a misguided preoccupation with "things."

As the north end found more status, the south end felt its self-esteem take a beating. We knew that First Class had to break down the cultural barrier and promote a sharing and appreciation of cultural differences so that each group could benefit from the best of the other group. But national statistics kept getting our attention. We learned that guns kill more than 15 teenagers every day, and, within a recent 10-year period, teenage homicide increased well over 200%. We learned that 25% of the nation's students are victimized by their schoolmates and that 10% of teachers are victims of violence. Fortunately, none of these statistics had touched our school—not yet, anyway.

As shocked and as saddened as we were by stories of prejudice and violence in our schools, they strengthened our resolve to develop a program that celebrated differences among students and that represented our best attempt to help develop character in them. Although celebrating differences among students was only one of our focuses, it was one of the most important because it was among the most visible and it promoted valuable interaction among so many of the students.

WHY WE NEED TO CELEBRATE DIFFERENCES IN OTHERS

We decided that one of the big responsibilities of teachers is to help children recognize that diversity within our society is one of its greatest strengths. The very differences that sometimes separate us give life its zest and its intrigue—as well as its inspiration. Every difference we find, even those we fear, widens life's perimeters. Our worlds become larger, more complex, more interesting, and much more fulfilling. We knew that the key for our students was to realize that we must be united by much of what seems to divide us!

This is no easy task. Many of us have been conditioned to fear what is different, to seek a predictable sameness in our lives, our activities, our surroundings, and especially our relationships with others. Isn't it ironic that this very sameness, once found and secured, leads to boredom and dissatisfaction with the routine—with the sameness? Further ironic are some people's solutions: excitement found in materialism, vices, even violence.

We wanted our students to realize that variety is, in fact, the spice of life and that the stimulation we require is found in other people, sometimes even the most unlikely people. Such people offer stimulation, even inspiration. Thirty-plus years of coaching taught this lesson to one of our football coaches. Bill learned it during his sophomore year in football from one of his teammates, Rich.

THE STORY OF RICH

Only a junior in high school, Rich already had a scraggly beard and a paunch that defied the best efforts of his shirts. His stomach regularly hung out, drawing attention not only to itself but to the ketchup and mustard stains that dotted his T-shirts. Rich liked the school cafeteria. He spent most of his free time there. Before he joined the football team, he usually sat alone, surrounded by candy wrappers and empty potato chip bags.

During his first two years in high school, many of the kids picked on him but now, in his junior year, everyone left him alone, including the teachers. During Rich's first two years in school, teachers had tried to talk to him several times, but Rich would only stare at them. After several attempts to get to know him, even the most caring of the teachers gave up.

Rich was in special education, for a variety of reasons. Even the special education teachers and counselors had a tough time talking to Rich, until he decided to join the football team. The team had a no-cut policy, so Rich participated in every practice, even though he dragged behind everybody in sprints and in most drills. But he kept working, struggling to do his best, to keep up with everyone else on the team. He rarely played, even in practice. The coaches were afraid that he might hurt himself. But he became an inspiration to Bill.

The coaches often praised Rich for his effort, and the players admired him for having the guts to stick it out. The object of more than a few smiles when he first walked onto the field, Rich worked harder than anyone else on the team. Smiles of derision gradually turned into smiles of approval and respect as the players watched a teammate with such obvious limitations commit himself so completely to practice.

Rich's teammates even insisted that he sit with them in the cafeteria, and they watched over him in school. His appearance even improved. Still bearded and occasionally mottled with ketchup, Rich walked a little taller and even started talking to teachers, often initiating friendly if short conversations. The team's affection and admiration for him reached its high point during the final game of the season when they found themselves behind by ten points at the end of the first quarter.

Just before an important third-down play, the quarterback told the players in the huddle to look over at Rich on the sidelines. Beard and paunch evident even in his helmet and pads, he was standing next to the coach shouting encouragement. Before calling the play, the quarterback said, "If he can do it, we can do it." They made the first down and went on to win the game.

It may not have been a state championship season, but even an average year has many sources of inspiration. Rich certainly was an inspiration for this team and, by extension, for our school. Bill and most of his teammates will always remember not only the thrill of that final victory, but how the courage of the worst player on the team became their greatest inspiration.

Rich will never forget it either.

This team understood that if we are to *do* something worthwhile, we must first *be* something worthwhile—and in order to be something worthwhile, we must recognize and accept what is worthwhile in everyone around us. Our Steering Committee wanted our students to realize that differences define our uniqueness and give us a sense of who and what we are. We had already accomplished freedom of individual and cultural expression with our Jubilee program. We developed the following activities to complement it.

Index of Activities for Understanding and Celebrating Differences in Others

Activity Number	*Name*	*Description*
6-1	Search	Getting to know each other as individuals
6-2	Silly Similes	Distinguishing among prejudice, discrimination, and harassment
6-3	Daffy-nitions	Understanding prejudice, harassment, stereotyping, and discrimination
6-4	Make a Motto	Promoting synthesis-level thinking about prejudice, discrimination, and harassment
6-5	Looking Closely at Stereotypes	Understanding stereotyping
6-6	Stereotyping, So What	Understanding the positive and negative effects of stereotyping
6-7	Combating Stereotyping	Shifting thinking toward an acceptance of differences
6-8	Who Are You?	Exploring the effects of stereotyping
6-9	Stereotyping and Discrimination	Understanding stereotyping and discrimination
6-10	You Be the Judge	Introducing the basics of discrimination
6-11	Up Close and Personal	Exploring the school setting for the effects of discrimination
6-12	Racial Stereotypes	Emphasizing the hurtfulness of stereotyping

Activity Number	Name	Description
6-13	Not Just About Race	Encouraging students to think before they act
6-14	Young vs. Old	Exploring age stereotyping
6-15	It's Your Call	Analyzing a situation involving stereotyping
6-16	Take Your Pick	Promoting reflection and critical thinking
6-17	Prejudice and Discrimination	Showing how both of these lead to disrespect
6-18	What Do You Think?	Analyzing a situation involving discrimination
6-19	Being Physically Disabled	Understanding physical disabilities
6-20	Sexual Harassment	Providing a definition and selected behaviors of what constitutes sexual harassment
6-21	More About Sexual Harassment	Continuing the definition of sexual harassment and analyzing a situation involving it
6-22	What Will You Do?	Analyzing a situation involving harassment
6-23	Jubilee, a Celebration of Diversity	The Jubilee program
6-24	A Challenge to the School Community	More about the Jubilee program
6-25	General Activities and Thought Questions	Questions arranged according to Bloom's Taxonomy (Junior High or Upper Elementary level)

Activity 6-1: Search

PURPOSE: To eliminate judging one another on the basis of race or ethnicity, we must be offered the opportunity to get to know each other as individuals. This personal knowledge helps us begin to break down the barriers of prejudice and discrimination that prevent us from valuing and celebrating those who are different from ourselves. Friendships begin by discovering that, although we are different in many ways, we share much in common. Those commonalities provide healthy nutrients for friendships to grow no matter what our ages, colors, communicating languages, or physical characteristics.

MATERIALS: Worksheets 6-1A and 6-1B; pencils

PROCEDURE:

- Give a copy of Worksheet 6-1A to each student. Instruct participants to ask a question from Worksheet 6-1A of any other member of the group.

- If the answer is "yes," the person answering the question signs his or her name on the sheet of the person asking the question.

- If the answer is "no," the person asking the question must continue to circulate among the members of the group until he or she receives a "yes" answer to a question before returning to the person who answered "no."

- The questions may be asked in any order.

- Each participant must personally interview the other members of the group.

- Give each student a copy of the discussion questions on Worksheet 6-1B.

- Encourage all students to share their reactions to and ideas for the discussion questions.

- As a whole class, come to a consensus on question 5 of the discussion questions by listing on the board the five best ways of starting a new friendship with someone you would like to get to know.

6-1A   **First Class Search**

Find someone:

1. who speaks a language other than English at home.   1. _____

2. whose parent(s) were born in a country other than
    the U.S.   2. _____

3. who has a grandparent who emigrated from Europe.   3. _____

4. who knows how to do the polka.   4. _____

5. who knows how to do the rumba.   5. _____

6. who can trace his or her family tree back to the
    Caribbean.   6. _____

7. who has blue eyes.   7. _____

8. who has brown or black eyes.   8. _____

9. whose family celebrates the Seder meal.   9. _____

10. who has a grandparent who emigrated from South
    or Central America.   10. _____

11. whose family observes Ramadan or who can
    explain what Ramadan is.   11. _____

12. whose eyes are shaped differently from yours.   12. _____

13. whose skin is darker or lighter than yours.   13. _____

14. whose last name is one syllable.   14. _____

15. whose last name is three or more syllables.   15. _____

16. who often celebrates Easter later than our
    calendar does.   16. _____

17. who can explain the season of Lent.   17. _____

18. who can name the national anthem of a country
    other than the U.S.   18. _____

6-1B   ## Search: Discussion Questions

Share your results of the Search activity by answering the following questions. Jot down your answers on this sheet.

1. Tell the class some of the information you discovered through the interview.

   _____

   _____

   _____

2. What do you have in common with one or several other people in the group?

   _____

   _____

   _____

3. How does learning something unusual about a person sometimes give insight into what the person is like?

   _____

   _____

   _____

4. How does knowing something about another person, rather than guessing about him or her, provide a springboard for friendship?

   _____

   _____

   _____

5. What could you do today to start a friendship with someone in this group you feel you would like to get to know?

   _____

   _____

   _____

(If you need more room to write, use the back of this sheet.)

Activity 6-2: Silly Similes

PURPOSE: To enable students to distinguish among the characteristics of prejudice, discrimination, and sexual harassment. Students enjoy this activity. It's fun as well as informative. It gives students a chance to be creative. Most important, it provides a thorough analysis of the terms and opens the door to the remaining activities in this section.

MATERIALS: Worksheet 6-2; pencils

PROCEDURE:

- Arrange the students in groups of three or four. Distribute Worksheet 6-2 and tell students to work together to answer the following questions:

  1. Think about the characteristics of prejudice. Brainstorm the first words that come to mind. Make sure everyone in your group contributes. Maybe jot down your ideas. Then answer this question: "Prejudice is like what household appliance?" Be creative; be funny. The appliance can be broken or old-fashioned. Just be sure to communicate something about prejudice. Finally, in one or two sentences, indicate why prejudice is like that household appliance.

  2. Next, think about the characteristics of discrimination. Again, brainstorm the first ideas that come to mind and write them down. Answer this question: "Discrimination is like what tool?" The tool can be broken or used incorrectly. Just be sure to say something about discrimination. Be creative, but accurate. In one or two sentences, indicate why discrimination is like that tool.

  3. Finally, think about the characteristics of sexual harassment. Brainstorm and jot down your ideas, then answer the question: "Sexual harassment is like what animal?" In one or two sentences, indicate why sexual harassment is like that animal.

- Have each group read their similes, followed by their brief discussion of why they developed the simile the way they did. When all the groups have finished the prejudice section, ask the class: "Based on everything we've heard from the different groups, what do we know about prejudice? What are its characteristics and its effects on people?" Write their reactions on the board.

- Next, do the discrimination section, then ask: "Based on everything we've heard from the different groups, what do we know about discrimination? What are its characteristics and what are its effects on people?" Write their reactions on the board.

- Finally, do the sexual harassment section, then ask: "Based on everything we've heard, let's talk about sexual harassment. What are its attributes and what effects does it have on people?

- If time permits, ask the class: "What do all these terms have in common? What is similar about them? What is different?"

- Conclude with: "Considerate people don't do any of these things to other people. Sometimes it takes guts to be considerate. Try it!"

6-2   # Silly Similes

Prejudice

Prejudice is like what household appliance? _____

_____

Why is it like that appliance? _____

_____

_____

Discrimination

Discrimination is like what tool? _____

_____

Why is it like that tool? _____

_____

_____

Sexual Harassment

Sexual harassment is like what animal? _____

_____

Why is it like that animal? _____

_____

_____

Activity 6-3: Daffy-nitions

PURPOSE: To enable students to understand and distinguish among prejudice, harassment, stereotyping, and discrimination. Students will enjoy this activity. Telling teenagers to try to mislead someone else capitalizes on one of their greatest strengths, certainly one of their most enjoyable diversions! This activity promotes competition to earn points by creating *almost* accurate definitions of discrimination, harassment, prejudice, and stereotyping. Your students will have fun creating the definitions and playing with the concepts, and the discussion that follows virtually guarantees their understanding of the terms.

MATERIALS: Worksheets 6-3A and 6-3B; pencils

PROCEDURE:

- Divide the class into groups of three or four.
- Distribute worksheet 6-3A.
- Tell students that the purpose of this activity is to mislead the rest of the class by creating close but incorrect definitions of the four terms: prejudice, discrimination, stereotyping, and harassment.
- Tell students to create their own definitions for each term, but close enough to their understanding of the real definition to be misleading.
- Tell students you have the dictionary definition for each of the four terms and will read it along with their misleading definitions:

    Discrimination: A showing of partiality or prejudice in treatment, specifically against the welfare of minority groups.

    Harassment: To trouble, worry, or torment as with repeated questions or unwanted advances.

    Prejudice: A judgment or opinion formed before the facts are known, usually unfavorable.

    Stereotyping: A fixed notion or conception allowing for no individuality or critical judgment.

- Tell students that after you read all the definitions, one of which will be the dictionary definition, each group will vote on which definition they think is the right one.
- If they guess the dictionary definition, they get one point. If one or more of the other groups guesses their definition, they get a point for each incorrect guess.
- In other words, if Group A guesses the dictionary definition and gets one group to "bite on" its misleading definition, Group A get two points. If Group B gets three groups to "bite on" its definition, Group B get three points. If Group C gets no one to "bite on" its definition, and fails to guess the dictionary definition, Group C gets no points.
- Follow the process for each of the four terms and tally all the votes. Announce the winning group, then distribute the questions on Worksheet 6-3B and discuss the questions as a whole class.

6-3A   # Daffy-nitions

Use this worksheet to record your daffy-nitions of the following terms. Remember to create definitions that come close to your idea of the real definitions, but that mislead everyone else in class so that you can win points for your group. Be sure to make the definition sound as if it came right out of the dictionary!

DISCRIMINATION _____

_____

_____

HARASSMENT _____

_____

_____

PREJUDICE _____

_____

_____

STEREOTYPING_____

_____

_____

6-3B   # Daffy-nitions: Discussion Questions

1. Why are discrimination and harassment sometimes hard to define and to recognize?

    _____

    _____

    _____

2. What is the most important and revealing element in the definition of prejudice?

    _____

    _____

    _____

3. Explain your understanding of "allowing for no individuality" in the definition of stereotyping.

    _____

    _____

    _____

4. If the class had difficulty with one or more of the definitions, why do you suppose this was?

    _____

    _____

    _____

Activity 6-4: Make a Motto

PURPOSE: To enable students to refine their understanding of prejudice, discrimination, and sexual harassment. This activity promotes synthesis-level thought process by asking your students to create a mascot and a motto for the current school year. Use this activity at the beginning of the school year to promote interest and commitment to the program. Classes or advisories can create their own mascots and mottoes and submit them to your school's Steering Committee for possible selection as the school's mascot and motto for the current school year.

Your students will get excited about creating the entire school's motto for the school year. This activity requires them to integrate everything they know about character and First-Class behavior, and results in a better understanding of what the school is trying to accomplish. It introduces freshmen to the basics of character and reintroduces all the other students to the importance of the program.

MATERIALS: Worksheet 6-4

PROCEDURE:

- Arrange the students in groups of two, three, or four. Tell them to consider all the characteristics of prejudice, discrimination, and sexual harassment. In essence, what do all these terms have in common?

- Next, tell them to identify or create a mascot: an animal, a person, a talking inanimate object. (Use Worksheet 6-4.) This mascot will represent their position on these three issues. It should be appealing and, through its appearance, embody some of what they are trying to say. For example, a panda might correspond to the motto: "Hey, black and white work for me!"

- Next, have students develop the motto. This is a synthesis-level activity, so the motto should incorporate much of what has been discussed about these three issues, and should reflect the unique character of the school.

- Finally, and as time permits, have the groups select a popular tune—nothing of questionable taste!—and write a jingle that synthesizes the school's position on the issues of prejudice, discrimination, and sexual harassment. Tunes like "Jingle Bells," the Notre Dame "Fight Song," or any of several popular songs would work.

- Conclude the session by having each group perform their jingle in front of the class. Vote on the best one.

6-4   **A School Motto**

Create a motto for the school. Write it on the banner.

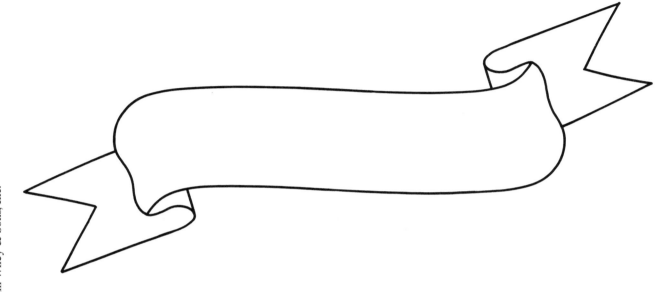

Next, identify and try to draw a mascot for the school Take your time; work with your group to come up with a good one.

Activity 6-5: Looking Closely at Stereotypes

PURPOSE: To promote an understanding of stereotyping.

MATERIALS: Worksheets 6-5A and 6-5B; pencils

PROCEDURE

- Read the following aloud to your class:

  "Imagine you are at an all-school dance. Imagine also that you're a people watcher. Standing on the outside edge of the dance floor, you watch kids go on and off the dance floor. Suddenly the D.J. calls for a line dance. Some kids just stand on the outside edge of the dance floor and snap their fingers to the beat of the music. These are the INVESTIGATORS. Others, the EXPERIMENTERS, place themselves in the middle of the line dance where they will be able to follow the lead of the kids in front of them. A third group, the ADVENTURERS, take their places at the lead points of the line dance. You get into the music and feel like dancing. What will you be, an INVESTIGATOR, an EXPERIMENTER, or an ADVENTURER?"

- Identify three areas of the classroom where the groups can meet and have the students sit with the group with which they identify.

- Hand out one copy of Worksheet 6-5A to each group.

- Ask each group to choose a recorder for its group who will write down the group's answers to the three questions on the chart: our description of ourselves, our description of the other two groups, and the other two groups' likely descriptions of us.

- When the groups have completed their charts, have someone from each group read what the members thought of themselves: the INVESTIGATORS, the EXPERIMENTERS, then the ADVENTURERS.

- Next, have someone from the INVESTIGATORS read *what they thought* was the EXPERIMENTERS' opinion of them. Then have the EXPERIMENTERS read their *actual* opinion of the INVESTIGATORS. Then have the person from the INVESTIGATORS read *what they thought* was the ADVENTURERS' opinion of them. Then have the ADVENTURERS read their *actual* opinion.

- Finally, have the EXPERIMENTERS and the ADVENTURERS follow the same procedure of sharing opinions as the INVESTIGATORS did.

- To conclude, give one copy of the discussion questions on Worksheet 6-5B to each group.

- Have the recorder in each group write down the group's answers to the questions. Allow the groups enough time to complete the questions.

- Have the groups share their answers to the questions as a springboard for discussion.

6-5A

Stereotyping Chart

Group Name	Words we use to describe our group	Words we use to describe the other two groups	Words we think the other two groups used to describe us
INVESTIGATORS			
EXPERIMENTERS			
ADVENTURERS			

Students' Names _____ **Date** _____

6-5B **Looking Closely at Stereotypes: Discussion Questions**

Answer the following questions in your groups. The recorder for your group will write the group's answers on this sheet.

1. How close were the other two groups to your opinions of your own group?

   _____
   _____
   _____
   _____

2. Why do you think they were so close?

   _____
   _____
   _____
   _____

3. What was it about the opinions of the other two groups regarding your group that most disturbed you? Why?

   _____
   _____
   _____
   _____

4. Were you looking forward to what the other two groups had to say about your group?

_____

_____

_____

_____

5. How did you feel when the opinions of another group differed from your opinion of them?

_____

_____

_____

_____

6. Which of these three groups is the best group?

_____

_____

_____

_____

Activity 6-6: Stereotyping, So What?

PURPOSE: To understand the positive and negative effects of stereotyping.

MATERIALS: Worksheets 6-6A and 6-6B; scissors; pencils

PROCEDURE:

- Give each student a copy of Worksheet 6-6A and have the students cut out the design so it can be used on both sides as ME and WE.

- Participants decide which group or groups they belong to. For example, a participant might be Mexican-American and a soccer player or African-American and a member of the jazz band at school.

- Using the ME side of the design, the participants write down all of the stereotypes (positive and negative) they have heard about the group or groups to which they belong.

- Set a time limit of approximately 3–5 minutes for this part of the activity. When 5 minutes are up, have the participants share with the class what they have written. Use the discussion questions for the ME part on Worksheet 6-6B.

- Now have the participants turn their designs to the WE side and repeat the same process, writing down the positive things they want others to know about the group or groups to which they belong.

- When the time has elapsed, have the participants share what they have written with the class and then follow up with the discussion questions for the WE part on Worksheet 6-6B.

ME/WE Design

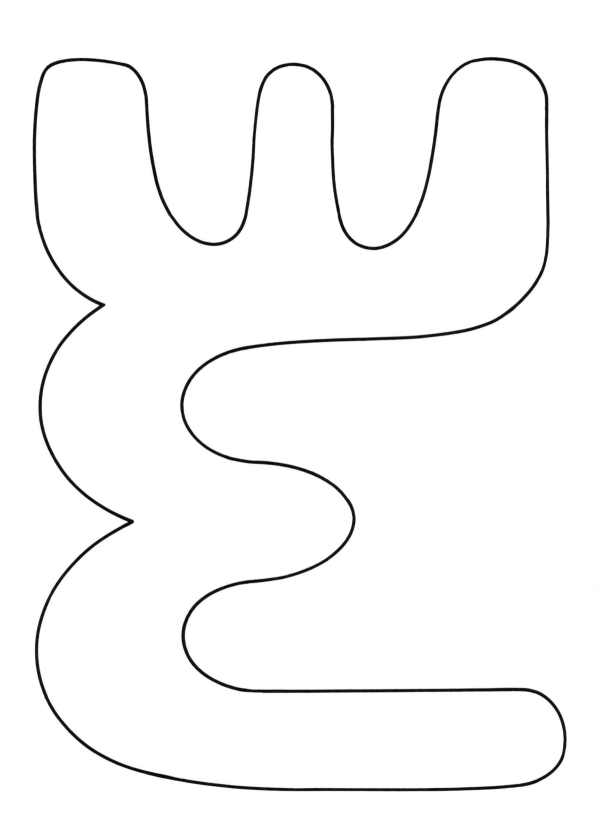

6-6B   # Stereotyping, So What?: Discussion Questions

ME

1. Which were more difficult to think of, positive stereotypes or negative stereotypes?

_____

_____

_____

_____

2. How do the stereotypes you have written make you feel?

_____

_____

_____

_____

WE

1. Have you ever felt you've been treated differently because of who you are or the group you represent?

_____

_____

_____

_____

2. How did that treatment make you feel?

_____

_____

_____

6-6B *(continued)*

3. Why do you think people stereotype?

_____

_____

_____

4. Do you think stereotyping is a good thing or a bad thing? Why?

_____

_____

_____

_____

5. Do we ever perpetrate stereotypes by the way we act?

_____

_____

_____

_____

Activity 6-7: Combating Stereotyping

PURPOSE: To shift thinking toward acceptance of differences.

MATERIALS: Worksheet 6-7; several peanut M&M's®; enough individual snack-size bags of plain or peanut M&M's® for each participant in the class; two blindfolds; pencils

PROCEDURE:

- Ask two students to volunteer to participate in a taste test in front of the class.
- Blindfold the two students.
- Give the two volunteers each a peanut M&M®. After the students have put the M&M® in their mouths and tasted them, ask them to describe what they tasted (e.g., candy, crunchy, nutty, chocolate, delicious).
- Ask what color the candy was that they ate.
- Discuss questions on Worksheet 6-7.
- Finish the activity by giving any student in class who wants one an individual snack-size bag of M&M's®.

6-7 ## Combating Stereotyping: Discussion Questions

1. Was the color of the M&M's® important? Why?

   _____

   _____

   _____

   _____

2. What message does this activity convey?

   _____

   _____

   _____

   _____

   _____

Activity 6-8: Who Are You?

PURPOSE: To demonstrate the universality of stereotyping and to explore its effects

MATERIALS: Worksheets 6-8A and 6-8B; an ethnic identification tag for every student; pencils

PROCEDURE:

- Copy an ethnic identification tag onto a stick-on label for each participating student.

- Place the stick-on label on the back of each student. Don't let the student see it! Students should have no knowledge of what their tag says.

- Give each student a copy of Worksheet 6-8A.

- Begin the activity by having students share with each other the first descriptor that comes to mind when they see each other's ethnic tag. Each student should be hearing a variety of descriptors from his or her classmates. None of the descriptors should involve off-colored language, but they can be inappropriate without being too obvious.

- Tell the students to write on their worksheet the descriptors that provide the best insights into who they are.

- Finally, tell students to guess who they think they are by writing the term on the space provided on the sheet.

- Only then may they remove the tags on their backs.

- After students have all made their guesses and removed the tags, use the questions on Worksheet 6-8B to stimulate discussion.

Ethnic Identification Tags

NATIVE AMERICAN FEMALE	**NATIVE AMERICAN MALE**
ASIAN-AMERICAN FEMALE	**ASIAN-AMERICAN MALE**
HISPANIC FEMALE	**HISPANIC MALE**
MIDDLE EASTERN FEMALE	**MIDDLE EASTERN MALE**
WHITE FEMALE	**WHITE MALE**
JEWISH FEMALE	**JEWISH MALE**
IRISH FEMALE	**IRISH MALE**

6-8A   **Clue Sheet**

Things people are saying (clues) to help you figure out who you are:

1. _____

2. _____

3. _____

4. _____

5. _____

6. _____

7. _____

8. _____

9. _____

10. _____

11. _____

12. _____

13. _____

14. _____

15. _____

WHO ARE YOU?

_____

6-8B   # Who Are You?: Discussion Questions

1. What did you learn from this activity?

    _____

    _____

    _____

2. How did you feel when you heard some of the clues others were giving you about
    who you are?

    _____

    _____

    _____

3. Was it easy coming up with the clues for everyone else?

    _____

    _____

    _____

    _____

6-8B *(continued)*

4. Let's identify at least five examples of stereotypes on television or in the movies. Do questions 4 through 6 as a class.

_____

_____

_____

_____

_____

5. What kinds of stereotypes do you run into here at school?

_____

_____

_____

6. How does the use of stereotypes relate to prejudice and discrimination?

_____

_____

_____

_____

Activity 6-9: Stereotyping and Discrimination

PURPOSE: To promote an understanding of stereotyping and discrimination

MATERIALS: Worksheets 6-9A and 6-9B; pencils

PROCEDURE:

- Randomly divide the class into small groups of three.
- Read aloud Worksheet 6-9A (or give a copy to each student).
- Give one copy of Worksheet 6-9B to each small group.
- Tell each group to select a recorder who will write the group's answers to the discussion questions.
- Have each group share its responses to the questions and allow the discussion to flow.

Erik's Ride

Erik, a recent International Business graduate of the University of Iowa in his first job as a mortgage broker with a Chicago firm, boarded the train at Ravenswood for the hour-long commute home. He was tired, but it had been a productive as well as a comfortable day in the office. Fridays were traditionally spent catching up on paper work and didn't require meeting with clients. So, the firm officially deemed Fridays "casual attire" days.

That morning Erik had chosen to wear his comfortable cords, a soft flannel shirt open at the neck, and his favorite baseball cap turned backwards. He carried a backpack for the materials he needed to review over the weekend before returning to work on Monday morning. Backpacks were a college habit he hadn't yet traded for an expensive attaché case.

As he got on the train, he noticed another man dressed in a three-piece business suit getting on with him. Remarking to himself that the man's stiffly starched collar and tie seemed to be cutting off the circulation to his head, Erik felt very relaxed, even though he was tired. He chose a seat near the window and looked around the car as the train began slowly to move.

The conductor was checking tickets at the other end of the car. As he moved toward where Erik was sitting, he greeted the three-piece suit benevolently and offered polite conversation about the weather while validating the man's ticket. Then he was standing in front of Erik.

"Ticket," he demanded.

"I'll need to purchase a ticket from Ravenswood, please," replied Erik.

The conductor looked Erik up and down from his comfortably worn shoes to his baseball cap and backpack.

"You didn't get on at Ravenswood," boomed the conductor. "You got on in Chicago. That'll be $3.50 more."

"Sir, I did get on at Ravenswood," replied Erik.

"You're lying," shouted the conductor. "I saw you get on in Chicago myself. You either pay the $3.50 more, or I'll throw you off this train!"

People in the car began turning around to see who the conductor had caught cheating. Erik felt his face begin to turn red. The three-piece suit turned to look over at him. Erik looked at him expectantly, hoping the man would speak up in his defense since they had boarded the train together at Ravenswood. The three-piece suit didn't say a word and went back to reading his paper.

Erik tried one more time.

"Sir, I got on at 6:40 P.M. at the Ravenswood stop. If I had been in Chicago, I would have purchased a ticket there."

"That's enough out of you, kid," shouted the conductor. "You pay, or you're out!"

Erik, thoroughly embarrassed by this time and not wanting to cause a scene, paid the extra $3.50 and the conductor strode on down the aisle.

6-9B   Stereotyping and Discrimination: Discussion Questions

Respond to the following questions in your small groups. The recorder will write your group's answers to the questions on this sheet. Be prepared to share your answers with the rest of the class.

1. What happened in this incident?

   _____

   _____

2. Why did the conductor question Erik?

   _____

   _____

   _____

3. Why didn't he question the man in the three-piece suit?

   _____

   _____

   _____

4. Why didn't the man in the three-piece suit defend Erik?

   _____

   _____

   _____

5. What would you have done if you had been the person in the three-piece suit?

   _____

   _____

   _____

6. What is stereotyping?

_____

_____

_____

7. What is discrimination? How could we define it?

_____

_____

_____

8. What's wrong with discrimination?

_____

_____

_____

9. Is it fair? Explain briefly.

_____

_____

_____

10. Is anyone hurt by it? Explain?

_____

_____

_____

Activity 6-10: You Be the Judge

PURPOSE: To introduce the basics of discrimination. On Bloom's Taxonomy, this is an application-level activity, excellent for helping students apply their understanding of discrimination to a real-life situation.

MATERIALS: None

PROCEDURE:

- Arrange your class into groups of two or three, then read the following to them:

  "You are the judge. A local business has come to you asking your advice about the kinds of questions they ask during employment interviews. Listen to each question, discuss it in your group, then let me know whether it is legal or illegal; in essence, whether it is discriminatory or nondiscriminatory. I'll pass your decisions onto the local business."

- Here are the questions. (The answers have been provided for you in parentheses.)

  1. "What is your native language?" Legal or illegal? (*illegal*)
  2. "Have you ever been convicted of a crime?" Legal or illegal? (*legal*)
  3. "Have you ever used a different name in your current job?" Legal or illegal? (*legal*)
  4. "Of what professional organizations are you a member?" Legal or illegal? (*legal*)
  5. "What is your religion?" Legal or illegal? (*illegal*)
  6. "Are you married?" Legal or illegal? (*illegal*)
  7. "Where does your spouse work?" Legal or illegal? (*illegal*)
  8. "Should we call you Mrs. or Ms.?" Legal or illegal? (*illegal*)
  9. "How old are you?" Legal or illegal? (*illegal*)
  10. "What is your nationality?" Legal or illegal? (*illegal*)
  11. "What societies or lodges do you belong to?" Legal or illegal? (*illegal*)
  12. "What languages do you speak fluently?" Legal or illegal? (*legal*)
  13. "What's your maiden name?" Legal or illegal? (*illegal*)
  14. "Are there any jobs you cannot perform because of any mental, physical, or medical disabilities?" Legal or illegal? (*legal*); *this would be illegal if the interviewer asked: "Are you disabled, or have you ever had the following diseases?"*

- Tally all the votes in order to determine a winner. Remind students of their votes during the discussion of the questions.

DISCUSSION QUESTIONS

1. What do all the legal questions have in common? (*They are job-related.*)

2. Why, then, are the other questions illegal? (*They don't relate to the job, and they question areas of personal life that have no bearing on work. As such, they are potentially discriminatory.*)

3. What are some of the reasons an interviewer might ask a candidate a potentially discriminatory question, such as "How old are you?" (*The interviewer obviously wants information. Will the woman leave the job soon because of a pregnancy? Does he believe that women are just not forceful or strong enough to handle the job? Is the man too old for the job? Might he not have the energy and the drive to do the job right?*) **(If the kids don't mention these as possibilities, you bring them up because they reflect the real world and they give you a lead-in to the following facts.)**

    • Genetic engineers are reporting that many of you will live to be 100. They're also saying that a child born today can expect to live to 125. How will you feel at age 65 if someone suggests that you aren't energetic or vibrant enough to handle a job? At 65, you'll be a middle-ager! Maybe you won't *want* to work, but you certainly won't want someone telling you that you *can't!*

    • What about gender discrimination? Look at it this way. In the early 1950s, a sportswriter for the *New York Times* wrote that "any self-respecting school boy could beat the records of the greatest woman champion." He argued that women should not compete in the Olympics. A few short years later, Bobby Morrow won the men's 100-meter run in the 1956 Olympics in a time of 10.5 seconds. Later, Florence Griffith-Joyner won the women's 100-meter run in a time of 10.49 seconds. Sounds like women can be pretty talented.

4. Let's find five ways that discrimination in the workplace is bad. Let's start with race discrimination. What's wrong with it? (*Then go to gender and age discrimination. This should take you to the end of the period.*)

Activity 6-11: Up Close and Personal

PURPOSE: To discover if discrimination exists in your school setting and its effects.

MATERIALS: The video you will produce

PROCEDURE:

- Ask for volunteers from different ethnic groups in your school to try out for the Cultural Diversity video you are going to produce.

- Interview and simultaneously practice videotaping the volunteers in order to select those who are willing and able to speak openly and honestly for the round-table video.

- A group of 12 students representing all of the ethnic groups in your school provides a lively round-table video. Too many students limit the amount of time students can speak.

- Use the following discussion questions to help you select the candidates for the video production:

  1. Do you think white people are privileged?
  2. Do you think people who are not white are underprivileged?
  3. Do white people benefit from their skin color?
  4. Do white people worry about how they are treated based on stereotypes?
  5. Do people from minority groups worry about how they are treated based on stereotypes?
  6. Do the actions of one member of a minority group have an affect on all members of that minority group?
  7. What are the stereotypes about your ethnic background?
  8. Has anyone treated you based on a stereotype? Give an example.
  9. What does "sell out" mean?
  10. Do you think people give up who they are when they assimilate to America?
  11. How easy is it to be accepted by two cultures?
  12. Do you ever feel like you have to choose between white culture and your ethnic culture?
  13. Do you think people from certain minority groups separate themselves here at our school?
  14. Do you think people from certain minority groups get treated differently based on their ethnic background? Give examples.

15. Are teachers' expectations the same for every racial group? Elaborate.

16. How does it feel to be the only member from your ethnic group in a class?

17. Is life good for minorities?

18. Is racism declining?

19. Can we be a colorblind society?

20. What do you want others to know about your ethnic group?

21. What do you never want to see, hear, or experience again as a member of your ethnic group?

22. What do you want your allies to do?

- Once you have selected the participants for your panel discussion, select an adult mediator who is versed in multicultural experience to conduct the panel discussion.

- Choose a comfortable, well-lighted room in which to conduct the discussion and taping of the video.

- Have the mediator explain the procedure for the panel discussion. For example, one person speaks at a time. Everyone listens until that person has finished. Another person may then pick up on the discussion and continue. When the group has pretty well covered one question, the mediator will move the discussion along with another question. The above questions can serve as a good springboard for discussion.

- Use the homemade video for classes, group discussions, or group counseling sessions in your school. When people from your own school speak of actual experiences, the impact is strong.

- Use these questions to allow students watching the video to react to it:

  1. Do you agree with someone in the video? Why?

  2. Do you disagree with someone in the video? Why?

  3. Do you identify with someone in the video? Who? Why?

  4. Why do you think these students were willing to do this video?

  5. Have you ever been the racial minority in a group? Explain how you felt.

  6. Have you ever been the minority in a group? Explain how you felt.

  7. If you're comfortable, share an incident where you caught yourself stereotyping another person or persons. (*Example:* Think of the first day of term 1 in your classes. "Uh oh, I'm the only _____ in here."

  8. Describe what it's like to be in the racial minority. (*Example:* You're the only person of your racial group in the classroom)

  9. Describe what it's like to be in the racial majority. (*Example:* Everyone in class is a member of your racial group.)

10. Do you think it's easy or difficult to assimilate into the American culture? Why?

11. Do you think people give up who they are when they assimilate to America?

12. Is it easy to be accepted by two cultures?

13. Do you think people from certain minority groups separate themselves at our school? Why or why not?

14. Do you think people from certain minority groups get treated differently based on their ethnic backgrounds? If yes, give examples.

15. Are teachers' expectations the same for every racial group? Elaborate.

16. Is life good for minorities here in our school? In our community?

17. Is racism declining?

18. Can we be a colorblind society?

Activity 6-12: Racial Stereotypes

PURPOSE: To realize how hurtful stereotyping can be.

MATERIALS: Worksheets 6-12A and 6-12B; pencils

PROCEDURE:

- Randomly divide the class into small groups of three.
- Read Worksheet 6-12A (or give a copy to each student).
- Give one copy of Worksheet 6-12B to each small group. Instruct the small groups to choose a student from the group to serve as the recorder to write the group's answers to the discussion questions.
- Allow the groups enough time to complete the discussion questions.
- Go over the discussion questions one at a time, allowing each group to share its answer to the question being discussed. Use the questions as a springboard for discussion.
- As a class, come to a consensus on question 6.

That Spring Afternoon

Greg, an African-American professional football coach, was working in his yard one spring afternoon in the northern town in which he lived and worked. On this particular afternoon, he realized the hedge trimmer he was using was simply worn out and was leaving the hedge in his backyard looking ragged instead of neat and trim. He pitched the old hedge trimmer in the trash and hopped into his car for the short drive to the local do-it-yourself store in his town.

Once in the store, Greg began wandering down the aisles looking at all the great tools he'd like to buy, but just didn't have the time to use because his job kept him traveling a great deal as well as working on weekends. He had picked up, admired, and put down a number of shiny new tools when he noticed two clerks were suddenly busily arranging tools in the same aisle where he had been alone just minutes before. Then a third and fourth clerk joined the first two, and they seemed to move everywhere Greg went. He began to feel uncomfortable, so he picked up the hedge trimmer he had come to purchase and went to the check-out counter.

One of the clerks who had been in the aisle with Greg stepped up to the cash register, rang up the sale, and asked suspiciously, "Will you be paying for this with a credit card?"

"No," Greg replied, "I prefer to pay with a check." The employee looked disgusted and said, "We only accept local checks and I must require three forms of identification." Greg indicated that would be fine and opened his checkbook bearing the stamped name and address of his business, the local professional football team. The employee, seeing the checkbook and the team name, suddenly looked embarrassed and said, "Oh, Coach, I didn't recognize you! Don't bother paying for this little hedge trimmer. Consider it a gift from our company to you."

"Thank you," replied Greg, "I appreciate your offer, but I prefer to pay for it."

6-12B   **Racial Stereotypes: Discussion Questions**

Choose one person from your group to serve as the recorder. He or she will write your entire group's answers to the questions below. Be ready to share your answers with the entire class.

1. Have you ever been in a situation where you were discriminated against because of your race or ethnic background? Please share your experience.

   _____

   _____

   _____

   _____

   _____

2. How did the treatment you received make you feel?

   _____

   _____

   _____

3. What's wrong with discrimination?

   _____

   _____

   _____

   _____

4. Is anyone hurt by it? Explain.

   _____

   _____

   _____

   _____

5. Why do you think people treat other people differently when their skin is of another color or their ethnic background is different?

_____

_____

_____

_____

6. What is the right thing to do in the situation in "That Spring Afternoon"?

_____

_____

_____

_____

_____

_____

Activity 6-13: Not Just About Race

PURPOSE: To encourage everyone to think before we just react

MATERIALS: Props (either real or pictures) to depict a set of tools, a six-pack of beer, skis, a make-up kit, gardening tools, a rocking chair, a rap music CD, sunglasses, symphony tickets (if time does not permit, simply write the list of things on the board or on kraft paper); Worksheet 6-13; pencils

PROCEDURE:

- Ask for two boys and two girls to come to the front of the room. Tell the class that these are four of your friends and give each of them a sign to hold telling their name and age (**Jack, 24, cab driver; Margie, 26, suburban homemaker; Yuri, 30, construction worker; Adele, 72, retired teacher**).

- Group the remainder of the students in the class into small groups of three. Tell the groups to pick one gift from the items pictured or listed to give to each of the four people at the front of the room. Have one person in each group be the recorder and write each of the four people's names and the gift the group decided on for each person.

- Go through the list of gifts. Ask, "How many groups gave Jack the set of tools? The six-pack? The skis? etc. Then repeat with Margie, Yuri, and Adele until each has a gift from the groups in the class.

- Give one copy of Worksheet 6-13 to each group of students.

- Instruct the groups to complete questions 1–3. The recorder for each group will write the group's answers on the sheet.

- After the groups have completed the first three discussion questions, have them share their answers with the entire class.

- Now tell the students a little more about Jack, Margie, Yuri, and Adele. After sharing the following information about each person, ask the groups of students what they now believe would be an appropriate gift for each one.

    Jack drives a cab during the day, but at night he goes to the community college where he is studying the violin.

    Margie has always loved all kinds of music.

    Yuri works as a construction worker during the day, but he also donates his time to the local hospital where he dresses like a clown and visits sick children.

    Adele is a retired P.E. teacher and was also on the 1976 Olympic Ski Team.

- Have the groups complete the last two questions on the discussion sheet and then let them share their responses with the whole class.

- As a whole class, come to a consensus on question 5. Write the suggestions on the board.

6-13   # Not Just About Race: Discussion Questions

In your small groups, respond to questions 1–3. The recorder for your group will write your group's answers on this sheet. Be prepared to share your answers with the rest of the class.

1. How did you decide which gift to give to each person?

_____

_____

_____

2. Was making that decision difficult? Why or why not?

_____

_____

_____

3. Why do you think people stereotype?

_____

_____

_____

Now finish the discussion questions by responding to questions 4 and 5. Again, be ready to share your group's answers with the rest of the class.

4. What would be a better way of selecting gifts for these people?

_____

_____

_____

5. What would be some things we could do to help dispel stereotypes?

_____

_____

_____

Activity 6-14: Young vs. Old

PURPOSE: To expand upon the concept of stereotyping.

MATERIALS: Worksheets 6-14A and 6-14B; pencils

PROCEDURE:

- Give a copy of Worksheet 6-14A to your students, Instruct them to read each statement and then indicate if the statement was said by a Young Person (YP) or an Old Person (OP).

- Use the following questions as a springboard for discussion:

  1. As a teenager, have you ever experienced or known anyone who has experienced prejudice or discrimination based on age? (i.e., being followed in a store because you are young, not getting a job, trying to participate in an activity intended for another age group)

  2. Both younger and older people can be the victims of prejudice based on age. In what ways is growing up *similar* to growing old?

  3. In what ways is growing up *different* from growing old?

  4. Why do people make statements like those on the sheet you just read?

  5. How do you think your grandparents would feel if they heard the statements about older people?

  6. As a teenager, how do those statements make you feel?

  7. What is the term we use for grouping people without taking their individual differences into account?

  8. What is the term we use for acting on those oversimplified ways in which we group people?

- Now, randomly divide your students into small groups of three.

- Give each group one copy of Worksheet 6-14B. Ask each group to choose a recorder from the group who will write the group's answers for the worksheet questions.

- After the groups have completed the worksheet, have them share their responses with the entire class. List their responses on the board.

6-14A   # Young vs. Old

Read each statement below and indicate if it is a Young Person (YP) talking about an old person, or an Old Person (OP) talking about a young person.

_____ "They always stick together and keep their distance from other age groups."

_____ "I hate the way they drive! They're a menace on the road."

_____ "They're always taking and never giving. They think the world owes them."

_____ "They're so opinionated. They think they know it all!"

_____ "They're never satisfied, always complaining about something."

_____ "Don't hire them because you can't depend on them."

_____ "They always hang around the parks and shopping malls."

_____ "They certainly don't remember anything for very long!"

_____ "I wish I had as much freedom as they have."

_____ "They should act their age."

6-14B　　　**Stereotypes: Young vs. Old Worksheet**

Choose one person from your group who will serve as the group's recorder to write
your answers to the questions below. Be prepared to share your responses with the
entire class.

1. What can you do as younger people to dispel age-based stereotyping and
   discrimination?

   a. _____

   _____

   b. _____

   _____

   c. _____

   _____

   d. _____

   _____

   e. _____

   _____

2. What are some ways in which younger people can work together with older people
   to dispel age-based stereotyping and discrimination?

   a. _____

   _____

   b. _____

   _____

   c. _____

   _____

   d. _____

   _____

   e. _____

   _____

Activity 6-15: It's Your Call

PURPOSE: To enable students to analyze and evaluate a situation involving prejudice.

MATERIALS: Worksheet 6-15; paper; pencils

PROCEDURE:

- Distribute Worksheet 6-15 and give the class enough time to read it. Then arrange students in groups of three or four to discuss it. Tell them to discuss the questions, then seek a consensus among themselves for answers. Tell them to write their answers in order to share them later with the entire class.

- After the groups have had enough time to discuss the situation and answer each question, have them share their answers with the entire class. After each group shares its answers, ask the entire class for a reaction.

- After every group has shared its answers, tell the class to choose the best from each group and establish a consensus opinion for the entire class.

It's Your Call

The Down Side of Being Vertically Challenged

You're a junior boy at Milford High School. You're about 5′2″ and you weigh under 100 pounds. You're the smallest person in a family of small people. Your dad is barely 5′6″. The beginning of the school year is always a pain in the neck. The start of the second semester is not much better, given all the new faces and not-so-new wisecracks you encounter. Invariably, you're called everything from "chicken little" to the runt of the litter and someone is always interested in what the air is like "down there."

Today was the worst day of the year. On your way to the cafeteria, you took a short-cut across the commons and found yourself in the middle of a group of senior boys who seemed always to take special delight in tormenting you. Today, they went too far. Two of the boys decided to play catch with you, seeing how far they could throw you and still catch you. After each successively longer throw, the other boys—and many of the girls in the area—would cheer.

Finally, you managed to get free and walked as fast as you could to the cafeteria, where you sat alone thinking about the whole incident.

FIRST OF ALL:

- Describe you feelings. How did you feel as you were being tossed back and forth? How did you feel when you heard and saw some of the senior girls cheering?

- Why do you suppose the senior boys picked on you? Was it your fault?

- Why do you suppose the senior boys acted as they did? How would you describe their behavior?

- How does this incident relate to discrimination? Harassment?

WILL YOU . . .

- Stay away from the commons and turn the other way whenever you see the senior boys?

- Just try to forget the incident and hope that it doesn't happen again?

- Laugh along with them and pretend to be having fun?

- Get a couple of your friends from the football team to "straighten them out"?

- Try to reason with the senior boys individually when you get the chance?

- Have your parents contact their parents?

- Report them to the Dean of Students?

- Have your parents get a lawyer and initiate a lawsuit?

- Other. What else might you do?

Activity 6-16: Take Your Pick

PURPOSE: To promote reflection and critical-thinking skills.

MATERIALS: Worksheets 6-16A and 6-16B; pencils

PROCEDURE:

- Organize the class into groups of three.
- Give each group copies of Worksheets 6-16A and 6-16B, and provide time for students to read them.
- Have students individually answer the questions on Worksheet 6-16B.
- After each student writes his or her reactions to the situation, have them discuss the situation as a group and try to reach group consensus.
- After the class has achieved or approximated consensus, have a spokesperson for each group read the answers to the rest of the class. Discuss all the answers as a class and try to determine a "best" answer.

Sue's Dilemma

Earlier in the school year, you were elected by the student body as the senior representative to the Homecoming Court and attended the dance with the starting fullback on the football team. The Christmas Ball is about a month away, and you're wondering if the fullback is going to ask you again. Frankly, you're not worried about a date because, without being self-serving, you know that you're one of the most popular girls in school and, yes, one of the prettiest!

It's Thursday. School has ended, and you're on your way to the parking lot to meet two of your girlfriends. You're suddenly approached by Bill Thompson, a recent transfer to the school and one of the basketball team's best players. Bill is also in your AP European History class and obviously is very intelligent. Frankly, you've noticed him and have been attracted by his good looks and personality. He's also African-American in a school that is predominantly white and more than a little confused about race relations. Bill says hi and, without any hesitation, asks you to the Christmas Ball.

You indicate to him that you're a little surprised because you know him only through projects on the Homecoming Parade and Varsity Club meetings, but he says that he's enjoyed your comments in class and thought that a date to the Ball might be fun.

He also says: "You didn't know Mike before the Homecoming Dance, did you? He's a nice guy. I'll bet you had fun. We will, too!"

You smile and nod your agreement and, still surprised, ask if you can give him an answer tomorrow.

He says, "Fine. I'll see you tomorrow. Have a nice night, Sue."

On your way to the parking lot, several different thoughts race through your mind. Your first thought is to simply refuse him because a date with an African-American kind of scares you. You're not afraid of Bill; he's a nice guy. Everyone who knows him says he's very smart and super considerate. It's just that this whole Black/White thing seems a little too much for you.

But then, you think: "Hey, what's the big deal. He's a nice guy and we'll be triple dating with Sally and Joan, so being alone won't be an issue."

Then you think of your mother. Sally had been asked out by a black student last year from another school and had refused. Your mother told her that she had been smart to do so, that high school is not the place for breaking down social barriers. It was a time to have fun; besides, "their" culture is just too different from ours.

You aren't sure how your dad feels about such things, but you don't think this is the time to find out. Even if he goes along with it, what will your friends think? What will the rest of the school think? How will Sally react? Wouldn't it just be easier to say no and avoid the whole thing? But you're not sure, so on the way to the parking lot, you find yourself doing a lot of thinking.

6-16B   **Take Your Pick**

First, Two Questions

1. As Sue, were you correct to ask yourself so many questions? Explain.

_____

_____

_____

_____

_____

2. How might you have responded if Bill were not African-American? If this "whole race issue" didn't scare you? Explain.

_____

_____

_____

_____

_____

The Search for Alternatives

In the space provided, write down each alternative available to you. Underneath each alternative, write at least two consequences of that decision.

ALTERNATIVE 1: _____

_____

   CONSEQUENCE: _____

_____

   CONSEQUENCE: _____

_____

ALTERNATIVE 2: _____

_____

   CONSEQUENCE: _____

_____

   CONSEQUENCE: _____

_____

ALTERNATIVE 3: _____

_____

   CONSEQUENCE: _____

_____

   CONSEQUENCE: _____

_____

ALTERNATIVE 4: _____

_____

   CONSEQUENCE: _____

_____

   CONSEQUENCE: _____

_____

MORE ALTERNATIVES AND CONSEQUENCES? Write them on the back of this sheet.

Activity 6-17: Prejudice and Discrimination

PURPOSE: To show how prejudice and discrimination lead to disrespect.

MATERIALS: Worksheet 6-17; pencils

PROCEDURE:

- Hand out a copy of Worksheet 6-17 to each student. Have them choose one or both of the situations to role-play.
- Draw a long line on the board or on butcher paper taped to the wall.
- Label the line from left to right "Strongly Agree, Agree, Disagree, Strongly Disagree."
- Have the class role-play or read the situations.
- Ask each member of the class to come to the board and "sign the line."
- Use the questions below to discuss the role-play.
    1. How typical is this situation in your school?
    2. Why did you "sign the line" where you did?
    3. Imagine that the participants in these situations could replay them. What, in your opinion, would be a better response?
- Repeat the discussion above for the other situation if time permits.
- Have the students answer the two questions at the bottom of Worksheet 6-17.
- As a class, come to a consensus about the best ways to make a difference.

6-17   # Role-Play

Situation 1: The Fiestada Fiasco

Frank accidentally knocks his fiestada off the table and onto the floor while gesturing wildly about his new class. Meanwhile, other students walk by Frank's table and squish the fiestada into the floor. Carrie turns to Frank and says, "Aren't you going to pick that up?" Frank replies, "No! That's why we have janitors around here. Without us, they wouldn't have jobs."

Situation 2: Show Me the I.D.

Heather pays for her ham and cheese on a Kaiser, grabs her milk, and exits the lunch line into the cafeteria. As she exits, Mrs. Juarez, the lunchroom supervisor, asks her for her I.D. Heather turns to Mrs. Juarez and says, "That's soooo stupid! Besides, *you* can't make me."

Answer the following questions regarding situations—like the ones above—that happen every day.

1. What can I do to make a difference?

   _____

   _____

   _____

   _____

2. What can we do to encourage others to make a difference?

   _____

   _____

   _____

   _____

Activity 6-18: What Do You Think?

PURPOSE: To enable students to analyze and evaluate a situation involving discrimination.

MATERIALS: Worksheet 6-18; paper; pencils

PROCEDURE:

- Distribute Worksheet 6-18 and give the class enough time to read it. Then arrange them in groups of three or four to discuss it. Tell them to discuss the questions, then seek consensus among themselves for answers. Tell them to write their answers in order to share them later with the entire class.

- After they have had enough time to discuss the situation and answer each question, have students share their answers with the entire class. After each group shares its answers, ask the entire class for a reaction.

- After every group has shared the answers, tell the students to choose the best from each group and establish a consensus opinion for the entire class.

What Do You Think?

Discrimination Hurts All of Us

You're a senior at Happy Valley High School, a predominantly white school in an upper-middle class community, and this is your fourth year serving on the Executive Board of the Girls' Intramural Association. You're embarrassed to admit it, but you're one of the school's best athletes, owning at least three school records in track and starring on the school's conference championship basketball team. It's late in the school year, and you, your activity sponsor, and the rest of the Executive Board are selecting new members for next year's Board.

One of the candidates for the Board is a teammate of yours, an excellent student, a gifted athlete, an accepted member of the basketball family, and fast becoming a good friend of yours. She's also black, one of only three or four African-Americans in your school. You've been singing her praises for the past five minutes, guaranteeing your fellow Board members that Haley would be an excellent choice.

The activity sponsor seems convinced, but three of the four other members of the Board are more reserved. Mandy said, "I really think Haley is sweet, but is she respected enough around the school to relate to the other girls?" Two of the other girls nodded their shared concern. One of them responded, "I agree, and I'm not sure Haley sees things the way we do." At which point, you asked, "What do you mean the way *we* do?"

Mandy replied, "You know what we mean. Haley hasn't fit in for a couple of years now. How do we select her for our Board?"

"*Our* Board?!" you asked. "Well, I . . ."

WILL YOU . . .

- Take a deep breath and, without confronting them, ask to discuss the three girls' concerns?

- Tell the other three members that they are sounding discriminatory and ask them to clarify their positions?

- Get angry with the three girls and give them a piece of your mind?

- Acknowledge their apparent discrimination and ask the activity sponsor to do something about it?

- Seek intervention from the principal if the activity sponsor fails to help?

- Go to the Director of Student Activities and say that you think the Board is being discriminatory?

- Resign from the Board?

- Think about it. What else might you do? As important, *why* will you do it?

Activity 6-19: Being Physically Disabled

PURPOSE: To promote an understanding of physical disabilities

MATERIALS: Worksheet 6-19; pencils; blindfolds; masking tape; a snack for everyone involved in the activity

PROCEDURE:

- Divide the class into small groups of three or four.
- Assign each student a "pretend" physical disability (i.e., one student is deaf, one student is blind, one student has no use of hands or feet).
- Arrange physical limitations to match the assigned disability (e.g., blindfold the "blind" student, tape the hands together of the student who can't use hands).
- Send one "handicapped" student from each group to a central location in the building to obtain and bring back a snack for himself or herself and the other members of his or her group.
- The group must help each other, as the disability necessitates, to eat the snack.
- Distribute Worksheet 6-19 and have students respond individually to the questions. Then discuss the questions as a whole class.

6-19   # Being Physically Disabled: Discussion Questions

1. How difficult was it to maneuver with your "disability"?

   _____

   _____

   _____

2. How did you feel as you tried to accomplish your tasks?

   _____

   _____

   _____

3. How did this experience help you better understand the daily experiences of a person with disabilities?

   _____

   _____

   _____

4. How will you change your attitude and behavior toward people with disabilities?

   _____

   _____

   _____

Activity 6-20: Sexual Harassment

PURPOSE: To define what constitutes sexual harassment and to identify behavior that can be construed to be sexual harassment.

MATERIALS: Worksheet 6-20; pencils

PROCEDURE:

- Using the chalkboard or butcher paper, have the participating students brainstorm their definition of sexual harassment.

- Give each student a copy of Worksheet 6-20 to complete.

- Divide the students into small groups of three or four to discuss the results of their worksheets and come to a consensus regarding the suggested behaviors.

- Ask the groups to select a spokesperson for each group to share the findings of the groups with the entire class. Allow the groups to defend or justify their answers.

- Conclude with the following questions:

    1. How does sexual harassment resemble flirting?

    2. How does sexual harassment differ from flirting?

    3. Based on your discussion, what is a viable definition for sexual harassment?

Students' Names _____ Date _____

6-20   # Flirting vs. Sexual Harassment

Indicate with an **F** those behaviors you think are flirting and an **S** those you think are sexual harassment.

_____ smiling across the hall

_____ pinching

_____ grabbing

_____ talking

_____ showing an interest in someone

_____ staring

_____ making sexual comments

_____ unwanted touching

_____ making eye contact

_____ waving at someone

Activity 6-21: More About Sexual Harassment

PURPOSE: To continue to define sexual harassment and to enable students to analyze and evaluate a situation involving sexual harassment.

MATERIALS: Worksheets 6-21A, 6-21B, 6-21C, and 6-21D; pencils

PROCEDURE:

- Divide the class into small groups of three or four.
- Distribute one copy of Worksheet 6-21A to each small group.
- Ask the students to read and discuss the case studies in their small groups, decide if the case is flirting or sexual harassment, and give reasons why they decided what they did.
- Ask each group to select a spokesperson to share with the whole class the consensus of the group and the reasoning behind its decisions.
- Follow-up with the discussion questions on Worksheet 6-21B.
- After the students have answered the discussion questions, give each student copies of Worksheets 6-21C and 6-21D.

Sexual Harassment: Case Studies

Case Study 1

Several high school girls are standing in the hallway talking before school one morning when Bill, the captain of the football team, walks by. One girl whom Bill thinks is pretty cool yells out, "Nice buns! Call me sometime." Bill, embarrassed, laughs and says, "Sure. I'll do that."

Case Study 2

Elise's seat is in front of Rich in their History class. While the teacher is talking, Rich snaps Elise's bra strap, which is visible through her white T-shirt. Elise feels humiliated and embarrassed.

Case Study 3

Mr. Johnson, an older teacher, is walking towards the cafeteria one day for lunch. He sees a small group of students watching him and laughing. As he gets closer he realizes they are making sexual comments about him. Very embarrassed, he hurries on, pretending to be engrossed in the mail he just picked up from his mailbox in the main office.

Case Study 4

Jerry, an excellent band member, isn't very good in P.E. When teams are chosen, Jerry always seems to be the last one picked. Some of the kids in the class tease him about how unathletic he is, call him things like "faggot" or "wimp," and tell him he throws a ball "like a girl." Every day before P.E. class, Jerry begins to feel nauseated and anxious. It takes all of his willpower to get himself to go. He'd rather cut the class and take a detention.

6-21B   **More About Sexual Harassment:**
Discussion Questions

1. How do you think the "victim" feels in each case study?

_____

_____

_____

_____

2. Why do you think people engage in sexual harassment?

_____

_____

_____

3. What do you think "eye of the beholder" means?

_____

_____

_____

4. What would you do if you were the person being harassed in each case study?

_____

_____

_____

_____

6-21C   # Sexual Harassment vs. Flirting*

Sexual Harassment   **Flirting**
Makes the receiver feel: Makes the receiver feel:
    Bad   Good
    Angry/sad   Happy
    Demeaned   Flattered
    Ugly   Pretty/attractive
    Powerless   In control

Sexual Harassment   **Flirting**
Results in: Results in:
    Negative self-esteem   Positive self-esteem

Sexual Harassment   **Flirting**
Is perceived as: Is perceived as:
    One-sided   Reciprocal
    Demeaning   Flattering
    Invading   Open
    Degrading   A compliment

Sexual Harassment Is: **Flirting Is:**
    Unwanted   Wanted
    Power-motivated   Equality-motivated
    Illegal   Legal

*Susan Strauss, *Sexual Harassment and Teens* (Minneapolis: Free Spirit Publishing, 1992).

What to Do If It Happens to You*

Follow the sexual harassment policy and procedure that is used by your school, district, or workplace. If there is no existing policy and procedure, use this one.

Step 1: Communicate to your harasser (1) what you are feeling, and (2) that you expect the behavior to stop. You may do this verbally or in writing. If you choose, you may get help and support from a friend, parent, professional, or other trusted adult.

Step 2: If the behavior is repeated, go to a person in authority, such as a principal, counselor, complaint manager, or supervisor. Document exactly what happened. Give a copy of your written record to the authority, and keep one for yourself.

Your documentation should include the following information. Use exact quotes where appropriate and whenever possible.

- what happened
- when it happened
- where it happened
- who did the harassing
- who the witnesses were (if any)
- what you said and/or did in response to the harassment
- how your harasser responded to you
- how you felt about the harassment

Step 3: If the behavior is repeated, go to a person in higher authority, such as a school board member, the superintendent of schools, the company president, etc. Keep documenting the behavior.

At any point in this process, you may choose to contact the Office of Civil Rights, your State Department of Education, your State Department of Human Rights, an attorney, or a police officer.

*Susan Strauss, *Sexual Harassment and Teens* (Minneapolis: Free Spirit Publishing, 1992).

Activity 6-22: What Will You Do?

PURPOSE: To enable students to analyze and evaluate a situation involving harassment.

MATERIALS: Worksheet 6-22; pencils; paper

PROCEDURE:

- Distribute Worksheet 6-22 and give the class enough time to read it. Then arrange students in groups of three or four. Tell them to discuss the questions, then seek a consensus among themselves for answers. Tell them to write their answers in order to share them later with the entire class.

- After students have had enough time to discuss the situation and answer each question, have them share their answers with the entire class. After each group shares its answers, ask the entire class for a reaction.

- After every group has shared the answers, tell the students to choose the best from each group and establish a consensus opinion for the entire class.

The Situation

Flirting or Harassment?

You're sitting in English class. Tom, two rows over, is smiling at you. Because this is just the start of the first semester, you barely know him. Reflexively, you smile back, then turn your head toward the teacher as class starts.

After class, Tom approaches you in the hall. "Hey, Cathy, got a second?"

You respond hesitatingly: "I guess . . . but just a second. I have another class."

"The football team's having a party this weekend, and I was wondering if you would like to go."

"With you?" you ask. "I hardly know you."

Tom smiles, winks at you, and says: "No big deal. We'll have lots of time to get to know each other at the party."

"Oh, I don't think it would be right . . .," you respond.

"Why not?" asks Tom. "You smiled back at me, didn't you?"

"Well, yes," you explain, "but it didn't mean anything."

"Smiles," explained Tom, "always mean something. Come on, I got the message."

"What message?"

Said Tom, "We obviously have a little chemistry going here."

You smile again and say, "Oh, I don't think so. I'd better be going to class."

At which point, Tom grabs your arm and says, "Wait a minute. Maybe if the chemistry isn't here now—it will be." Then he gives you a long look, starting at your feet and slowly moving up your body.

What Will You Do?

First of all:

- Does this episode involve flirting or harassment or both?

- If it involves harassment, at what point in the conversation did the harassment start?

- Why do you think it was harassment at that point?

Will you . . .

- Ask him nicely to let go of your arm, smile, and walk away?

- Pull your arm from his grasp and, without smiling, tell him to leave you alone?

- Slowly pull your arm away and tell him that you are offended by his behavior and that you would prefer not to talk to him when he acts this way?

- Slowly remove your arm, tell him you're offended, and instruct him not to talk to you again?

- Laugh and, after calling him a jerk, tell him to stay away from you?

- Walk away, saying, "Stay away from me"?

- Report him to the Dean of Students?

- What else might you do, and why would you do it?

Activity 6-23: Jubilee, a Celebration of Diversity

PURPOSE: To celebrate the cultural diversity of the school community

MATERIALS: Poster (sample is given); Worksheet 6-23; participants provide their own equipment (e.g., boombox, TV/VCR); the school provides tables and extension cords

PROCEDURE:

- Organize committees to handle applications, publicity, set-up, and clean-up. Display posters around the school.

- Have those wishing to participate complete the application process (see Worksheet 6-23).

- Hold an informational meeting with the participants to clarify all the details and stipulations of your Jubilee.

- Decide and announce how members of the school community may visit the Jubilee (with their Social Studies classes, during their lunch period, during their Physical Education classes).

- One school used Jubilee participation accompanied by a written paper as the equivalent of its final exam in Social Studies or Foreign Language.

Let Your Heritage . . . Sparkle

You are invited
to
participate in the
FIRST CLASS JUBILEE

When?	**May 3, 2002**
Where?	**North Gym**
What time?	**Period Two**
	Participants will set up Period One **and take down their displays Period Three**
Who?	**You and a friend (or 2)**
	You, your friends, and **. . . a teacher (what an idea!)**
	A teacher . . . and another teacher!
What?	**Celebrate our cultural heritage!**
Why?	**Because it's fun**
How?	**Get your group together** **and** **Begin thinking and planning**

Complete the application and return it
to the Guidance Office during the week of April 8–12.

First Class Jubilee Application

Name(s): _____   Culture/Country: _____

_____

_____

_____

Due: _____
Turn in to Guidance Office

Draw (as best as possible) a picture or diagram of what your display will look like. Displays should be no larger than 4- by 3-feet. Project display boards are available at office supply stores.

NOTE: You/your group need(s) to provide your own equipment (boombox, TV/VCR, etc.). The school will provide tables and extension cords.

- -

For Jubilee Committee use only.

Proposal: _____ Accepted   _____ Not Accepted

Activity 6-24: A Challenge to the School Community

PURPOSE: To challenge students to create "something" that celebrates the diversity of the school community. Through a variety of activities it becomes apparent that the school community is a complex mixture of people. The mixture varies in ethnic backgrounds, in physical make-up (size, shape, color, height), in social skills (very popular, quiet, date a lot, date no one, go everywhere do everything, homebodies), in economic status (rich, poor, works and goes to school, doesn't work and has money to spend), and in expertise (in the arts, sports, volunteering, academics, and leadership).

MATERIALS: Worksheet 6-24; items needed for "creations"

PROCEDURE:

- Say to your class, "Clearly, differences make us unique and who we are. Therefore, how can we share this with others?"

- Divide the class into groups of three or four. Each group is to create "something" to *celebrate* who we are as a school community.

- Some ideas include, but are not limited to: a huge mural, a rap song, a poem, a photo, a photo collage, a written belief statement, a video, a quilt.

- Allow several class sessions for groups to work on this project.

- Submissions can be judged by a team of students, staff, and administration. (See Worksheet 6-24.)

- The top five entries after the first judging can be shared with the entire school body through closed-circuit TV or public display, and then voted on by all staff and students. Appropriate prizes could be awarded and the best entries may be adopted by the school.

First Class Challenge

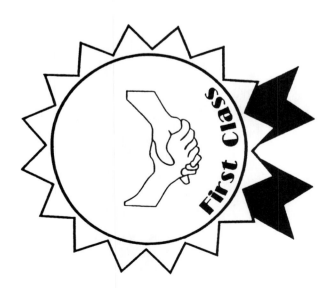

Advisory entries celebrate the diversity and unity of our school community by:

- **Communicating the theme**   4   3   2   1

- **Revealing meaningful insights**   4   3   2   1

- **Using creative and original approaches**   4   3   2   1

- **Displaying quality craftsmanship**   4   3   2   1

Key:

4	Fabulous!
3	Groovy!
2	Getting there!
1	Nice try!

Judges' Notes:

_____

_____

_____

Activity 6-25: General Activities and Thought Questions

PURPOSE: To understand and celebrate differences in others.

MATERIALS: Worksheet 6-25

PROCEDURE:

- Divide the class into groups of three or four.
- Give each group a copy of Worksheet 6-25 and have the students discuss the questions.
- After the groups have had enough time to discuss the questions, have them share their answers with the entire class. After each group shares its answers, ask the entire class for a reaction.
- Tell the students to choose the best from each group and establish a consensus opinion for the entire class.

General Activities and Thought Questions: "Understanding and Celebrating Differences in Others"

Comprehension Level

- What differences in others cause problems that you might see on the news on TV?
- Name two or three differences in others that you hear about on TV or in the movies.

Application Level

- To accept differences in others, sometimes you have to go against what your friends want. How do you feel when you do that?
- Explain what your school would be like if everyone could accept the differences in everyone else. What would it be like if they *couldn't* accept the differences in everyone else?

Analysis Level

- In what ways are people different? Arrange them according to looks and actions.
- In what ways are you just like your friends? In what ways are you different?

Synthesis Level

- Create the perfect friend, someone who would accept the differences in you. List what he or she is like.
- Join with your classmates to bring to class and to put on the bulletin board pictures that show how people are different.

Evaluation Level

- Accepting the differences in others is important, but sometimes it's very hard. Explain.
- Which is more important—being different or accepting the differences in others? Why?

SECTION 7

UNDERSTANDING AND CELEBRATING DIFFERENCES IN MYSELF

"If a man does not keep pace with his companions, perhaps it is because he hears a different drummer. Let him step to the music he hears, however measured or far away."

HENRY DAVID THOREAU

More of the Story:

Our students are individual works of art that come to us in a variety of sizes, shapes, and colors. Like all art, they define the scope and direction of our creative energies and reveal what is culturally important to us. Looking at our children this way provided a focus for our Steering Committee. As artists in our own right, we asked ourselves an important question. Was our job to create artifacts, tools for a growing technological society? Or was it to create masterpieces, triumphs of whatever genius we possessed?

We decided to create masterpieces. Creating masterpieces, however, is much easier said than done. To be successful, we must first find genius, then focus it exclusively on our subjects. Finding genius was not difficult. You will find it, too, if you accept Christopher Quill's belief that "genius is the infinite capacity to take life by the scruff of the neck." We decided to grab hold and persevere.

First, we accepted the fact that, by definition, masterpieces are unique. No two can be alike. Any attempt to homogenize them, therefore, was inconsistent with our purposes. This belief provoked the reconsideration of existing traditions in our school, such as ability grouping, and it underscored our idea that children must learn to celebrate their uniqueness. Most of these activities do just that.

We also recognized that good art can be dangerous. It challenges and questions. It destroys existing boundaries. It often forces us to look at the truth. Art doesn't simply

305

reproduce reality. It provides new and penetrating views of reality. We knew that our masterpieces would do exactly that, and we welcomed their insights and their challenges, even asked for them, recognizing that students provide important perspectives about schools and their operation. Some of the materials regarding student input are provided in Sections 8 and 9 of this book.

An obvious benefit to all of us was that our students, no matter their size or shape, began to think of themselves as masterpieces. Karen shares a story:

"Two of my freshmen students were arriving late to class at least once or twice a week. I asked them one day what the problem was.

"Said one, 'We have to go to the bathroom sometimes, and we have to go to the other end of the building to find one.'

"'Why?' I asked. 'What's wrong with the bathroom around the corner?'

"'A couple of seniors are smoking in there all the time, and it stinks. Once, they even told us to keep our mouths shut.'

"So I asked, 'Why don't you just tell them they aren't being first class?'

"In my zeal to promote the program, I completely overlooked the fact that both boys were 'vertically challenged,' victims of their own developmental delays, fairly typical freshmen boys!

"'Oh, we couldn't do that! They'd pound on us! Could you just watch the bathroom for us?'

"'I'd prefer if you guys would stand up for yourselves, but I'll see what I can do.'

"So I started keeping an eye on the bathroom but couldn't do much about the smoking because I couldn't smell anything outside. But one day, only a few minutes before class started, I heard two squeaky voices scream from inside the bathroom, 'THAT'S NOT VERY FIRST CLASS!' Then I watched my two freshman boys scramble through the bathroom door like two puppies tumbling out of a bushel basket.

"I smiled, certain that the two seniors hadn't seen them. When the seniors ran out, I noticed that they also were two of my students, so I said, 'I don't think it's very first class either.' They just scowled at me and walked away.

"Later in the day, when the seniors came to class, both actually apologized for their behavior.

"I smiled, recognizing that some masterpieces take a little longer than others."

Index of Activities for Understanding and Celebrating Differences in Myself

Activity Number	*Name*	*Description*
7-1	Taking a Closer Look at Me	Promoting a positive self-concept
7-2	Finding the Real Me	Promoting self-discovery
7-3	Self-Acceptance	Identifying the positive qualities of the students
7-4	Is What You See What You Get?	Focusing on who students really are as opposed to how they are perceived by others
7-5	Self-Criticism: What Must Happen First?	Looking at what is needed to be self-critical
7-6	Self-Criticism: How Do I Do It?	Considering the processes of self-criticism
7-7	A Bump on the Way	Looking at failure as an opportunity for personal growth
7-8	The Kingdom of Perfect Happiness	Looking at our accomplishments in life and relating them to happiness and self-worth
7-9	Building a Better Me	Promoting the development of a positive attitude
7-10	To Get Friends, Be One	Exploring the process of making friends

Activity 7-1: Taking a Closer Look at Me

PURPOSE: To help students develop a positive self-concept. In order to understand and celebrate differences in others, kids must be able to understand and like themselves. A positive self-concept accepts limitations and promotes personal growth. Positive character traits are directly linked to a strong sense of self-worth.

MATERIALS: Worksheets 7-1A, 7-1B, and 7-1C; pencils; glue or tape; an individual photo of each student in the class

PROCEDURE:

- Have each student complete #1 on Worksheet 7-1A. You, too, should complete it.
- When the class has completed the task, begin by sharing the three things you have written.
- The class will vote on which one of the three statements was invented. (Allow comments or questions if they come up naturally.)
- Call on each student one at a time to follow the same procedure. After each sharing, the class members will vote on the statement they think is *not* true.
- Follow-up with discussion questions 1–8 on Worksheet 7-1B.
- Divide the class into small groups of three and ask each group to complete question 9 of the discussion questions.
- Ask each group to share the responses to the question. List them on the board.
- Finish by giving each student a copy of the snowflake (Worksheet 7-1C), a symbol of their celebrated uniqueness.
- Have the students write their names and attach their pictures to the center of their snowflakes.
- Display the "unique" snowflakes on a wall in the classroom.

7-1A   **Taking a Closer Look at Me**

1. Write three things about yourself. *One of the three things must be invented.*

    a. _____

    b. _____

    c. _____

2. Write the invented thing about each of your classmates.

    Name   **Invented Thing**

    _____

    _____

    _____

    _____

    _____

    _____

    _____

    _____

    _____

    _____

    _____

    _____

    _____

    _____

7-1B   ## Taking a Closer Look at Me: Discussion Questions

1. Why did you write the particular untrue statement about yourself?

   _____

   _____

   _____

2. Why do we often feel compelled to impress or shock others with who we are, what we know, who we know, what we have?

   _____

   _____

   _____

3. How do the two true statements you shared about yourself make you the same as one other or some of the others in the class?

   _____

   _____

   _____

4. How do the two true statements you shared about yourself make you unique?

   _____

   _____

   _____

5. The dictionary defines unique as being the only one of its kind. What are the advantages of being unique? How do the things that make you unique help you understand things that others might not understand?

   _____

   _____

   _____

   _____

7-1B *(continued)*

6. What are the disadvantages of being unique?

_____

_____

_____

7. Since everyone can be both unique and the same simultaneously, which is easier to celebrate and appreciate—being unique or being the same? Why?

_____

_____

_____

8. Since we know that our uniqueness makes each of us one of a kind, how can we best celebrate and appreciate the uniqueness of others?

_____

_____

_____

9. Come to a consensus in your small group on three good ways to develop a positive self-concept. Be prepared to share your ideas with the rest of the class.

_____

_____

_____

_____

_____

_____

Taking a Closer Look at Me

Activity 7-2: Finding the Real Me

PURPOSE: To promote self-discovery

MATERIALS: Worksheets 7-2A and 7-2B; pencils

PROCEDURE:

- Distribute these worksheets two days before doing Activity 7-3, *Self-Acceptance*. Have the students complete Worksheet 7-2A and have them give 7-2B to their parents to complete. Provide students and their parents and/or siblings sufficient time to complete the worksheet.

- It is important for the students and their parents to complete their worksheets before Activity 7-3. Encourage the students to compare their self-perceptions with the perceptions of their parents and, ultimately, their classmates.

- Be sure to remind students well in advance to bring these results to class on the day you plan to use Activity 7-3.

Finding the Real Me: Student Copy

Three Little Words:

Write the first three words that come to mind to describe yourself. Jot them down quickly without giving them a lot of thought.

_____

_____

_____

Three More Words:

OK, those three words represent the "surface" you, the person you think everyone else sees. They may also be the person you *want* everyone else to see. But now take a moment to think about the *real* you, the person many of us don't see. Think about the "you" that consists of likes and dislikes, feelings, wants and desires, hopes and fears. Use three nouns to describe this "you."

_____

_____

_____

The Bigger Picture:

Now provide even a clearer picture of you. Add an adjective to each noun that describes you. Again, give it some thought.

_____

_____

_____

The Active You:

Finally, jot down three "ing" words that describe you. They can involve everything from "fishing" to "caring." Don't worry if you find yourself repeating one or more of the words you have already used to describe yourself. Repeated words are sometimes the best descriptors.

_____

_____

_____

Finding the Real Me: Parent Copy

Please answer the following questions and return the sheet to your child. Your child needs your reactions in order to participate in a follow-up activity in our character education program. Thanks for your help.

Three Little Words:

Write the first three words that come to mind to describe your child. Jot them down quickly without giving them a lot of thought.

_____

_____

_____

Three More Words:

Those three words probably represent the child you or your child thinks everyone else sees. They may also represent the child you *want* everyone else to see. But now take a moment to think about the hidden part of your child, the person that many of us don't see. This is the child consisting of likes and dislikes, feelings, wants and desires, hopes and fears. Use three nouns to describe this child.

_____

_____

_____

The Bigger Picture:

Now provide even a clearer picture of your child. Add an adjective to each noun that describes him or her. Again, give it some thought; maybe talk it over with others in the family.

_____

_____

_____

Your Active Child:

Finally, jot down three "ing" words that describe your child. They can involve everything from "fishing" to "caring." Don't worry if you find yourself repeating one or more of the words you have already used to describe your child. Repeated words are sometimes the best descriptors.

_____

_____

_____

Activity 7-3: Self-Acceptance: Knowing the Better Me

PURPOSE: To identify and explore our many positive qualities.

MATERIALS: Worksheet 7-3; white paper plates or sheets of notebook paper; string, tape, or paper clips; pencils; crayons

PROCEDURE:

- Introduce the activity by sharing the idea that our self-perceptions are some-times different from the perceptions of others. It's surprising how often the per-ceptions of others can give us insights into ourselves. Sometimes we're a whole lot better than even we think we are!

- Start the activity by having the students help each other attach the paper plates or the sheets of paper to the *backs* of their shirts. They should not be able to see the plates or the sheets of paper at any time during the activity.

- Next, give students 10 to 15 minutes to circulate about the room in order to write words or phrases on everyone else's plates with crayons. The words or phrases should describe the wearer's positive personal qualities. *Only positive terms can be used,* for example: good-looking, friendly, athletic, good student, caring, honest, funny, hard-working, sharp dresser, sensitive, helpful.

- Use more time as needed. When students have no more to write, tell the stu-dents to return to their desks and to remove or to get help removing the plates or sheets of paper.

- Next, give the students time to look carefully at their plates and to think about the words and phrases. Then distribute Worksheet 7-3 and have the students answer each question. Encourage them to be as honest and as sensitive as pos-sible. They will *not* be expected to share their answers with the rest of the class.

- Finally, tell them to compare their classmates' perceptions with their self-perceptions as well as the perceptions of their family members. (Refer to Activ-ity 7-2.) Tell students to take the plates and the worksheets home to share with their families.

Self-Acceptance: Knowing the Better Me

1. Review the words and phrases your classmates used to describe your personal qualities. Which of them surprises you? Why?

   _____

   _____

   _____

2. Which of the descriptions do you most agree with? Why?

   _____

   _____

   _____

3. Which of the descriptions do you most disagree with? Why?

   _____

   _____

   _____

4. Do you think your family members will agree with these descriptions? Explain your answer.

   _____

   _____

   _____

5. What words did you expect to see—and didn't? Why do you suppose no one wrote them down?

   _____

   _____

   _____

TAKE YOUR CLASSMATES' DESCRIPTIONS AND THIS
FORM HOME TO DISCUSS WITH YOUR FAMILY. HAVE YOUR
FAMILY REACT TO EACH QUESTION.

Activity 7-4: Is What You See What You Get?

PURPOSE: To help students think about who they are in contrast with how they are perceived to be. This activity is designed to help students look at and accept themselves for who they really are.

MATERIALS: Worksheet 7-4; a coin for each pair of students; pencils

PROCEDURE:

- Pair each student in the class with a partner he or she does *not* know.
- Ask the partners to introduce themselves to each other (*names only*).
- Hand out Worksheet 7-4 to all members of the class. Instruct students to answer the questions about their partners just by observing their partners without asking them any questions. They should write their answers in the column marked **PERCEIVED ANSWERS**.
- Give each pair a coin.
- Tell one partner to be "heads" and the other partner to be "tails."
- One partner flips the coin. If it lands heads up, the partner who is designated "heads" answers the first question on the worksheet.
- Partners continue flipping the coin and answering the questions until all the questions on the worksheet have been answered. If heads (or tails) turns up more times than there are questions, the partner asking the questions may make up more questions.
- The partners compare the **PERCEIVED ANSWERS** with the **REAL ANSWERS** and give themselves one point for each answer they perceived correctly about their partner.
- The person in each group who scores more points is the winner.
- The groups will take turns, using the information they learned from the worksheet, introducing each other. The winning partner will begin by introducing his or her partner. Then his or her partner will introduce him or her. Continue until the entire class has been introduced.

7-4　　　　　　　　**Is What You See What You Get?**

A. Answer the following questions about your partner by **guessing** how you think he or she might respond. Write your answers under the column marked **PERCEIVED ANSWERS**.

　　1. What is your favorite rock group?

　　2. What is your favorite class?

　　3. What is your favorite song?

　　4. What color describes you?

　　5. What song describes you?

　　6. What two characteristics ending in "able" (e.g., likeable) best describe you?

　　7. Of what two things are you proud?

　　8. In what two community causes or school activities are you involved?

　　9. What two things make you feel uncomfortable?

　10. What two things do you value?

B. Now interview your partner to find out his or her real answers to the same questions and write them under the column marked **REAL ANSWERS**. If the **PERCEIVED ANSWER** matches the **REAL ANSWER**, give yourself one point.

PERCEIVED ANSWERS	REAL ANSWERS	POINTS
1. _____		
2. _____		
3. _____		
4. _____		
5. _____		
6. _____		
7. _____		
8. _____		
9. _____		
10. _____		

C. Now that you have interviewed your partner, how has your perception of him or her changed? Based on what you've learned about him or her in your interview, introduce your partner to the class.

Activity 7-5: Self-Criticism: What Must Happen First?

PURPOSE: To help students explore the personal qualities necessary for self-criticism. By the end of this activity, students should recognize and understand that true self-criticism requires security, sensitivity, self-confidence, and courage. Such qualities promote a willingness to look carefully at our own behavior, to recognize shortcomings, and to have the strength to correct them.

MATERIALS: Worksheets 7-5A and 7-5B; pencils

PROCEDURE:

- Introduce the activity by discussing self-criticism. Tell the students that the focus of this activity is not on whether or not they like their eyebrows, their hair, or their complexions! That's not the kind of criticism we're seeking. Nor are we talking about self-loathing, the general dislike of self that sometimes plagues all of us. This activity looks at the ability of each of us to reflect on our behavior, to see and accept that we may have done something wrong, then to do something about it.

- Select three students to role-play the episode on Worksheet 7-5A. The Narrator should be one of your best and most demonstrative students, maybe a student who is interested in acting. While informing the rest of the class of the process you will follow with this activity, have the three students rehearse the episode to determine how they will handle their roles.

- Next, divide the class into groups of four or five. Distribute Worksheet 7-5B to every student and have the groups work on Section A. Tell them to try to reach a consensus on the three qualities. Then discuss their decisions as a class. If necessary, help them see that self-confidence, sensitivity, and courage are essential before anyone can be self-critical. Self-criticism takes guts!

- Finally, have them go on to Section B. Follow the same process as with Section A. Try to achieve consensus with the entire class. Be sure they dialogue about the question, trying to build on each other's ideas. One opinion should not be encouraged to prevail over another. This is not a debate. It is a collaborative attempt to mutually agree on the qualities that are needed to be self-critical.

- For older students, paraphrase Polonius in *Hamlet* by quoting, "To your own self be true. Because it follows, you won't then be untrue to others." What did Shakespeare mean? How does the quote relate to this activity?

Self-Criticism:
A Role-Playing Episode

MARY: Isn't Phil Brown cute? I don't even like basketball, but I'll go anywhere to see him in those shorts!

CAROL: Is he ever! I hear he likes Diane Simms. How lucky is she?!

MARY: Well, why not? Diane gets just about everything she wants, doesn't she?

CAROL: (A little hesitatingly) Yeah, I guess so . . .

NARRATOR: It's time for the plot to thicken! Carol was just invited to Diane's birthday party on Saturday. Mary wasn't asked. Carol jumped at Diane's offer. Carol isn't very popular in school. In fact, she doesn't have a lot of friends, but she and Diane are on the same intramural softball team. Diane invited everyone on the team.

MARY: Well, Diane can have Phil if she wants him. But we can still dream, can't we?!

CAROL: Yeah, there's always dreaming.

MARY: Hey, by the way, don't worry about dressing up for the banquet on Saturday. It's pretty informal. I'll have to wear a dress, but you don't have to. I'm pretty nervous about getting this award. I'm really glad you're coming. At least I'll see one friendly face in the audience!

NARRATOR: Here it comes! What's a story without conflict? Carol promised Mary three weeks ago that she'd go with her to the banquet, but now she's accepted Diane's offer to go to the birthday party on the same day. Something's got to give. What do you think it'll be?

CAROL: I forgot to tell you! My mother told me that I have to stay home with my little brother on Saturday. She has to go somewhere with my dad.

NARRATOR: She's lying through her teeth! Her mom's going to be home all day. But Carol thinks it's the perfect excuse. If Mary discovers that she went to the party, Carol will just say that her mother changed her mind and that she received a late offer to go to the party.

MARY: (*Dejected*) Oh, no! I was really looking forward to having you with me. This award is really important to me, and I wanted you there. Are you sure you can't make it?

CAROL: I don't see how. My mom really needs my help.

NARRATOR: So, what's the deal with Carol? Friendship is not one of her strengths, is it? Maybe she'd benefit from a little self-criticism.

7-5B   # Self-Criticism: What Must Happen First?

Section A: Important Qualities

The Narrator probably is right. Carol needs to take a good look at herself. But before she can do that, what qualities does she need as a person? Work with your group to identify at least three qualities each of us must have before we can be self-critical.

Quality One: _____

Why is it important?

_____

_____

_____

Quality Two: _____

Why is it important?

_____

_____

_____

Quality Three: _____

Why is it important?

_____

_____

_____

Section B: You Have the Power

You have the power to create the perfect friend. Think about if for a moment, then list four characteristics of the perfect friend.

1. _____

2. _____

3. _____

4. _____

Next, what kinds of influences does this person need to be the perfect friend? The influences in our lives help to make us who we are. List four family and/or social influences we all need to be the perfect friend.

1. _____

2. _____

3. _____

4. _____

Finally, create a slogan, the kind you might find on a bumper sticker, that indicates how being a good friend relates to being self-critical.

Activity 7-6: Self-Criticism: How Do I Do It?

PURPOSE: To explore and promote the process(es) of self-criticism. This is a very effective activity; however, it is designed primarily for older students. You are encouraged to develop similar episodes and questions for younger students.

MATERIALS: Worksheets 7-6A, 7-6B, 7-6C, and 7-6D; pencils

PROCEDURE:

- Select several of your most outgoing students to dramatize the episodes on Worksheet 7-6A. Encourage them to create their own special interpretations of the roles.

- Divide the class into groups of three to watch and react to the episodes. After the first episode, tell them to respond to the questions on Worksheets 7-6B and 7-6C.

- Next, have students write their own follow-up episodes. The episodes should represent the group's ideas of what self-critical students *would* do next.

- Select two or three groups to role-play their own scripts. Two or three groups are enough to reflect the students' diversity and important principles. Try, however, to get everyone involved during the entire activity.

- After students dramatize their own episodes, distribute Worksheet 7-6D and have students summarize what they saw by reacting to the general questions.

- Follow the same procedure with the second episode.

- Conclude the activity by mentioning that sometimes our surroundings encourage good people to do bad things. Consider with your students the following examples:

    — The need for soft money in politics and how it corrupts formerly good government officials.

    — The growing pressure on students to get into college and how it has tempted even good kids to cheat.

    — Parental over-control, causing rebellion in good children.

    — Peer groups and the temptations they sometimes impose, causing even good kids to do dumb things.

- Emphasize that the first thing we must do when we sense a problem is LOOK IN THE MIRROR and ask ourselves, "What are the gains? The losses?" and "What did I do to help cause this problem?" Self-reflection and self-criticism are always the first steps.

Self-Criticism: Role-Playing Episodes

EPISODE ONE:

TOM: That's 40 miles away!

JIM: So what? They don't check IDs, and the place is loaded with chicks!

BILL: Is that the place in Smithville? Isn't that a biker bar?

JIM: No. There may be a couple, but it's mostly high school kids.

TOM: Who's gonna drive?

JIM: I am. I told my parents we were going to a flick. Use the same line on your parents.

TOM: *You* are? You already got one DUI. Are you goofy?

JIM: Then you can drive my car. What's the big deal?

**Go to Worksheet 7-6B to answer the questions
that apply to this episode.**

EPISODE TWO:

SUE: I'm not going.

JANIE: Why? Her counselor's a good guy.

MANDY: I agree with Sue. She'll kill us if she finds out.

SUE: Yeah, and let's get real. The counselors in this place are a bunch of clowns!

MANDY: Well, I don't know. Mine's pretty good. I like him.

JANIE: What if we just tell her that we know and we think she needs help?

SUE: Yeah, that'll go over big. You know Tina. She'll be so embarrassed she'll never talk to us again.

JANIE: We have to do *something!* I followed her after lunch yesterday. I could hear her throwing up in the bathroom.

SUE: Not me. Hey, maybe her parents know.

**Go to Worksheet 7-6C to answer the questions
that apply to this episode.**

7-6B # Self-Criticism: How Do I Do It?

Questions for Episode One: Tom, Jim, and Bill

1. Any form of criticism needs information. You are Tom. What additional information do you need to be effectively self-critical in this situation? Identify at least two pieces of information you should have.

   _____

   _____

   _____

2. All self-criticism requires that you ask yourself, "What are the gains for me? What am I going to get out of this?" Then, you must ask yourself, "What are the potential losses?" What are the gains for Tom and Bill in this episode? For Jim? What are the potential losses for Tom and Bill? For Jim? For all of them? Write your answers.

   _____

   _____

   _____

3. In order to be effectively self-critical, we must always be willing to look in an imaginary mirror and ask ourselves, "What would a reasonable person do in similar circumstances?" As important, we must ask ourselves, "What am I doing to contribute to a potential problem here?" Answer both these questions as if you were Tom; then as if you were Bill. Use the back of this sheet as needed.

   _____

   _____

   _____

Now that you've answered these questions, write your own follow-up episode. How would one or more self-critical students handle this situation? Show how they would handle it!

7-6C   ## Self-Criticism: How Do I Do It?

Questions for Episode Two: Sue, Janie, and Mandy

1. Is there a need for any additional information here? What is it?

    _____

    _____

    _____

2. Consider once again the gains and losses. What are the gains for all the girls if:

    - They tell Tina's counselor? _____

      _____

    - They confront Tina? _____

      _____

    - They tell Tina's parents? _____

      _____

    - They don't tell anyone? _____

      _____

    What are the *losses* for all the girls if they don't tell anyone? What are the losses
    for Tina if they all keep quiet?

    _____

    _____

    _____

3. Look in the mirror again.

    - What would a reasonable person do here?

      _____

      _____

      _____

    - You are any one of the girls. What are you doing to contribute to a potential
      problem? Use the back of this sheet as needed.

      _____

      _____

      _____

**Now that you've answered these questions, write your own follow-up episode. How would
one or more self-critical students handle this situation? Show how they would handle it!**

7-6D   # Self-Criticism: How Do I Do It?

Answer these questions after watching each follow-up episode developed by your classmates.

1. Based on what you saw in these follow-up episodes, how would you summarize the self-reflection and self-criticism needed by the characters?

    _____

    _____

    _____

2. Did you see any responses or statements from one group and not the others that seemed to make a lot of sense?

    _____

    _____

    _____

3. What do all the groups seem to be saying about self-reflection and self-criticism? Did you see one or more responses that seemed common to all the groups? Based on your own observation and thinking about these episodes, what general statements can you make about self-reflection and self-criticism?

    _____

    _____

    _____

    _____

    _____

Activity 7-7: A Bump on the Way

PURPOSE: To help students understand that failure is an opportunity for personal growth and development. Everyone experiences failure, it's a part of life. What is important is how students look at failure and its effect on their character development.

MATERIALS: Worksheets 7-7A and 7-7B; pencils; a skier for each player; one die for each group

PROCEDURE:

- Divide the class into groups of three.
- Give each group a game sheet (Worksheet 7-7A), one die, and a set of cut-apart Bump Cards. The Bump Cards should be turned face down on the desk or table where the game is being played. Also give each player a skier.
- Give each group a copy of Worksheet 7-7B.
- Read aloud the children's rhyme written around the Wishing Star and ask the students if they remember the rhymes from their younger years. Ask for a show of hands from those who believe that wishing for something makes it happen.
- Tell the students that today, for the moment, they are all wishing to be expert skiers.
- Give students the following instructions on how to play "A Bump on the Way." Allow enough time to complete the game.

GAME INSTRUCTIONS

1. Each player rolls the die. The player with the highest number begins. He or she advances his or her skier the number of spaces rolled.

2. The other two players follow the same procedure.

3. If a player lands on a bump, he or she draws a Bump Card and follows the instructions.

4. The object of the game is to be the first skier to reach SUCCESS at the bottom of sWISHing Mountain.

- When the students have completed the game, discuss the following questions:
  - — As you headed for Success at the bottom of sWISHing Mountain, what interrupted your progress?
  - — What advanced your progress?
  - — Does wishing make a dream come true? Why or why not?
  - — Tell the students that the Wishing Star has five points. In their groups, the students decide on and fill in the points of the Wishing Star with the traits they must develop as a person of strong character that will turn "bumps on the way" into challenges they can meet and overcome without fear or self-doubt. (An example of a completed star is given.)

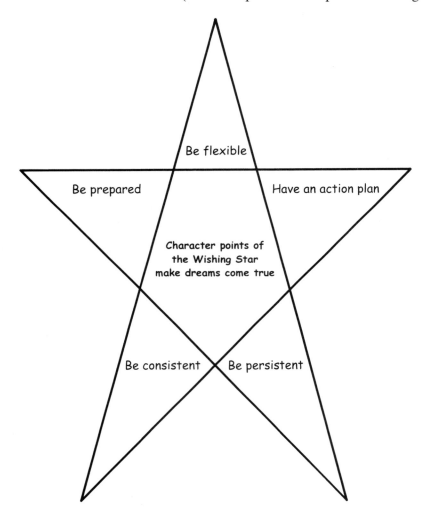

- Have each group share with the entire class its completed 5-point Wishing Star.
- Post the stars on the wall or on a door where they can be seen regularly.

Skiers

Bump Cards

You hit the bump and wipe out. Your skis fall off. *Skip your next turn while you put them back on.*	You are so angry when you fall on the bump that you sit in the snow and pound your skis. *Skip your turn.*
You don't wear your goggles and can't see the bump well. You wipe out. *Go back 1 space.*	You hit the bump perfectly and use it to propel yourself downhill. *Advance 3 spaces.*
You follow your plan for attacking the bump and master it with grace and form. *Advance 2 spaces.*	Your skis lock together when you try to do a spread eagle. *Skip your turn while the wind you knocked out of yourself comes back. Do better next time.*
While showing off, you take the bump off balance and wipe out. *Skip your turn.*	Your skiing is controlled and consistent. You are poetry in motion on the bumps. *Advance 3 spaces.*
You become totally discouraged when you wipe out on the bump. You take off your skis and threaten to give up skiing forever. *Go back 4 spaces and try that bump again.*	You become furious when you wipe out on the bump. As a result you take out your anger on your ski pole and break it in half. *Go back to start and learn from your mistakes.*
You wipe out because you're way over your head up here on the bumps. *Skip 2 turns to do more practicing on the lower slopes.*	Coming into the bump, you rotate your skis too soon and wipe out. *Go back 2 spaces and try it again.*

A Bump on the Way: Game Sheet

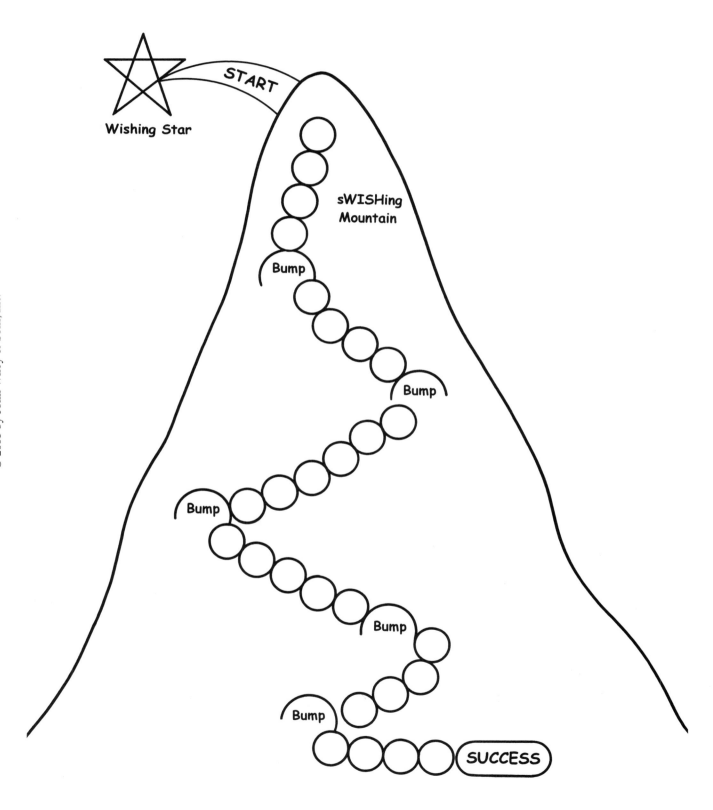

7-7B

A Wishing Star

Star light, star bright
First star I see tonight,
I wish I may, I wish I might
Have this wish I wish tonight.

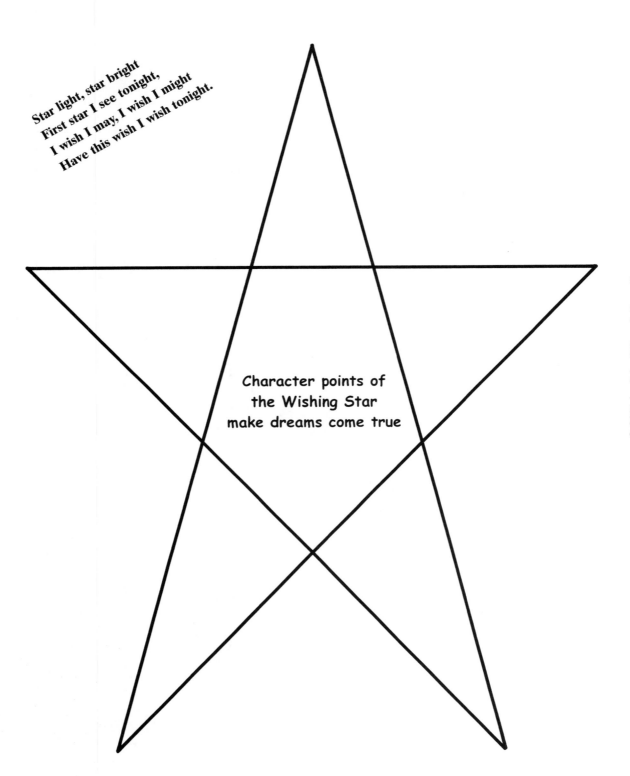

Character points of
the Wishing Star
make dreams come true

Activity 7-8: Eric Hanson and the Kingdom of Perfect Happiness

PURPOSE: To explore and discuss the accomplishments in life that bring us the greatest happiness and the strongest sense of self-worth.

MATERIALS: Worksheets 7-8A through 7-8J; pencils

PROCEDURE:

- Introduce the general activity by emphasizing to your students that all of us need a sense of accomplishment, which is one of our most important ego needs. Some accomplishments, however, may be more worthwhile than others. These activities are designed to explore happiness and to help students reevaluate the relative importance of what they consider to be the most important accomplishments in their lives.

- These activities may be used individually, or they may be combined, but be sure to sequence them. You may use one or more in each class period based on time requirements. Normally, one activity is appropriate for each class period.

    — Part One: To identify important accomplishments
    — Part Two: To relate sensitivity to accomplishment
    — Part Three: To relate "doing good" to happiness
    — Part Four: To explore the term "happiness"
    — Part Five: To relate self-worth to happiness

- Distribute Worksheets 7-8A and 7-8B, and tell your students to complete them during the class period. Encourage the students to read the section of the story deliberately and to think carefully about each question. Give the students at least half the period to read the story section and to think about their answers. Use the rest of the period to discuss their answers as a class. Use additional story sections during that period as needed; you may even discover that one section runs over to another class period.

- Circulate among the students while they are reading each segment and answering the questions. Encourage them to use you as a resource and to dialogue with you as needed.

- When they have read and thought about each segment and have answered the questions, have as many students as possible share their answers with the entire class. Their insights are often quite remarkable.

Eric Hanson and the Kingdom of Perfect Happiness

Part One: The Story Begins

Eric had come a long way. He had learned how to walk and talk. Each of these accomplishments in itself was a remarkable feat. He had learned about being with others, about sharing, caring, and being cared for. He had learned how to think for himself, and he marveled each time he discovered exciting new knowledge. His journey through life had been filled with one intriguing moment after another, and now he found himself on the Plateau of Wonderment.

He hadn't come upon the plateau suddenly. It had involved a gradual and sometimes difficult climb, but it had been full of interesting turns and unpredictable experiences, each involving a new and challenging decision. Now, walking along the plateau and approaching the Brink of Self-Discovery, he wondered what would lie ahead.

Standing on the Brink, he surveyed the next part of his journey. Far ahead he could see his ultimate goal, the Kingdom of Perfect Happiness. What he saw surprised him. He had expected to see a golden place, a land of bright sunshine and incredible beauty. But it looked very normal, little different from his hometown and other communities he had seen.

To get there, he must first climb the Mountain of Accomplishment, an imposing set of peaks that loomed large before him. They were intimidating, and Eric doubted his ability to make the climb. He even wondered if the climb was worth it. After all, the Plateau of Wonderment was comfortable, and he was generally satisfied with the success of his journey so far. Just the thought of the prodding he had received from his parents and teachers to make the journey in the first place disturbed him. He would rebel. "To heck with this place of Perfect Happiness," he thought. "I'm tired of everyone telling me what to do."

So thinking, he studied the Mountain of Accomplishment. The more he looked at it, the bigger it grew. Maybe it was the challenge that caused him to reconsider. Eric decided that he would make the climb, but he knew that he would need help. Suddenly, three horses appeared to his right. Magically, they could talk. The first, big and strong, said his name was "Athletic Ability." The second, smaller but obviously intelligent and persistent, said his name was "Good Grades." The third seemed passive and soft-spoken. She said her name was "Good Deeds." One of the horses would be the perfect choice to help Eric climb the Mountain of Accomplishment.

7-8B   # Questions for Part One

Decision Time: Carefully think about your answers to the following. Use the back of this sheet and another sheet of paper if you need more space for your answers.

- If you were Eric Hanson, which of the horses would you choose to climb the Mountain of Accomplishment?

- In essence, what accomplishment in life is most important to you?

- Why is it so important?

- What is it about your other accomplishments that makes them less important to you?

- Why does your journey of self-discovery sometimes cause you to wonder if it's all worth it? (We'll discuss this later as a class.)

_____

_____

_____

_____

_____

_____

_____

_____

_____

_____

_____

_____

_____

Eric Hanson and the Kingdom of Perfect Happiness

Part Two: The Story Continues

It worked, but Eric again was surprised. The climb had been quite simple. Some of it was tough going, but much of it was fun. His stallion proved to be very helpful. He no longer wondered if he chose the right one. Good Grades, though smaller than Athletic Ability, had the drive to get him to the top of the mountain. Now he stood atop the Mountain of Accomplishment. But Eric was smart. He had pulled the other two horses behind him up the mountain in case he needed them in the future.

He was so happy to have climbed the Mountain of Accomplishment that he forgot what he had to do to reach the Kingdom of Perfect Happiness. In fact, he wondered why he even needed Perfect Happiness. He was very satisfied right now. He also was very tired. The climb, though relatively easy, had taken most of the day. So he decided to sleep, knowing that he would need all his strength for the journey ahead—should he choose to continue.

Eric awoke the next morning to the Dawning of Awareness. It brightened his day and revealed much of the journey ahead. It found him rested, once again interested in doing whatever it took to reach the Kingdom. He also felt stronger. Sitting atop the Mountain of Accomplishment made him feel good, eager to continue the journey, maybe to find greater satisfactions.

So he pushed Good Grades a little harder. The stallion started down the mountainside, at first moving very carefully. Eric held on to the horse's neck, fearful that he might fall off. About a third of the way down the mountainside, Eric spied the Forest of Feelingood immediately ahead. Both he and Good Grades were anxious to get there, so they forgot about being careful. Almost immediately, Good Grades stumbled and fell. Eric fell off the mighty stallion, and both of them tumbled head over heels down the mountainside, landing hard on the sandy ground.

When Eric came to his senses, he could see all around him the signs of others who had fallen from the Mountain of Accomplishment. Broken saddles, shattered eyeglasses, discarded shoes and boots, even a skeleton or two suggested how easy it was to fall off the Mountain of Accomplishment when you stopped being careful. He knew that his desire to get to the Forest of Feelingood caused his fall off the Mountain of Accomplishment. He vowed to be more careful in the future.

So he again prodded Good Grades and, in a matter of moments, reached the edge of the forest. Soon among the trees, he understood why it was called the Forest of Feelingood. Eric felt wonderful. He had climbed the Mountain of Accomplishment and, as a result, now found himself in the Forest of Feelingood. It was a very satisfying moment. But no sooner did he enter the forest than he got lost. He wandered aimlessly among black and gnarled trees until darkness obscured his way.

Eric soon realized that without a sense of direction, feeling good didn't feel very good. As darkness and growing fear surrounded him, Eric jumped off Good Grades and sat disconsolately on the trunk of a fallen tree. "What will I do now?" he wondered. Just then, a squirrel jumped down from a tree and asked Eric, "Why so glum?" Eric told him that he was lost.

The squirrel said, "Oh, don't worry; we get lost all the time!"

To which Eric responded: "*All* the creatures in this forest get lost?"

"No," said the squirrel. "All the other creatures are fine. Only squirrels want to feel good *all the time,* so they often lose their way." The squirrel continued, "But to find your way out of the Forest of Feelingood is to see with your eyes *and* with your heart!"

Eric wasn't sure how to "see with his heart."

Looking down at the squirrel, he asked, "I don't understand. How do I see with my heart?"

The squirrel told him: "You have to get out of your head! Your eyes are too close to your brain. They make you think too much. At least that's what I've discovered. Your heart helps you *feel.* Once you get out of your head and you start to feel, you begin to see things more clearly."

"Oh, I think I understand," said Eric. "My eyes help me see, but my heart helps me see things more clearly!"

"Right!" said the squirrel.

So Eric forgot about being lost and thought instead of his parents and of how much he missed them. When feelings and thoughts of love overcame his fear of being lost, he suddenly saw the light! An arm of brilliant sunlight muscled its way through the trees and illuminated a path out of the forest.

"I see the light!" said Eric. The squirrel smiled and quickly scampered back up the nearest tree. Eric jumped on Good Grades, and the two of them followed the pathway out of the forest.

7-8D

Questions for Part Two

Decision Time: Take your time with these questions. Provide complete answers.

- Why did Eric and Good Grades fall off the Mountain of Accomplishment when they thought only about feeling good?
- What did Eric mean when he said, ". . . without a sense of direction, feeling good doesn't feel very good"?
- What did the squirrel mean by "only squirrels want to feel good *all* the time"?
- What does the squirrel mean by "see with your heart"?
- How does "seeing with your heart" help people who lose themselves in their search to feel good?
- List five characteristics of people who see with their hearts.
- What does it mean "to see the light"?
- Why did seeing with his heart enable Eric to see the light?

_____

_____

_____

_____

_____

_____

_____

_____

_____

_____

_____

_____

Eric Hanson and the Kingdom of Perfect Happiness

Part Three: The Story Continues

No sooner was he out of the forest than Eric heard and saw the raging waters of the Ego Grande River. It was a torrent of white water cascading over thousand-pound boulders, surging, swirling, thundering danger. Eric knew that the Ego Grande was the single biggest obstacle people faced when trying to get into the Kingdom of Perfect Happiness. He also knew that not even Good Grades could swim the river. He and his mighty horse would have to jump over it.

"Well, big fella," said Eric, "it looks like we'll need a running start. The bigger the Ego Grande gets, the more dangerous it can be."

But Good Grades just backed away from Eric, saying, "I don't do rivers. I can't do rivers, especially that one."

"What are you talking about?" asked Eric. "You've been everything I've needed up to this point!"

"Yeah, yeah, I know," said the stallion. "I can't help you any more. I've helped build your ego. I get along well with Ego Grandes. But you need to break your ego down to get into the Kingdom of Perfect Happiness."

When Eric reached for Athletic Ability's reins, that horse said the same thing: "No, no, I'm an ego-builder, too. I'm not very good at helping you get rid of it. There's no way you'll get me over that river! I've never been very interested in the Kingdom of Perfect Happiness anyway!"

With that, Good Deeds stepped forward, saying, "Jump on, Eric. I've negotiated this river a hundred times. I knew sooner or later you'd have to choose me. I'm one of the few things that can get you into the Kingdom of Perfect Happiness."

7-8F   # Questions for Part Three

Decision Time: Think carefully about your answers!

- What is it about Ego that causes it to be "the single biggest obstacle people face when trying to get into the Kingdom of Perfect Happiness"?
- Why is Good Deeds the only horse that can jump into the Kingdom of Perfect Happiness?
- Why are Good Grades and Athletic Ability unable to help Eric?
- How do Good Grades and Athletic Ability lead to accomplishment but not necessarily to *perfect* happiness?
- What are the relationships among good deeds, love, and happiness?

_____

_____

_____

_____

_____

_____

_____

_____

_____

_____

_____

_____

Eric Hanson and the Kingdom of Perfect Happiness

Part Four: The Story Continues

Eric was pleased with Good Deeds's ability to jump the Ego Grande. Just a few seconds earlier worried about getting into the Kingdom, Eric suddenly found himself standing just outside the massive bronze gate that now barred his way.

"What do I do now?" Eric wondered out loud.

Said Good Deeds: "Knock. All anyone can do is knock at the door of Perfect Happiness."

Eric knocked. In a matter of seconds, the massive bronze door swung open and a little man with thick eyebrows and an enormous handlebar moustache stepped forward.

"What do you want?" he demanded.

Eric looked down at him and couldn't help but laugh. "My, you're a funny little man," he said.

Immediately the little man backed inside, and the big bronze door slammed in Eric's face.

"What the heck happened?" shouted Eric.

Good Deeds responded: "Well, that's simple enough! That's not the way you talk to people in the Kingdom of Perfect Happiness. They're not used to that kind of talk."

"So what do I do now?" asked Eric.

"Knock again," said Good Deeds. "You goofed, so try again. Every time you goof, you try again."

So Eric knocked again.

The little man swung the big door open and once again demanded, "What do you want?"

"I would like to enter the Kingdom of Perfect Happiness," answered Eric.

"Why do you want to do that?" asked the little man.

"I guess because I want to be happy," said Eric.

ERRRRRRRRRRRKK.

Eric jumped when he heard the big buzzer go off and looked around to see where it was, but all he saw was the little man scowling in front of him.

"Wrong answer," he shouted and once again slammed the big bronze door in Eric's face.

Astonished, Eric turned to Good Deeds and raised his hands as if to ask, "Now what did I do wrong?"

Good Deeds understood the gesture and simply pointed to the door.

So Eric knocked a third time.

Immediately the big door swung open and again the little man asked, "Yes, what do you want?"

"I want to enter the Kingdom of Perfect Happiness," said Eric.

"Why?" asked the little man.

"I want to feel good about myself," said Eric.

ERRRRRRRRRKK.

Again the invisible buzzer sounded and, completely exasperated, the little man shouted, "Wrong answer!" and slammed the big door.

Eric stood silently before the big door, staring at it. Finally, he turned to Good Deeds and asked, "What am I doing wrong?"

Good Deeds responded immediately, "I think I can help you. I've had a lot of experience with the Kingdom of Perfect Happiness."

"Good," said Eric. "I need all the help I can get."

"It's really quite simple," said Good Deeds. "Your happiness is never your direct goal. Your direct goal should always be to help others. Perfect happiness comes to you when you care about and help others. Can you do that? Can you say that to the little man and mean it?"

"I'm pretty sure I can," said Eric. "I've learned a lot on this journey."

So Eric knocked on the big bronze door one more time, and the little man emerged and asked, "Yes, what do you want?"

Eric answered, "I'd like to get into the Kingdom of Perfect Happiness."

Once more the little man asked, "Why?"

This time Eric said, "I seek to live in perfect harmony with others and to do what I can to make the world a better place."

"Good answer!" shouted the little man as he pushed the door open wider and stepped aside. "Enter the Kingdom of Perfect Happiness!"

7-8H   ## Questions for Part Four

Decision Time: Think carefully about your answers!

- Why did Eric get the door slammed in his face the first two times he knocked?
- What did Eric learn about the relationship between happiness and caring about others?
- What did Good Deeds mean when she said, "Every time you goof, you try again"?
- Why did Good Deeds say, "I think I can help. I've had a lot of experience with the Kingdom of Happiness"?
- Based on Eric's most recent experience, how would you define perfect happiness?
- What is it about some "happinesses" in our lives that mislead us, that don't make us so happy as we think they should? Name some.
- Name at least two personal qualities that are essential to finding happiness.

_____

_____

_____

_____

_____

_____

_____

_____

_____

_____

_____

_____

Eric Hanson and the Kingdom of Perfect Happiness

Part Five: The Story Concludes

Well, Eric did it. He finally entered the Kingdom of Perfect Happiness. But when he got inside, he stopped almost immediately and stared slack-jawed at what lay before him.

After a moment, he turned to the little man and asked, "Is this a trick? Are you tricking me?"

"Why do you ask?"

"Because this is the neighborhood where my home is. I'm back home!"

"Well, what did you expect?" asked the little man. "Palm trees, fountains, and gold-lined streets?"

Said Eric, "No, but . . ."

"Come on, get real," said the little man. "Perfect happiness doesn't have anything to do with where you live or what you have. Haven't you learned anything yet?"

"Well, yeah," said Eric, "but . . ."

The little man interrupted, "Perfect happiness has everything to do with who you *are*! Come on, Eric old boy! Do you *deserve* perfect happiness? Are you *good* enough?"

"Well, I get good grades and I'm good at sports . . . ," said Eric.

"That's not what I'm talking about!" shouted the little man. "Those are good accomplishments, but they don't make you a good person. We want you to be a good person if you want to get into the Kingdom of Perfect Happiness."

"Wait a minute!" said Eric. "Are you telling me that Perfect Happiness is right in my own backyard?"

"You got it," said the little man. "Sounds hokey, doesn't it? Like it's right out of Hollywood? But it's true!"

Eric smiled, remembering when the little squirrel in the Forest of Feelingood told him to see with his heart. He also remembered thinking incorrectly that Good Grades was all he needed to get into the Kingdom of Perfect Happiness.

"I sure have come a long way," he thought—and he smiled again.

7-8J   # Questions for Part Five

Decision Time: Take your time answering these questions. Your answers will reveal what you learned from Eric.

- What did Eric mean by "happiness is right in my own backyard"?
- Why did the little man distinguish between good accomplishments and being a good person?
- What does the term *self-worth* mean to you? Define it.
- How does it relate to happiness?
- Is happiness possible without a sense of self-worth? Explain your answer.
- What are some of the surest and best ways to find self-worth?

_____

_____

_____

_____

_____

_____

_____

_____

_____

_____

_____

_____

_____

Activity 7-9: Building a Better Me

PURPOSE: To develop and maintain a positive attitude. Everyone has problems, and adversity can win if we let it. The trick is to think optimistically.

MATERIALS: Worksheets 7-9A and 7-9B; pencils

PROCEDURE:

- Divide the class into small groups of three or four.
- Give each group one copy of Worksheet 7-9A.
- Instruct each group to choose a recorder who will record the group's responses on the worksheet.
- Have the groups complete each statement on the worksheet with a positive reason beginning with the word *because*.
- When the groups have finished, go over the statements on the worksheet one at a time. Have a spokesperson from each group share his or her group's responses with the entire class.
- Follow up with the discussion questions on Worksheet 7-9B.
- As the teacher, if you are truly an optimistic person, try following the Experiment. The experiment underscores the point that if you believe you are going to fail, your subconscious mind will help you to fail. However, if you believe you will succeed, your subconscious mind will help you to succeed.

Experiment

1. Choose a person in the class who is (or considers himself or herself) to be physically strong.

2. Invite that person to come to the front of the class.

3. Ask the student to hold out his or her arm straight to the side and to resist as you try to push down on it. The challenge for the student is not to let you push the arm down to his or her side. (You will probably find that the student can do this quite well and you will have difficulty pushing it down.)

4. Now tell the student that you want him or her to look at the members of the class and say 10 times in a row, "I am a bad person." Tell the student that you will count so that he or she doesn't have to worry about that part of the task. His or her task is to convey the message "I am a bad person" to the classmates.

5. When the 10 times are up, ask the student to again hold his or her arm out to the side and to resist as you push down on it. You will find that the arm pushes easily down to his or her side.

6. Ask the class what happened. (Negative thoughts entered the student's mind and the subconscious mind helped him or her to fail the task.)

7. Next, tell the student and the class that you can't leave this student in his or her present state. So, the student must now say 10 times to the class, looking directly at them, "I am a good person." Again, tell the student you will count the number of times he or she says, "I am a good person" so that he or she needs only to concentrate on getting the message across to the class.

8. At the end of the 10 times, ask the student once again to extend his or her arm and resist while you push down on it. You will find that the student's strength has returned and that it is difficult to push the arm down.

Note: I am 5'2" tall and weigh 100 lbs. I have never had this experiment fail even with athletes who were 6'4" and weighed 250 lbs.

7-9A   # Building a Better Me Worksheet

In your small groups, complete the following statements by adding a **positive** reason for each statement beginning with the word *because*. Be prepared to share your responses with the entire class.

Example:

> I am thankful for my alarm that goes off early in the morning because
> _____ *I know I am alive.* _____

1. I am thankful for having to park at the train station six blocks from school due to a shortage of spaces in the student parking lot because

   _____

2. I am thankful for the pile of homework I have each night because

   _____

3. I am thankful for aching and tired muscles at the end of my day because

   _____

4. I am thankful for the chores I am required to do at home each day because

   _____

5. I am thankful I have to baby-sit my little sister/brother every afternoon after school because

   _____

6. I am thankful I got a deans' detention for smoking in the washroom because

   _____

7. I am thankful that I was the only member of my racial/cultural group in my social studies class last semester because

   _____

8. I am thankful that I got turned down the first time I asked a girl to a school dance because

   _____

9. I am thankful that I have to shovel the driveway for my grandparents each time it snows because

   _____

10. I am thankful for the teacher who made me stop and do 50 push-ups in the hallway when she caught me roughhousing because

   _____

7-9B   # Building a Better Me: Discussion Questions

1. What did you do in this activity to overcome everyday obstacles or failure?

   _____

   _____

   _____

2. How does this approach help overcome what can be perceived as obstacles or failures?

   _____

   _____

   _____

3. Does this mean you are supposed to close your eyes to problems and obstacles in your life? Explain.

   _____

   _____

   _____

4. Author Michael Levine says, "A pessimist is someone who complains about the noise when opportunity knocks." What's the difference between a pessimist and an optimist? Which one—a pessimist or an optimist—succeeds more often? Why?

   _____

   _____

   _____

   _____

Activity 7-10: To Get Friends, Be One

PURPOSE: To help students understand that having friends is not just a matter of collecting. Friendship is a two-way street. The true rewards of friendship come from giving of yourself, your time, and your talents.

MATERIALS: A sheet of 8-1/2 by 11 plain white paper for each group; a large piece of butcher paper or packing paper for each group; old magazines; scissors; colored markers or crayons; glue

PROCEDURE:

- Divide the class into groups of three or four.

- The challenge is to design a graphic organizer for the word *friendship*. A graphic organizer is a pictorial way of showing how various words can be related or associated with one another. Sometimes it is called "webbing." Students begin with the word *friendship* and brainstorm all the pertinent words that come to mind as they consider this word.

- Have each group sketch its ideas for their graphic organizer on an 8-1/2 by 11 sheet of plain white paper.

- When the groups have completed their sketches, have them transfer their ideas more formally onto large pieces of butcher paper, adding decorative effects and magazine pictures to highlight their word associations.

- Ask each group to take turns sharing and explaining its graphic organizer to the rest of the class.

- Post the finished products on the walls, windows, etc., where they can be seen.

- Follow up with the discussion questions below.

    — In all the posters you created, what are the common ingredients for friendship? (*List them on the board.*)

    — How do we get friends?

    — Is getting friends hard or easy? Why?

    — Are friends necessary in our lives? Why or why not?

    — Does getting and keeping friends involve giving or taking? Explain.

    — What are the ingredients for being a good friend that you need to work on? (*Allow individuals to answer if they choose. Don't force students to answer the question aloud.*)

SECTION 8

BEHAVING IN A FIRST CLASS WAY

"Our deeds determine us, as much as we determine our deeds."
GEORGE ELIOT

More of the Story:

Our Steering Committee learned quickly that character should be much more than an intellectual response to the world around us. It must be a conditioned reflex, an intuitive, almost unconscious willingness to do the right thing. We all agreed that to promote such character in our students, they must not only understand appropriate behavior; they must have it drilled into them—like well-coached athletes. We must be like coaches who drill fundamental skills into their players.

Parents and teachers must drill character into their children. Drilling positive behaviors into children means encouraging and expecting them to volunteer for local activities, to be considerate of others, to speak respectfully to friends and acquaintances, to use language appropriate to the setting, and to reflect good upbringing. These are just a few of the "fundamentals" we chose to drill into our students. We also chose to promote a respect for the environment, for the elderly, and for their own appearance.

We believe that by drilling such behaviors into our students, their character becomes almost intuitive. It happens spontaneously, like a good habit. It is similar to the well-trained athlete who finds himself or herself "in the zone," sinking a succession of three-pointers or grooving a fast ball unconsciously. Ask the gymnast why she nailed that perfect ten, and she'll tell you she doesn't know; it just felt right—and it felt *good*. So it must be with character. Character is impossible without a sense of self-worth.

This meant that everyone in our school had to be "on the same page." All of us had to reward good behavior and acknowledge bad behavior. We certainly didn't need to punish kids every time they got out of line. We just wanted them to know that someone, maybe several "someones," was watching them. We also knew that those "someones" had to be students as well as teachers. Mundelein High School was our school, everyone's school, and we all shared a responsibility to make it the best place it could possibly be.

Consider another story from Karen:

> "Most of the kids in my advisory were seated before the bell rang to start the period. A few students in the front of the room near the door were shouting into the hall. One of them, Tom, was quite loud: 'Hey, why don't you get a room?'
>
> "I asked them who they were talking to. Tom told me that the same couple spends at least 20 minutes every day in an alcove down the hall kissing and fondling each other. Then he said, 'Hey . . . give us a break! These guys are X-rated!'
>
> " 'Why don't you say something to them?' I asked.
>
> " 'Hey, you're the teacher. That's your job! Why don't you say something?'
>
> " 'Because this is *our* school,' I said. 'If something bothers you, you have as much right—and responsibility—to say something as I do.'
>
> " 'OK,' said Tom, 'let's go.' With that, he stood up, beckoned everyone in the class to follow, and started for the door.
>
> "I said, 'Hey, wait a minute! What's the plan?'
>
> "Tom said, 'Let's all just stand around them and tell them they're not being very first-class.'
>
> "I said, 'OK, but no other comments—right?'
>
> "In unison the class responded, 'Right,' and we filed quietly out the door into the hall.
>
> "The couple in the alcove were so lost in the moment that they failed to notice the class forming a semi-circle around them. Moments after forming the line, the students all said, 'That's not very first class!'
>
> "Startled, both students turned quickly, smiled shyly, and walked as quickly down the hall as their dignity would allow. My class then filed back into our room, and I used the first few moments of the period to talk about open displays of affection and self-worth. A few minutes later, we got into the French lesson for the day."

Karen also made sure later that day to go to the Dean of Students to find the two students in the yearbook and to ask him to talk to each of them. She didn't want them to be punished, just to have the chance to talk about personal freedom and social responsibility. Both Karen and the Dean understand that punishment simply puts the punished act on hold for a while. What students need to develop genuine character, especially these two, was a more appropriate way of behaving!

Accepting this principle as a guide to our own behavior, the Steering Committee focused on two fundamental questions for our students. Recognizing that most students are preoccupied with their independence and freedom, we decided to ask them two important questions: "Independent *of* what?" and "Free to *do* what?" These are important questions, and they give rise to some very important and revealing dialogue. The following activities address these issues.

Index of Activities for Behaving in a First Class Way

Activity Number	Name	Description
8-1	The First Class Pledge, Part One	Defining and promoting the 3R's of First Class
8-2	The First Class Pledge, Part Two	Helping students integrate first-class behaviors
8-3	Bring the Outside In	Promoting communication between students and community adults
8-4	Volunteering: Something for Everyone!	Promoting school/community volunteer activities
8-5	A Teenager's Declaration of Independence	Exploring the characteristics of independence
8-6	School Washrooms	Promoting respect for the school environment
8-7	Familiar Places	Emphasizing an appreciation of familiar settings
8-8	Word Choice	Emphasizing appropriate speech
8-9	Considerate Communication	Promoting thoughtful communication with others
8-10	Show Your Pride	Emphasizing that first-class behavior leads to a sense of self-pride
8-11	First Impressions	Exploring how appearance creates first and sometimes lasting impressions

Activity 8-1: The First Class Pledge, Part One

PURPOSE: To define the 3R's of First Class and to encourage students to *live* the 3R's of First Class. The goal of this activity is to discuss what commitment to the 3R's really means. The discussion is designed as an opportunity for students to speak openly and freely about where they are in relation to how committed they feel to the principles defined in the 3R's. Your role is not to attempt to achieve closure or to get everyone to agree. Instead your role is to encourage students to converse.

MATERIALS: Worksheets 8-1A, 8-1B, 8-1C, and 8-1D; pencils

PROCEDURE:

- Discuss the definitions of the 3R's of First Class using Worksheets 8-1A and 8-1B with the whole class.

- Divide the class into small groups of three. Ask each group to select a recorder who will record the group's answers to Worksheet 8-1C.

- Give one copy of Worksheet 8-1C to each small group and allow the groups to discuss it openly and completely. Small groups work well in an activity such as this because students are more willing to share their real thoughts and feelings in smaller groups where they feel safe and know they won't be laughed at or made fun of.

- When the students have finished their discussions and completed Worksheet 8-1C, collect it from each group and save all of them for the next class session.

- Now give each student his or her own copy of Worksheet 8-1D. Ask each student to take it home to discuss and complete with a trusted adult (a parent, a grandparent, a teacher, a co-worker, a boss).

- Instruct the students to bring their completed worksheets for the next class meeting.

First Class Philosophy Statement

As members of the **First Class** community
we believe in and are committed to the philosophy
that every individual is valued and celebrated.

We understand that the success of our community
depends upon the 3R's:

Respect for self and others

Respect for our surroundings

Respect for the ways we communicate

First Class Expectations

Our school is outstanding because of its students, staff, and community. As we begin this school year, we would like to focus our efforts on making it an even better place in which to learn and work together.

- *Why should we?*

Since we spend at least 35 hours each week together, we owe it to each other to make this a quality experience.

- *How can we?*

We can be most successful by being aware of each other's expectations and ensuring that our actions reflect this understanding. In the past we may have made assumptions about each other's expectations, but as we begin this school year we see value in clarifying them.

- *What are we really talking about?*
  The 3R's

Respect for Self and Others

All members of the school community should conduct themselves with the dignity they deserve. This is reflected through actions and appearance. Respect should be shown to others by treating them as you would like to be treated. These roles and expectations as students and staff are not limited to the boundaries of the classroom. Everyone is expected to comply with requests in a spirit of mutual cooperation.

Respect for Our Surroundings

Our school's appearance is a source of pride for all of us. We all need to do our part in maintaining our campus including hallways, cafeteria, and washrooms.

Respect for the Ways We Communicate

We know our audience when communicating and always use appropriate verbal and nonverbal language. No one should be subjected to hearing offensive or profane language in our school.

Students' Names _____ **Date** _____

_____

8-1C   # The First Class Pledge

Answer the following questions in your small groups. The recorder for your group will write your group's answers on this sheet. Be prepared to share your group's responses with the rest of the class.

1. What does a commitment to *living* the 3R's mean?

_____
_____
_____
_____

2. Are you willing to sign a pledge to *live* First Class? Why or why not at this point?

_____
_____
_____
_____
_____

3. What would a pledge to live First Class really mean to you? Why would you be able to make that commitment at this time?

_____
_____
_____
_____
_____

4. If you are unsure or not willing at this time to pledge to live First Class, what conditions are necessary for you to make that commitment, to honestly take the step and make a pledge?

_____
_____
_____
_____
_____

Student's Name _____   **Date** _____

Name of Trusted Adult _____

Relationship to Student _____

8-1D   # The First Class Pledge

Answer the following questions. Share your answers with a trusted adult (a parent, a grandparent, a teacher, a co-worker, a boss). Ask that person for his or her advice for each question below. Bring your completed worksheet to your First Class advisory.

1. What does a commitment to *living* the 3R's mean?

   _____

   _____

   _____

   _____

   Trusted adult's opinion _____

   _____

   _____

   _____

2. Are you willing to sign a pledge to *live* First Class? Why or why not at this point?

   _____

   _____

   _____

   _____

   _____

   Trusted adult's advice _____

   _____

   _____

   _____

   _____

8-1D *(continued)*

3. What would a pledge to live First Class really mean to you? Why would you be able to make that commitment at this time?

_____

_____

_____

_____

_____

_____

Trusted adult's advice _____

_____

_____

_____

4. If you are unsure or not willing at this time to pledge to live First Class, what conditions are necessary for you to make that commitment, to honestly take the step and make a pledge?

_____

_____

_____

_____

Trusted adult's advice _____

_____

_____

_____

Activity 8-2: The First Class Pledge, Part Two

PURPOSE: To have 100% commitment to *living* First Class. The goal is not to force anyone to sign a pledge if he or she is not comfortable. It is appropriate for students and staff to sign at any point in time when they believe they are willing to "walk the talk" and live First Class. Meanwhile, the pledge card they sign remains visible for all to see just who is willing among the staff and students to make that commitment. For some, a trust level might need to be more in place for them to feel willing to sign the pledge. For others, when they see that their friends or those whom they respect are signing, they too might be willing to commit. A discussion about commitment sends a message that you are "institutionalizing" First Class—making it an expectation, a culture, a foundation from which the members of your school community live and work each day.

MATERIALS: Worksheet 8-2; First Class pledge sheet; First Class stickers like the sample shown here

PROCEDURE:

- Instruct the students to get back into the same small groups they were in for Activity 8-1.

- Return Worksheet 8-1C filled out in the last session by each small group.

- Ask the students to take out the worksheets they filled out individually and took home to share with a trusted adult. (Be aware of students with no trusted adult connection. Do they need guidance intervention?)

- Use the questions from those worksheets and the discussion questions on Worksheet 8-2 to engage the class in a discussion of the 3R's of First Class and what pledging to *live* the 3R's of First Class means.

- Invite each small group to share its opinions and reactions to the worksheet questions.

- When the discussion has concluded, invite everyone willing to "walk their talk" to come forward and sign a pledge sheet by conveying the idea that "talk is cheap." Anyone can say they will be respectful; but it is our actions that speak louder than our words. Tell them that they are being asked to act on their beliefs by signing their names to the First Class Pledge. By signing it, they are agreeing to demonstrate First Class behavior in their lives.

- You should come forward first and then invite students willing to sign the pledge to come forward to sign the document.

- As students sign the pledge, give them a First Class sticker to affix to their student I.D. cards. This sticker gives a message to anyone who has reason to look at a student's I.D. card (deans, hall monitors, and cafeteria supervisors). Those people checking I.D. cards should commend a student who conducts himself or herself appropriately in a First Class manner. A student whose I.D. card has a First Class sticker and is not conducting himself or herself in a First Class way can and should be called on his or her lack of First Class behavior. The student can be reminded in a proactive way that a pledge is binding and "walking the talk" is what is expected from the student.

- Be sure all faculty, administration, and staff have been invited to sign the First Class Pledge. It is important for students to see the signatures of staff members on the pledge as it is for staff to see the signatures of students.

- Display the First Class pledges in the same place in each classroom for all (students, faculty, staff, parents, and visitors) to see.

- Some schools might like to use a large banner for the First Class pledges (instead of the 8-1/2 by 11 pledge cards) to be displayed in a prominent area of the school.

We Pledge to Support the 3R's!

First Class

8-2   # The First Class Pledge: Discussion Questions

1. Why do people get upset when their name is mispronounced, shortened, or changed to a nickname they don't like?

_____

_____

_____

2. What is the most important thing you have had to sign your name to? How did you feel when you signed it?

_____

_____

_____

3. When people mention your name, what do you think are the three most important qualities your name represents? (Examples are honesty, trustworthiness, capability, reliability)

_____

_____

_____

4. What are you willing to sign your name to?

_____

_____

_____

Activity 8-3: Bring the Outside In

PURPOSE: To promote communication and understanding between community adults and teenagers. A valuable part of students' education is to bring the outside world into the school and to move what is happening in the school to the outside world.

MATERIALS: fliers, letters, outlines, and certificates (see samples)

PROCEDURE:

- Form a committee of teachers, students, and parents who will handle the various parts of developing and implementing a Community Speakers Day at your school. Your First Class Coordinators serve as the facilitators of the event.

- Divide your committee into subcommittees that will entice enough volunteers to successfully complete their part of Community Speakers Day. The more people who become involved in the process, the more the feeling of ownership in the event and in the program grows. The event requires approximately 6 weeks to plan and carry out. Mundelein High School's first Community Speakers Day brought in 80 volunteer speakers with requests to be invited back again the following year.

- The essential subcommittees are as follows:

Community Speakers

1. Get the word out into the community regarding the objective of the Community Speakers Day and solicit volunteers. This could be done by asking students to invite their parents to come to school to speak to a group of students about their profession and degree of education required to be in that particular profession, as well as their advice for young people today about education and the future. (Repetition in a varied way is a great way to drive home the point that education is important.) Other ways of soliciting volunteers is to call them on the phone at their business establishments and explain that the school would be honored by and appreciative of their help in the Community Speakers Day program. Brief pitches of the idea for a Community Speakers Day could be presented by a member of the Community Speakers Committee to the Rotary or Kiwanis Clubs in your community, as well as to other service organizations.

2. Volunteer speakers should be assured that they would be speaking to groups of 20–30 students, no more. Most adult volunteers are frightened by the idea of facing a group of teenagers and offer excuses why they can't participate. They must be reassured that their presentations can be informal and the ambiance will be comfortable.

3. Provide a timely letter thanking the volunteers for their willingness to serve. Include in the letter a suggested outline for their presentations. Do let them know how long you expect their presentations to be. The length of time they are required to speak seems to cause trepidation for some. (Experience has shown that these are the folks who are the first to volunteer to come back the following year!)

Student Leaders

1. Student leaders should receive careful instructions regarding their responsibilities to and for the volunteer speakers.

2. Student leaders should greet and introduce themselves to the volunteer speaker to whom they have been assigned, be sure the speaker has whatever he or she needs, and introduce the volunteer to the group of students he or she will be addressing. This will require the student leader to interview the volunteer speaker briefly in order to find some pertinent and interesting information to use for the introduction.

Student Body and Faculty

1. The student body and faculty should be informed with announcements, fliers, etc., about the event. Publicity should begin the week before the event.

2. This is an opportunity to emphasize that the volunteers will be looking as closely at the students, forming impressions about teenagers in general based on their morning's experience, as the students will be looking at the adult volunteers and forming their impressions. The 3R's of First Class (Respect for self and others, Respect for our environment, and Respect for how we communicate) are always important, and it is important for the students to remember they only get one chance to make a first impression.

Publicity

1. Contact the local newspapers for coverage of the event.

2. Cover the event in the student newspaper.

3. Invite the members of the Board of Education and the Mayor (if they are not already volunteer speakers). School administrators should support the event with their presence.

4. Send the school photographer(s) to photograph each volunteer in action.

5. After the volunteer speakers have arrived and before they are escorted away by the student leaders, provide an overview of your First Class initiative including a handout packet with your philosophy statement, goals and objectives, as well as some of the highlights of the program. This is an excellent opportunity to bring what is happening in your school back out into the community.

Reception

1. Plan some kind of thank-you reception for all the volunteers after their presentations.

2. The Community Speakers Committee (parents, teachers, and students), the faculty, student leaders, and the administration should attend.

3. Provide each speaker with a small thank-you gift (a certificate of merit, a coffee mug, etc.).

Follow-up

1. Send out a handwritten thank-you note. (Such a display of willingness to make a contribution to education deserves a handwritten note.) Include the picture of the volunteer taken in action by the school photographer(s) on Community Speakers Day.

2. In the note, mention your hopes for their continued support of Community Speakers Day by being a volunteer for next year. (You will be pleased and surprised at the number of positive responses.)

3. Keep an accurate list of the volunteer speakers, including the businesses they represent as well as their addresses and phone numbers.

First Class

Community

Speakers Day

March 18, 2002

Dear _____,

On behalf of the First Class committee at Mundelein High School, I would like to thank you for offering your time and expertise to help guide our students in their attempt to rekindle the 3R's—**Respect** for one another, **Respect** for our surroundings, **Respect** for how we communicate. We look forward to meeting you personally and to joining you in our First Class advisories on Monday, March 18, 2002. I have included a sample guideline for your presentation. Please feel free to modify it to fit your personality and your own story.

Mundelein High School is located at the corner of Hawley and Midlothian Streets. We would ask you to please plan on arriving at 9:00 A.M.

Parking will be available in the east parking lot as you enter the campus from Hawley Street.

Our guest sign-in area will be at the main east entrance to the building. A student leader will meet you there and escort you to your appointed room.

We would also like to extend an invitation to you for an informal coffee immediately after the First Class advisory at 9:45 A.M. in Room A106.

Sincerely,

_____

Karen Royer and
The First Class committee

Mundelein High School
First Class Program 2002

Suggested Guidelines for Community Speakers

Benefits of Education in Achieving Success

- Personal background
    — including education and type of student you were
    — add any stories from your childhood or other parts of your life that will grab your audience's attention
    — how did your education influence your success?
- How you found yourself where you are now
- Advice you can offer to high school students today
    — about schooling
    — about work
    — about their social life
- Bring anything that would be of a visual value
    — pictures, slides, artwork, etc.
- Did you experience any roadblocks to your success? Explain how you overcame them.
- If you could "turn back the clock," what would you have done differently?
- Allow 5–10 minutes for questions and/or comments

Thank you!

Certificate of Appreciation

Mundelein High School

recognizes

Greg Royer

for commitment to students in creating a First Class school

Spring 2002 Community Speakers Program

Activity 8-4: Volunteering: Something for Everyone

PURPOSE: To promote involvement in school and/or community volunteer activities.

MATERIALS: Worksheets 8-4A, 8-4B, and 8-4C

PROCEDURE:

- Introduce the activity by telling the class that recent studies indicate that students who engage in extracurricular and/or volunteer activities eventually enter some of the best colleges and are among the nation's most successful graduates. Involvement in school and/or community activities provides the experiences many young adults need to get perspective on the world around them. Maybe Confucius was right when he said, "He who wishes to secure the good of others has already secured his own."

- Have the entire class think about an appropriate volunteer activity. The activity can range from volunteering to play cards or games with the elderly in a nearby nursing home to maintaining waste receptacles inside and outside the school. Students can clean graffiti, assume responsibility for the cleanliness of the hallway just outside their classroom, police a certain part of the school grounds, or work with local junior highs or elementary schools to provide tutoring. Contact the local village/city hall for additional information and ideas.

- Once students decide on an activity, tell them to choose one of three groups to join: the contact group, the organizing group, or the public relations group.

- Be sure to keep the groups relatively well-balanced. One can be bigger than the others, but all should have enough members to perform the necessary tasks.

- Put students in their groups and distribute the appropriate worksheet to each member of the group.

- Circulate among the groups to provide advice and to keep them on target!

- Even though this activity is relatively unstructured, it can result in some excellent and very creative ideas. Trust the kids. In many more instances than not, they won't disappoint you. They also will learn a lot about organizations in the process!

Volunteering: Contact Group

Directions: Your group has the responsibility to contact everyone who has to approve the activity or to help you secure times, equipment, or other materials. For example, if our class is volunteering to work with the elderly, you will have to contact the administrator of the nursing home to get his or her approval, one or more of the nursing home's social workers to get ideas for activities, and any of the nursing home's assistants who will help us organize the actual visits. In addition, you may have to meet with one or more of these people to guarantee our interest in the activity.

The same is true of any activities that involve our school or neighboring schools. You might have to meet with our principal or assistant principal(s) to organize an in-school activity or with a local elementary school principal to organize a volunteer activity—perhaps tutoring—with his or her school. Consider the following items:

1. The person or persons to provide approval for our involvement:

   Name: _____

   Phone number: _____

   Address: _____

2. The development of an introductory letter to send to the organization to explain:

   - The suggested times of our involvement.
   - The number of students who will be involved.
   - The kinds of activities we would like to engage in.
   - Suggested times to meet to discuss our involvement.
   - The person or persons to respond to.
   - Consider including a stamped, self-addressed envelope for them.

3. The names and addresses of parents who might be able to provide transportation. Remember that such transportation must be approved by the school. If it isn't approved, an alternate form of transportation must be identified and organized.

4. The possibility of meeting with one or more of the other groups in our class to coordinate information and schedules.

5. You might have to meet once or twice outside the classroom to write letters or to organize your responsibilities. See me at any time for any help I can provide.

Volunteering: Organizing Group

Directions: Your group has the responsibility to recommend to the class the particulars of this activity. For example, if we are volunteering to work with a local nursing home, you will have to brainstorm ideas for possible activities with them. If we are working with a local elementary school, you will have to identify the subject matter strengths in this room and suggest processes to have the tutors work with the elementary students. Consider some of the following:

1. What are the particulars of the general activity we are planning? What *specifically* has to be done to make sure we accomplish this activity successfully?

   _____

   _____

   _____

   _____

   _____

2. How will we handle these particulars? _____

   _____

3. Who is best able to handle these particulars? _____

4. Do we need to develop any schedules? Is time a factor? _____

   _____

5. Do we need parent approval? You may need to develop a form to provide information to parents and to secure their approval.

6. What else do we have to do? Use the back of this sheet as needed.

   _____

   _____

   _____

   _____

   _____

   _____

   _____

Volunteering: Public Relations Group

Directions: Your group has the task of handling the public relations for the activity we are planning. It is important that school and community newspapers be given information periodically. If our activity is really unique, you might even contact larger metropolitan newspapers to share information. One or more of them might even want to send photographers, so be sure to contact them well enough in advance to give them time to schedule visits. Depending on the nature of the activity, you also might have to write periodical press releases to keep newspapers updated on the progress of the activity. Consider the following:

1. **Contact persons.** Get the names and phone numbers of all media people whom you will want to contact to share information. You will want the phone numbers because you might have to call them to provide information or to arrange personal meetings.

   Local newspaper people: _____

   Local radio people: _____

   Local television and local access cable people:

   _____

2. **Press Releases.** Look at the sample press release form and keep the following in mind:
   - Always provide a title for the release. Newspaper people call it a "slug." The slug is not a headline; just a word or two to describe what the press release is about.
   - Underneath the slug, indicate the release date of the information. You might indicate *For Immediate Release* or give a time in the future.
   - The press release then indicates the name of the contact person or persons here at school, the address of the school, and the fax and/or phone numbers.
   - Use only the front side of the release form and be sure to double-space the copy.
   - Be sure the release is well-written. The papers might just scan it and use it as written. Get help with the writing as needed.
   - Inform the reader(s) of the main point of the story as soon as possible.
   - Remember the journalist's love of "who, what, when, where, how, and why!" Answer these questions in every release.
   - Use correction fluid to erase everything but the relevant information on the attached release, then make duplicate copies of it. Develop several sample releases. Practice and get some feedback from me or another teacher. Keep the additional copies of the release forms for future use.

PRESS RELEASE

TITLE *(Slug)*

TO: *(The names of all the newspapers you intend to contact.)*

For Immediate Release *(or release date)*

Name:

Address:

City, State, ZIP:

Phone:

Fax:

(Use the rest of the page for the text of the release.)

Activity 8-5: A Teenager's Declaration of Independence

PURPOSE: To explore the characteristics of independence. What does it mean to students and, possibly, to all of us to be independent? Specifically, *of what* are we independent? In addition, what responsibilities accompany any new-found independence? An added purpose of this activity is to promote dialogue among students and their parents about the characteristics of independence.

MATERIALS: Worksheets 8-5A, 8-5B, 8-5C, and 8-5D; pencils

PROCEDURE:

- Begin the activity by mentioning that all young adults, when they mature, move from a state of dependence to a state of independence. "OK, most of us know that. But what does it mean?"

- Ask students to think about some of their past and current dependencies. "Who are you dependent on and for what? As you mature, who and what are you independent *of*—and *why*? Is independence something you deserve—or do you earn it? If you earn it, does it involve some responsibilities? What are they?"

- Involve students in general dialogue about these ideas. Tell them they will identify the specifics in their groups.

- Also inform them of the process. They will be expected to discuss dependence and independence in their groups and to develop a bumper sticker that summarizes their ideas. Then you will develop a total class response. They will take the class's ideas home for more discussion and to get ideas from their parents.

- They will return to class tomorrow (or the next time you meet) with their parents' ideas. They will share these ideas with the rest of the class and, using their parents' ideas, decide as a class on what young adults become independent of and what some of the responsibilities are that result from that independence.

- Once these decisions are made, each group will write a *Teenager's Declaration of Independence,* incorporating statements of independence as well as statements of responsibility. The best of these will be shared with the school newspaper for publication. When the entire activity is complete, you might even emphasize with the class the value of collaboration!

8-5A   A Teenager's Declaration of Independence

Directions: Discuss these questions. No one person's ideas are better than anyone else's. Use the best thinking of your group to develop your group's position on each question. Get a little pride in your group! See if your group can convince the rest of the class to go along with your ideas.

1. As children and teenagers mature, they move from a state of dependence to a state of independence. Exactly what does that mean? Think about and identify five dependencies you had as a child that you no longer have. List them:

   a. _____

   b. _____

   c. _____

   d. _____

   e. _____

2. What one or two reasons explain this change? Why do you no longer have these dependencies? Write your group's reason(s).

   _____

   _____

   _____

3. As you mature, you will outgrow additional dependencies. What are they? List the five most obvious ones:

   a. _____

   b. _____

   c. _____

   d. _____

   e. _____

4. What are the reasons for these changes? Why will you no longer have these dependencies? Write your group's reasons:

_____

_____

_____

_____

5. What does your growth away from these dependencies suggest about any responsibilities you will assume? Do you assume new responsibilities every time you become independent of something or someone? Why? Write your group's answer:

_____

_____

_____

_____

6. Finally, now that you and your group have answered all the questions, create a bumper sticker—something catchy—that explains in one sentence the relationship between independence and responsibility. Write it here:

_____
| |
| |
| |
| |
| |
| |
| |
|_____|

We will use the last several minutes of today's class time to identify the best of what each group has to offer. Then we will develop a list that represents agreement among all of us. Take that list home and, using the *Parent Input* form, get reactions from your parents to the class's ideas. Tomorrow, we'll add your parents' reactions to our ideas and come up with what we think are the best answers to the above questions. Then, your group will write a *Teenager's Declaration of Independence*. The best one will be shared for publication in the school newspaper.

8-5B

A Teenager's Declaration of Independence:
What Our Class Agrees on

Directions: We will discuss your worksheets as a class. As we agree on the best answers, write them below. You will be expected to take this home to share with your parents and/or brothers and sisters. You will also be expected to take a *Parent Input* form home to get their reactions and ideas.

The five additional dependencies we are likely to outgrow as we mature are:

a. _____

b. _____

c. _____

d. _____

e. _____

The reasons we will outgrow these dependencies are: (We will list at least three)

a. _____

b. _____

c. _____

The responsibilities I will assume when I outgrow these dependencies are:

a. _____

b. _____

c. _____

d. _____

Share this with your parents tonight and get their
reactions and ideas on the *Parent Input* form.
Bring it to class tomorrow or the next time we meet.

Student's Name _____ **Date** _____

Parent Input

Directions: Please review the form your child has brought home and discuss it with him or her. Then write your reactions and/or any additional ideas in the spaces provided. Thanks for your input. Parent ideas are very important to our Character Education program.

1. As my child matures, I expect that he or she will outgrow the following dependencies:

   a. _____

   b. _____

   c. _____

   d. _____

   e. _____

2. He or she will outgrow them for the following reasons:

   a. _____

   b. _____

   c. _____

   d. _____

3. I expect that when my child outgrows these dependencies, he or she will assume the following responsibilities:

   a. _____

   b. _____

   c. _____

   d. _____

PLEASE BE SURE YOUR CHILD BRINGS THIS FORM BACK TO SCHOOL!

Student's Name _____ Date _____

8-5D   A Teenager's Declaration of Independence

Directions: Today, we will list the class's ideas and the reactions of parents to these ideas, then decide on the five most likely dependencies we will outgrow within the next several years. Then we'll identify the three best reasons that explain this growth. We'll list the responsibilities we assume when we become increasingly independent. Finally, we'll write a TEENAGER'S DECLARATION OF INDEPENDENCE, share our declarations as a class, and submit the best one or two for publication in the school newspaper.

We will outgrow the following dependencies in the next several years:

a. _____

b. _____

c. _____

d. _____

e. _____

The reasons we will outgrow them are:

a. _____

b. _____

c. _____

By outgrowing them, we assume the following responsibilities:

a. _____

b. _____

c. _____

d. _____

8-5D *(continued)*

Now, put your heads together to write your group's *Declaration of Independence.* Good luck.

A TEENAGER'S DECLARATION OF INDEPENDENCE

We hold these truths to be self-evident, that all teenagers are created equal, that they are endowed by their Creator with certain unalienable rights, that among these are Life, Liberty, and the pursuit of Happiness. Also among these are:

_____

_____

_____

_____

_____

_____

_____

_____

WE'LL DISCUSS THESE AS A CLASS AND PICK THE BEST ONE(S)
TO SEND TO THE SCHOOL NEWSPAPER FOR PUBLICATION.

Activity 8-6: School Washrooms (A Farce in One Act)

PURPOSE: To encourage students to think about their responsibilities for treating the school environment with respect. Most school washrooms are intended to be smoke-free, litter-free, graffiti-free, and hygienic. Some schools have difficulty guaranteeing those standards. This activity is designed to help students understand that the school environment is not just the responsibility of the faculty and administration, but theirs as well. The school belongs just as much to the students as it does to the faculty and administration. Therefore, to have a healthy school environment they wish to live in, students must be willing to create it and protect it.

MATERIALS: Worksheets 8-6A and 8-6B; pencils; hall pass; keys; toilet paper; mask; sunglasses; air freshener

PROCEDURE:

- Select two students from your class who are willing and able to take part in this scenario.
- Be sure both students have rehearsed the scenario and get into it.
- Give the following instructions to the student actors playing the TEACHER and the STUDENT.

  1. This is meant to be humorous (think "Saturday Night Live").
  2. Don't use a script. Memorize the sequence. If you can't memorize the lines, improvise the dialogue. The goal is to get the meaning across. (If you've wanted to overact and be a big ham, here's your chance.)
  3. Use the actual teacher's desk in the classroom. Cross to the classroom door. The student playing the TEACHER should always let the student playing the STUDENT get almost to the classroom door and then stop him/her and require him/her to return to the teacher's desk.
  4. The student actor playing the TEACHER should always pull the props out from under the desk.
  5. The student actor playing the STUDENT has to really build the need to go to the bathroom. Make it funny.

- Give everyone in class a copy of the discussion questions on Worksheet 8-6B, and go over them as a class. Encourage students to say "That's not First Class" as the answer for question 9.

School Washrooms (A Farce in One Act): Script

STUDENT: (*Approaches teacher and asks politely and quietly*) May I go to the washroom?

TEACHER: You know the rules.

STUDENT: I know—but it's an emergency!

TEACHER: O.K., but you'll need this before you go. (*Writes a hall pass*)

STUDENT: Thanks. (*Starts across the room toward the door*)

TEACHER: You forgot this. (*Gives keys to the student*)

STUDENT: Oh, right. (*Again the student starts to leave*)

TEACHER: Wait, you need the bathroom survival kit, too. (*Gives the student a roll of toilet paper*)

STUDENT: Oh, yeah. (*Starts again—is in need of leaving soon!!*)

TEACHER: And smoke protection. (*Gives the student a mask*)

STUDENT: Right. (*Starts again—with urgency*)

TEACHER: And graffiti protection. (*Gives the student sunglasses*)

STUDENT: Check. (*Has to leave quickly!*)

TEACHER: Forgot-to-flush protection. (*Gives the student air freshener*)

STUDENT: CHECK!

TEACHER: Okay, be back quickly and quietly.

STUDENT: Yes. (*Goes to the door—stops—turns around—comes back to the teacher—gives back each item **one at a time***)

TEACHER: What's the matter? You're prepared now.

STUDENT: I know, but it took so long to get ready that I don't have to go anymore.

8-6B   ## School Washrooms: Discussion Questions

1. Why does the teacher give the student all of those items just to use a washroom at school?

_____

_____

_____

2. What else would you include in the kit?

_____

_____

_____

3. Should you need these items? Why?

_____

_____

_____

4. What would you put in a School Hallway Survival Kit?

_____

_____

_____

8-6B *(continued)*

5. Review the school's expectations for behavior in the washrooms and hallways.
   Summarize them here.

   _____

   _____

   _____

   _____

6. How can we encourage others to adhere to these expectations?

   _____

   _____

   _____

   _____

7. What can we say to people who disregard these expectations?

   _____

   _____

   _____

Activity 8-7: Familiar Places

PURPOSE: To demonstrate the appropriateness of language in different situations. We should know and be aware of our audience when communicating and always use appropriate language. No one should be subjected to hearing profanity expressed in school.

MATERIALS: Worksheets 8-7A and 8-7B; "Stash Verbal Trash" cards; paper; pens or pencils

PROCEDURE:

- Divide the classroom into four corners, each representing a familiar environment (e.g., a place of worship, home, school, a Friday night party).
- Divide the class into four teams.
- Divide each team into four small groups. Each small group of the larger team will have a letter name. The groups are C, U, S, S.
- Have each small group (C, U, S, S) select one of their members to serve as the recorder.
- Now, from each team, send the C members to a corner of the room representing a familiar environment. Continue by sending the U members to another corner and each of the S groups to the third and fourth corners.
- Explain to the C, U, S, and S groups what environment they are in.
- Have everyone in each corner carry on a typical conversation, as himself or herself, that would occur in this particular setting.
- The catch is that every time they feel the need to use a profane word, they are to substitute it with the word *marshmallow*.
- The group is to keep the conversation going for approximately 5–7 minutes.
- During this time, the recorders need to gather data on the conversation. They should try to record the conversation as it occurs and keep track of the number of times the word *marshmallow* is used.
- If you don't think the groups can sustain a 5-minute conversation, have them switch to a second location after 3 minutes.
- When time is up, the original teams should regroup to discuss the data that the recorders have gathered.
- Follow up with the discussion questions on Worksheet 8-7A.
- At the end of the session, give each student a copy of Worksheet 8-7B.
- Photocopy the Stash Verbal Trash cards onto sheets of stick-on labels and give them to students to put on their folders. Or enlarge the labels and use them on trash bins in the school.

Stash *VERBAL* **trash!**

Stash *VERBAL* **trash!**

Stash *VERBAL* **trash!**

Stash *VERBAL* **trash!**

Stash *VERBAL* **trash!**

Stash *VERBAL* **trash!**

Stash *VERBAL* **trash!**

Stash *VERBAL* **trash!**

Stash *VERBAL* **trash!**

Stash *VERBAL* **trash!**

8-7A   # Familiar Places: Discussion Questions

1. How typical was the different language being used in each corner?

   _____

   _____

2. Why did you feel the need to use *marshmallow* and how appropriate was it in that place?

   _____

   _____

3. Why do people swear?

   _____

   _____

4. What's wrong with swearing?

   _____

   _____

5. Imagine yourself back in your corner. What, in your opinion, would be First Class language?

   _____

   _____

6. What can you do to make a difference in your familiar places?

   _____

   _____

7. What can we do to encourage others to make a difference in their familiar places?

   _____

   _____

What's Wrong with Swearing?*

Swearing imposes a personal penalty

It gives a bad impression.
It makes you unpleasant to be with.
It endangers your relationships.
It's a tool for whiners and complainers.
It reduces respect people have for you.
It shows you don't have control.
It's a sign of a bad attitude.
It discloses a lack of character.
It's immature.
It reflects ignorance.
It sets a bad example.

Swearing is bad for society

It contributes to the decline of civility.
It represents the dumbing down of America.
It offends more people than you think.
It makes others uncomfortable.
It is disrespectful of others.
It turns discussions into arguments.
It can be a sign of hostility.
It can lead to violence.

Swearing corrupts the English language

It's abrasive, lazy language.
It doesn't communicate clearly.
It neglects more meaningful words.
It lacks imagination.
It has lost its effectiveness.

*Taken from *CUSS CONTROL, The Complete Book on How to Curb Your Cursing* by James V. O'Connor (Three Rivers Press, 2000). Used with permission.

Activity 8-8: Word Choice

PURPOSE: To help students understand how important is the way they speak. It is necessary for everyone to realize that the way they speak reflects who they are as the representative of their country, their community, their school, and their family. We should demonstrate respect for the ways in which we communicate.

MATERIALS: Worksheet 8-8; pencils

PROCEDURE:

- Divide the class into small groups of three.

- Instruct each group to choose a recorder who will write the group's answers to Worksheet 8-8.

- Begin by asking the students to come up with some personal examples they would be willing to share when they asked for something from their parents or teachers and didn't get it because of the way they communicated.

- Ask the students to come up with some personal examples they would be willing to share when some adult (a teacher, a hall monitor, a boss or fellow employee, a coach), using ineffective speech and ways of communicating, asked or demanded something from them. Then ask students to share the result of that situation.

- Ask the students, who were willing to share their experiences with ineffective communication, what might have happened in the cited situations if the language and the way of communicating had been different.

- Give each group a copy of Worksheet 8-8.

- Allow the groups sufficient time to talk through the questions.

- Go over questions 1–8 with the entire class. Have each group share its reflections on the questions.

- Use questions 9 to come up with a class-generated list of five suggestions each for *What We Can Do as Individuals* and *What We Can Do as a Group* to deal with inappropriate language and a lack of respect for the ways in which we communicate. List them on the board.

8-8   # Word Choice

Answer the following questions in your small groups. The group recorder will write
your group's answers on this sheet. If you need more space, use the back of this paper.
Be prepared to share your group's responses with the entire class.

1. Does your language change from when you are with your friend to when you are
    with your parents? Why?

    _____

    _____

    _____

2. In what ways do students verbally abuse each other?

    _____

    _____

    _____

3. Where do profanity and gutter language most often occur?

    _____

    _____

4. What do you consider to be inappropriate language?

    _____

    _____

    _____

5. Why do people swear?

    _____

    _____

    _____

6. How does your language represent your maturity and intellectual level?

_____

_____

_____

7. Since language is an indication of your maturity and intellectual levels, what message does inappropriate language give about you?

_____

_____

_____

8. How, then, is that message a reflection on your community, your school, and your family?

_____

_____

_____

9. What can we do, as individuals and as a school, to deal with inappropriate language and a lack of respect for the ways in which we communicate?

What We Can Do as Individuals	**What We Can Do as a Group**

Activity 8-9: Considerate Communication

PURPOSE: To identify ways to be considerate and respectful when communicating with peers and adults. Communication isn't conveyed through words alone. Tone of voice, body language, and facial expressions are equally important in the communication process.

MATERIALS: A large piece of drawing paper for each student; colored markers or crayons; sample drawing

PROCEDURE:

- If possible, have the students arrange their desks into a circle.
- Ask the students to close their eyes and silently recall their earliest childhood mental image between each question.
  1. Who was your teacher/principal?
  2. Who were your friends?
  3. What did your classroom look like?
  4. What activities filled your day?
  5. What were you taught about communicating with others?
- Give a large sheet of drawing paper and a colored marker or two to each student.
- Ask the students to draw a large face on their sheet of drawing paper.
- Instruct them to write inside the large face a list of things they learned in kindergarten about communicating with others. An example is given here.
- Have each student show his or her poster to the rest of the class and tell about it.
- Follow-up with these discussion questions:
  1. How can you apply the things you learned in kindergarten to the ways in which you communicate with others in your lives today?
  2. What changes can be made to encourage respectful communication here at school?
- Display the posters in the classroom so that other students can view the ideas throughout the week.

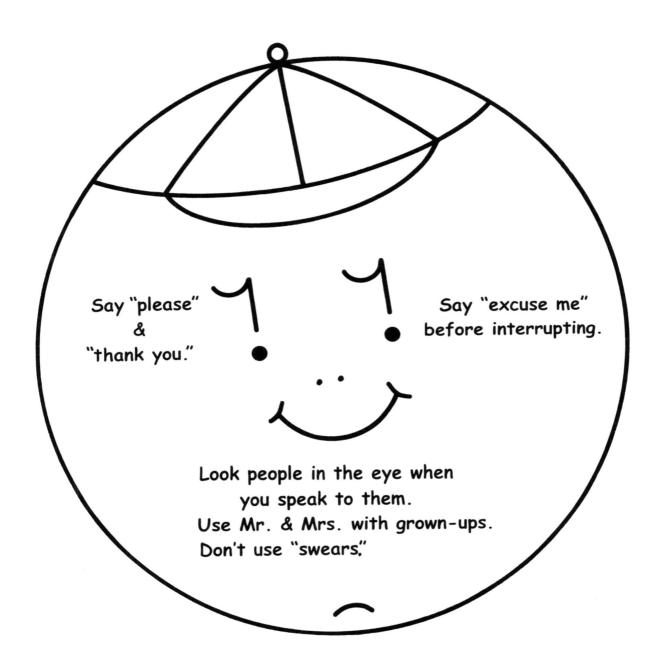

Say "please" & "thank you."

Say "excuse me" before interrupting.

Look people in the eye when you speak to them.
Use Mr. & Mrs. with grown-ups.
Don't use "swears."

Activity 8-10: Show Your Pride

PURPOSE: To think about how much your school has to offer. This activity is designed to encourage students to take pride in their school and to participate in the school community.

MATERIALS: Worksheets 8-10A and 8-10B; pencils; action cards; prizes

PROCEDURE:

- Duplicate the Action Reminders (cards) and cut them out.
- Divide the class into groups of three.
- Give each group one copy of Worksheet 8-10A turned printed-side down.
- At a given signal, have the teams begin the challenge. Allow an appropriate amount of time for the students, through collaboration, to complete as much of the School Trivia Challenge as possible
- When time is up, have the students stop and then go over the answers to the Challenge. Supply the correct answers for the questions the students don't know.
- Award prizes for the groups scoring the highest number of points. (Edible treats are always popular as prizes.)
- Next, have the students share aloud what they are most proud of about their school. It can be something repeated from Worksheet 8-10A, or a new idea altogether.
- Select one student to write the ideas on the board.
- Hand out one copy of Worksheet 8-10B to each group.
- Allow the groups enough time to brainstorm tangible ways that they can show their respect for and pride in their school.
- When the students have completed their worksheet, invite each group to share its ideas on one of the eight topics with the entire class.
- Distribute the Action Reminders cards. Tell the students the card is to remind them that they are to select one action to work on in order to demonstrate pride in their school and respect for their surroundings.

Action Reminders

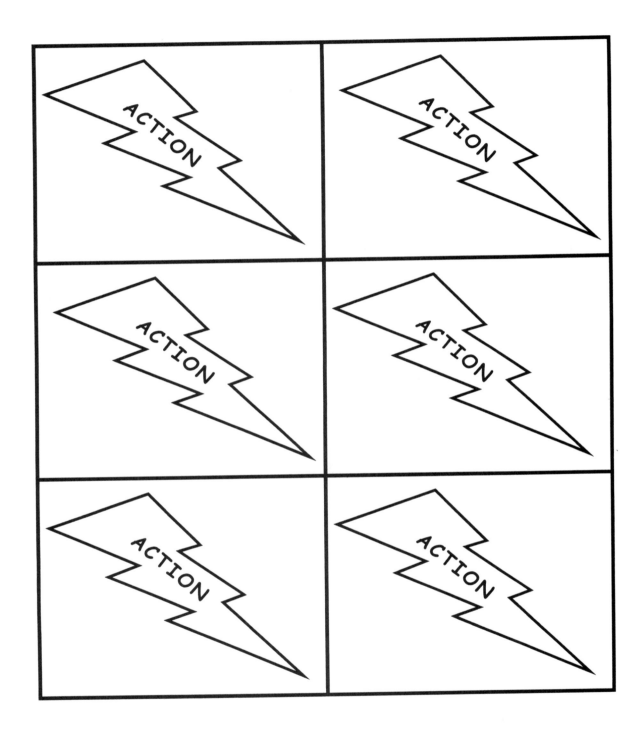

8-10A   # School Trivia Challenge

In your small groups, fill in the answers to the following questions about your school. Prizes will be awarded!

1. Name your school's head Custodian.   1. _____

2. In what year did your school first open?   2. _____

3. How many students attend your school this year?   3. _____

4. How any classrooms are there in your building?   4. _____

5. How many computers do you have in your building?   5. _____

6. What is the size of the school property?   6. _____

7. How many extracurricular clubs
   (athletic and nonathletic) are there in your school?   7. _____

8. How many new teachers are there in your school
   this year?   8. _____

9. What is the total number of teachers in your school?   9. _____

10. What is the capacity of the home bleachers in
    your stadium?   10. _____

11. What is the name of your school's Superintendent?   11. _____

12. What are the boundaries of your school district?   12. _____

13. What awards has your school won?   13. _____

14. How many books are there in your school library?   14. _____

15. How many seats are there in your school library?   15. _____

16. In what years and in what events has your school
    won conference and state championships?   16. _____

17. How many of your school's staff have served 20 or
    more years at your school?   17. _____

Students' Names _____ **Date** _____

_____

8-10B   ## Show Your Pride

There are many ways that we as students and faculty can demonstrate our pride and respect for our school building, surroundings, and community. In your small groups, list things you can do in the places and situations listed below to show respect and pride for your surroundings. Be prepared to share your ideas with the entire class.

1. I can take pride in my classroom by . . . _____

   _____

   _____

   _____

2. I can take pride in my locker by . . . _____

   _____

   _____

   _____

3. I can take pride in my media center by . . . _____

   _____

   _____

   _____

4. I can take pride in my computer lab by . . . _____

   _____

   _____

   _____

5. I can take pride in my sporting events by . . . _____

_____

_____

_____

6. I can take pride in my cafeteria by . . . _____

_____

_____

_____

7. I can take pride in my auditorium by . . . _____

_____

_____

_____

Activity 8-11: First Impressions

PURPOSE: To explore the initial and, sometimes, the lasting impressions of personal appearance.

MATERIALS: Worksheets 8-11A and 8-11B; pictures; pencils

PROCEDURE:

- Divide the class into six groups and give each group a different *Act It Out* picture.

- Instruct each group to look carefully at its picture. Then have students identify behaviors for the character and write a 30-second script of what this character might say to the class—and how he or she might say it. In other words, have students interpret the character based on appearance. You might say: "What might this character sound like?" "How would he or she talk?" "What would he or she say?"

- Give each group enough time—approximately 5 minutes—to develop the 30-second script and to select one person in the group to act it out for the rest of the class. Tell students to be (appropriately) creative!

- Then have the person from each group act out the script.

- Congratulate the students on their creativity and acting ability. Then distribute Worksheet 8-11A.

- Tell them to discuss and answer the questions in their groups.

- Following the discussion, select the two or three groups that created the most stereotyped characters and have them explain why they developed the characters the way they did. At least two or three of the groups will create characters that clearly match the appearance of the picture.

- After this initial discussion, distribute Worksheet 8-11B and have students discuss these questions as a class. Encourage them to develop a few principles they can use to guide their understanding of how personal appearance creates first and, sometimes, lasting impressions.

Act It Out

tax man

cowboy

student

worker

general

female boss

Students' Names _____   **Date** _____

_____

8-11A   **Lasting Impressions**

Answer each question regarding the script you created for the picture that was assigned to your group. We will discuss your answers as a class in a few minutes.

1. After looking at the picture that was assigned to your group, what were your first impressions of it?

     _____

     _____

     _____

2. What was it about the appearance of the picture that caused you to have such impressions and to create that particular script?

     _____

     _____

     _____

3. Why did the member of your group act out the character the way he or she did?

     _____

     _____

     _____

4. Did you like the character? Why or why not?

     _____

     _____

     _____

8-11B   # Lasting Impressions

We will discuss the following questions as a class.

1. Why does someone's appearance create first and, sometimes, lasting impressions on others?

    _____

    _____

    _____

2. Are these impressions always correct? Why or why not?

    _____

    _____

    _____

3. Do you care *now* about the impressions your personal appearance creates? Why or why not?

    _____

    _____

    _____

4. Can you think of any time(s) in the future when the impressions your personal appearance creates will be important?

    _____

    _____

    _____

5. *Take a minute to think about this last item, then write your answer.* Develop a guideline that explains when and why the impressions *your* personal appearance creates will be important to you.

    _____

    _____

    _____

    _____

EPILOGUE: TO THE TEACHER . . .

"Don't wait for the Last Judgment.
It takes place every day."
ALBERT CAMUS

A Final Story:

We knew the First Class program had officially arrived in Mundelein High School a few months ago when we were walking toward the school during the halftime of a Friday night football game. Two Mundelein players were walking just ahead of us unaware of everybody and everything around them. Even the clamor of the crowd and the halftime activities failed to muffle their excessively colorful descriptions of the referee who "robbed them of that first down"! Even in the dim light of early evening, we could see their invective turning the air blue. Sympathetic but exasperated, we got their attention:

"Boys, we agree with you, but maybe the language could be a little different?"

Surprised to see us right behind them, one of the boys responded: "Oh, sorry! Not very First Class, huh?"

"No," we said. "We agree with you about that ref, but maybe the language, especially out here, could be a little different."

This time, the other boy responded to us, "Sorry." Then, turning back to his friend, he said, "That goshdarned ref! His decision certainly was upsetting, wasn't it?"

To which his friend replied: "Yes, I must admit that I disliked it a great deal!"

Progress with the unfolding of such programs is like a baby's first steps. They're usually small, often tentative, and sometimes downright funny.

TAKING A QUICK LOOK AT EMPOWERMENT

Dr. Newbrough has been a long-time believer that the term "empowerment," so recurrent in the educational literature, requires a broader definition. He believes that teachers must share in the decisions traditionally limited to administrators. They must influence policy development, budget considerations, curriculum development, scheduling decisions, and their own professional growth. In a broader sense, however, he believes that teachers are already empowered. They may not have complete power to control the budget, execute policy, or evaluate personnel, but, without their support, programs such as the one emphasized in this book will never be successful.

Much of their power, therefore, is not to use; it is to *give*. That's why Dr. Newbrough believes that power is a two-way street. Administrators give it to teachers to create learning experiences for their students, to create and supervise their own professional growth, to control student behavior in their classrooms, to suggest and implement needed change in the building, even to influence administrative decision making.

But teachers also give power to administrators. They give administrators the power to implement programs such as the one in this book. Without their acceptance of such programs, the programs will never be successful. Mundelein High School is fortunate to have administrators who understand that teachers are inclined to give such power when they help develop and monitor school programs. That's why it's essential that teachers participate in the development of the program and eventually buy into it.

It's also important that they acknowledge that character education extends well beyond the activities in this book. Character education is only incidentally a set of activities. It is a total school focus on positive relationships among students, teachers, parents, and administrators. In fact, only through positive relationships can schools create the comfort levels and the awareness in students that result in character. Such relationships warrant further discussion. Consider the following points:

- *Recognition.* Comfortable interpersonal relationships involve recognition and some degree of affection. Recognition is especially important. Students *need* to be recognized; we all do. Some of us will go to extreme lengths to find such recognition, especially teenagers, many of whom have yet to develop or accept a set of protocols that govern dress, appearance, and behavior. At the extreme, some have discovered that being "freaky" and "geeky" is broadly recognized.

  Such students' predispositions toward bizarre, even violent behavior, are positively reinforced by such recognition. With some students, it is only a matter of time before their need for recognition results in thoughtless behavior, even senseless cruelty. Consider the 13-year-old middle-school student in Palm Beach who shot and killed a popular teacher. Prior to the shooting, he told a friend: "Just watch, I'll be all over the news tomorrow."

  It would be short-sighted to blame the media. Although the media provided immediate and nationwide recognition for this student, it wasn't the media that provoked his behavior. It was the student's need for recognition, a need that seeks satisfaction in either desirable or *undesirable* behavior, whichever is more likely to work. When the need is satisfied, the behavior that satisfied it is reinforced. When the class clown receives recognition for being a clown, he continues to be a clown. When the angry isolate receives recognition for being an angry isolate, he continues to be angry and an isolate.

A very angry Dylan Klebold wrote in his journal just before unleashing his violence in Columbine High School: "I swear like I'm an outcast and everyone is conspiring against me." It was this conspiracy that gave Klebold the recognition he needed. Such recognition, even when it's negative, satisfies the student's needs and becomes desirable in its own right. Klebold also wrote: "I'm full of hate, and I love it."

- **"Catch 'em being good!"** The recognition students receive and the relationships they develop with teachers should help them understand that the more good they do, the more recognizable they will be. Children need not be honor-roll students or all-conference basketball players to be recognized. They need only behave in ways that are consistent with the six facets of character mentioned in the introduction to this book. Being good students or outstanding athletes is necessarily subordinated to being good people.

Everyone can be a good person, and the school that seeks to develop character in its students must show affection for them and affirm their existence by following a maxim mentioned earlier in this book: "Catch 'em being good!" Recognizing students and showing affection for them is essential to the program; it will not be successful without the atmosphere such behaviors create. Student recognition goes well beyond the activities provided in this book. It is something that must influence all interactions with students.

- **Role Models.** We have already indicated that most of the activities in this book engage students in self-reflection, self-evaluation, and dialogue. We can't overemphasize the importance of the objective and reasoned consideration of sensitive topics such as prejudice, sexual harassment, stress, and anger. The more we encourage students to analyze such situations *before* they happen, the more likely they are to react to them rationally and dispassionately.

Having said that, however, we must emphasize that even reason takes a back seat to example. Good teachers have recognized for centuries that showing is more important than telling. Students need models more than they need critics. Like all of us, students imitate people they respect and admire. More specifically, they embrace not only the behaviors but the principles of the adults in their lives who impress them.

To be impressive, models must be successful and respected by others as well. They must be perceived as winners. Students are disinclined to imitate the apparent failure who loses the world but gains self-respect and inner tranquility. They seek out and admire people who enjoy prestige and success in the school community, winners who are respected by other teachers as well as the school's administration.

This suggests an important essential for the school seeking to implement an effective program of character education. Mundelein High School acknowledges that the school's most important purposes are realized in the classroom and that our teachers are the building's technical experts. The prestige that results from such a belief not only bolsters teachers' self-concepts and their sense of professional competency, but also establishes them as role models for students.

- **Reflection.** We realize that some children are so unreasonable that they leave their parents and teachers slack-jawed. We knew a teacher once who described teenagers as a pot full of uncooked noodles: rigid to the point of breaking and unwilling to do most anything until someone puts them in hot water. He indicated that they race through their young lives making arbitrary and self-focused decisions, yet demanding fairness at every turn.

  He may have had a point. Certainly, not all preteens and teens are as self-absorbed as he suggested, but the apparent contradictions in their behavior are real in one sense. They are rigid in their expectations of being treated fairly. This expectation may at times challenge the understandings and skills of teachers and parents, but it also provides a window of opportunity for the school interested in using the activities in this book as well as in the school's curriculum to promote character education.

  Good schools help students explore and understand their worlds in order to develop such character. Doing the right thing can be very hard. For example, fighting *for* a cause is noble, but, at times, so is fighting *against* one. Use the activities in this book, even develop more, to teach such lessons. Also emphasize similar experiences found in the analysis of history, literature, business affairs, married relationships, and the logic and inquiry inherent in math and science.

- **Keep the Students Involved.** Schools must help students analyze and evaluate their worlds and create their own realities. This is normally accomplished through the thoughtful and collaborative exploration of real-life as well as purely academic situations. When teachers trust students to examine complex issues and to identify reasonable alternatives to action, they are invariably surprised and pleased at their logic and sensitivity. Most important, such teachers understand that students will rarely "own" such judgments until they have the chance to make them themselves or to experience them directly.

  That's why it's important for schools to promote inservice and supervisory experiences for teacher that capitalize on education's growing body of research. Such research not only creates new knowledge, but it makes current knowledge obsolete at a rate never before experienced in human history. But the research does even more. It taps everything from the incredible potential of the human brain to stunning uses of new technology.

- **Observation Creates Reality.** Quantum scientists tell us that observation creates reality. Without getting into the mind-numbing subtleties of such a principle, let us emphasize one point. People who are involved in the creation of anything accept it more quickly than if they hadn't been involved. In other words, if you create it, it has relevance for you. If *we* create it, it has relevance for *us*. The input of students and teachers, therefore, is critical. It provides them a sense of involvement and control. It also underscores the relevance and timeliness of the activities and processes they suggest.

Schools interested in implementing any kind of program of character education are encouraged to organize a steering committee composed of teachers, parents, students, and, perhaps, an administrator. They are also encouraged to circulate among students, teachers, and parents opportunities to evaluate the program and to react to current concepts and recommendations for new ideas and processes.

Mundelein High School went so far as to train student leaders to assume the primary responsibility for delivering the program. The teachers who are responsible for the advisory, the homeroom, or the class are given the task of assisting the student leaders. This aspect of the program relieves teachers of another preparation and provides leadership training for students. The continued involvement of teachers and students as recipients of the program, evaluators, and leaders is essential to its continued success.

MORE ABOUT RELATIONSHIPS

The relationships between students and teachers are only one element in the success of the program. So are the relationships among students. Teachers can do much to foster positive relationships by overseeing the quality of student dialogue in the classroom. These activities will promote such dialogue; so will the facts, generalizations, and concepts found in the school's curriculum. *How* this information is dialogued will affect not only the quality of the learning experience, but also the way students learn to relate to each other.

Dialoguing about principles and appropriate behavior enables students to encounter a wide range of situations requiring reflection and a decision. Such dialogue provides a forum for sharing and building on each other's ideas, considering alternative solutions rationally and dispassionately, and seeking the best of several good ideas.

Teachers and student leaders, therefore, must understand the difference between "discussion" and "dialogue." Author and educator Peter Senge suggests that discussion usually involves conflicting opinions, one person trying to prevail over another. Sometimes the conflict gets personal, and it always tries to disprove or eliminate important aspects of opposing arguments.

On the other hand, dialogue seeks a win–win situation, in which everyone feels some responsibility and ownership for the group's decision. Such a decision represents the best thinking of everyone involved. Whereas discussion seeks to destroy conflicting opinion, dialogue uses it constructively, to create a position that represents the best thinking of everyone in the group. The difference between dialogue and discussion may seem only semantic, but Senge's thinking suggests important insights into the nature of school relationships.

Teachers and student leaders are encouraged to promote interactions among students that seek win–win situations and that capitalize on the best thinking of everyone in the class. The issue of character is too diverse and complicated to subject it to conflict rather than collaboration. Collaboration promotes a marriage of different but complementary opinion. It emphasizes the value of thoughtful interaction with others to develop mutually satisfying solutions to problems.

ONE MORE POINT ABOUT RELATIONSHIPS

Many of the activities in this book detail the roles of both students and teachers. They also clarify expectations of behavior. While mutual respect can't be mandated, it can be encouraged by looking thoughtfully at one's own behavior and acknowledging the needs of others. Respect is a two-way street, assumed to be free of potholes and unexpected turns. Students and teachers must practice mutual respect in order to function each day in a predictable and satisfying school environment.

The Mundelein High School staff, for the most part, recognizes that well-disciplined students are self-critical students. They are able to reflect on their own behavior, evaluate it, and make appropriate corrections. Certainly, this is not true of all students. We have the occasional characterless space cadet who satisfies his "me-first" mentality by trying to run roughshod over everyone else in the building. We deal with him, too.

But the important thing is that we don't anticipate such behavior from every student. We realize that most students are young men and women who deserve respect and will handle our requests maturely and sensitively. Even when they get out of line, we've learned that "Hey, knock it off!" doesn't work so well as "Tom, that kind of language bothers me in a school setting" or "Do you really think that's First Class behavior?"

Good teachers know, for example, that overt confrontation is as ineffective for kids as for adults. Experience and common sense have taught us that "Were you born in a barn?" and "Where's your brain?"—like most rhetorical questions—can result in some very surprising and unexpected responses! We've discovered that we're much better off assuming that all students have brains and, with a less confrontational approach, are more than willing to use them.

Consider a related issue—scolding. At one time or another during the school year, we all have to scold a student. Scolding is confrontational, sometimes negatively confrontational. *How* we scold students obviously has much to do with the student's willingness to listen and respond positively. Our attempts to discipline can be quite direct, but if we remember to discipline with dignity, we are more likely to improve student behavior.

More important, however, are the effects of scolding. Psychologists remind us that at the moment scolding stops, the student's behavior is reinforced. In other words, if the student is scowling or talking back, scowling and talking back will be reinforced when the scolding stops. In such a circumstance, the teacher not only fails to promote good behavior but actually intensifies negative behavior.

Teachers are well-advised, therefore, to reprimand in as positive a way as possible in order to provoke a smile of understanding or a nod of approval from students. Such a practice is consistent with the notion that punishment may momentarily restrain bad behavior, but that, in and of itself, it does little to promote good behavior. The key for schools is to help students replace poor behavior with good behavior. How we interact with kids will determine the success of our efforts.

Finally, teachers must recognize that a student's occasional snotty remark or lousy attitude is rarely directed to the teacher personally. Our knowledge of this fact helped us raise our children and relate to 30-plus years of students. We understood that a child's attitudes and thoughtless comments were not directed to us but to Mom and

Dad or to *teacher*. Looking at student behavior this way prevents us from taking things too personally and from reacting to students in anger. It is more important that evaluative and corrective comments from teachers shed light, not heat.

A FINAL LOOK AT MOTIVATION

We recently watched two television shows, one exploring the motivations of murderers on death row, the other declaring the effectiveness of "scaring kids straight." One show sensationalized the dark irrationality of murderers. The other showed youthful offenders being intimidated by prison inmates who were screaming the kids' likely futures behind bars. The child "experts" on both shows were convinced that such dramatic and provocative experiences do much to motivate kids to improve their behavior and to develop character.

What nonsense. Such shortsighted but commercially intriguing programs fall prey to their own misconceptions. They believe and they influence viewers to believe that motivation is something we *do* to kids. This is self-important silliness. Although we certainly have a role in student motivation, our task as teachers and parents is not to create or *control* their motivations. Our task is to help students *satisfy* their positive motivations.

A shortsighted focus on motivation as something *we* do obscures the fact that kids—all kids—have needs and that they are *motivated* to satisfy them. They will do anything, as indicated earlier in this section, to satisfy their need for recognition. They also will do whatever is necessary to satisfy their needs for achievement, safety, a sense of self, a sense of belonging, and, as prominent psychologist Abraham Maslow has indicated, food and water. The only thing a hungry child wants is food, and he will disregard his reputation, even his safety to get it.

At the risk of overstating the point, any school promoting character education must recognize motivation as the drive to satisfy such needs. In essence, the role of parents and teachers is to satisfy needs—the *kids'* needs. The needs of students must constitute the school's framework of motivation. Teachers and others in the building must operate inside, not outside, this framework.

They do so by developing and maintaining a caring atmosphere in the school, not by manipulating students or by "scaring them straight." Without such an essential atmosphere of mutual concern and support, even the best conceived program of character education and the most thoughtfully developed curriculum will be ineffective.

A FINAL THOUGHT

Schools devote countless time and money to activities that recognize and reward the academic and athletic accomplishments of students. Perhaps this is as it should be. Schools are educational institutions with wonderfully varied curricula and a wide range of opportunities for students to engage not only in academic but in extracurricular and cocurricular activities. That we reward accomplishment in these activities seems to be a very important part of our responsibilities as educators.

In fact, we have devoted so much time and energy to the academic and athletic accomplishments of some students that many kids now define their self-worth in terms of the honors they receive. Again, this may not be all bad. We want young people to make the effort to be the best they can be in every aspect of their lives. Achievement and recognition are powerful motivators. Academics and athletics, however, are only two aspects of their lives.

As indicated already, teacher and parent emphasis on straight A's and all-conference honors has resulted in the related need for students to get into the most prestigious universities or to receive athletic scholarships. Still, this is not all bad. It starts becoming bad when prestigious universities and athletic scholarships become ends in themselves. It becomes worse when the more important aspect of the student's personal development is deemphasized in school or at home and diminished in the eyes of the student.

Such a tendency is especially unfortunate because it is so easily avoided. If schools would reward good behavior as well as they punish bad behavior, we would realize a shift in our thinking that would benefit students, schools, homes, and communities. Imagine an end-of-the-year school banquet devoted to the recognition of student good deeds and volunteer activities. What a remarkable idea! What is additionally note-worthy is that *every student in the school,* not just the academically or athletically gifted, could earn such honors.

Imagine the new world that would open for all students. In such a school, all students would have the opportunity to define their self-worth in terms of the good they do instead of the scholarships and grades they receive. They would learn to temper competition with cooperation. They would focus on who they are as opposed to what they have. They necessarily would reach out to others, and they would go through the school day feeling good about themselves. In short, they would develop character.

But some of us persist in treating symptoms, rather than in dealing with the problem itself. Consider psychology's most recent emphasis—"oppositional defiance disorder." Is it surprising that the acronym for this euphemism is ODD? Odd can't even explain the tendency of some educators to use such esoteric terminology to describe plain, old misbehavior.

Maybe the confusion about the behavior and violence in our schools has caused some of us to reach deep into our bag of terms to find explanations. Maybe it's easier to create euphemisms than to confront and change mistaken priorities in our schools. Whatever the reasons, our schools and our society will continue to have problems until we decide to look at our students and our relationships with them realistically.

We can call it oppositional defiance disorder (ODD). We might even create our own term, one that comes closer to the truth—Behavioral Adjustment Disorder (BAD). Whatever we call it, we must first acknowledge that an absence of character is at the core of the problem and that the problem is not that hard to remedy, if we choose to complement our academic and athletic emphases with an equal focus on good deeds and compassionate and charitable behavior.